Power and influence in health care

A NEW APPROACH TO LEADERSHIP

Power and influence in health care

A NEW APPROACH TO LEADERSHIP

Karen E. Claus, Ph.D.

Assistant Research Psychologist and Lecturer,
Co-Director, Creative Leadership
Development Program, School of Nursing,
University of California,
San Francisco, California

June T. Bailey, R.N., Ed.D.

Professor and Associate Dean,
Co-Director, Creative Leadership
Development Program, School of Nursing,
University of California,
San Francisco, California

with 27 illustrations

The C. V. Mosby Company

Saint Louis   1977

The C. V. Mosby Company
11830 Westline Industrial Drive, St. Louis, Missouri 63141

Library of Congress Cataloging in Publication Data

Claus, Karen E   1941-
    Power and influence in health care.

    Bibliography: p.
    Includes index.
    1. Nursing service administration. 2. Power
(Social sciences). 3. Influence (Psychology).
I. Bailey, June T., joint author. II. Title.
RT89.C58   658'.91'61073   76-57769
ISBN 0-8016-0417-6

GW/CB/CB 9 8 7 6 5 4 3 2 1

CONTRIBUTORS

Jacquelyne Gorton, R.N., M.S.

Lecturer, School of Nursing,
University of California,
San Francisco, California

Jocelyne M. Nielsen, R.N., M.S.

Assistant Clinical Professor,
School of Nursing,
University of California,
San Francisco, California

PREFACE

Dynamic changes in twentieth century society present new concerns and challenges to professional nurses. A primary concern is the critical need for effective nursing leadership. We believe that to be effective leaders, nurses need to accept the reality and legitimacy of power. We want nurses to understand power as a positive force and to use power to influence health care.

The reader will find two major themes throughout the book that record our views as to what leadership is all about: the effective leader is conceptualized as having the capacity to use power wisely to influence goal attainment, and the leader is viewed as a planner, energizer, initiator, and humanizer who takes actions, accepts risks, and is responsible and accountable for the results. These two themes are interrelated and form the basis of our operational definition of leadership and the development of a Power/Authority/Influence Model.

Two major criteria were developed to guide us in making decisions as to what should constitute the most relevant content. First, we wished to share our perceptions as to what power and influence are all about. Second, we wished to provide nurses with an instructional tool—the Power/Authority/Influence Model—so that nurses can optimize their power and be more effective leaders.

Our basic assumption is that to optimize the use of power, nurses must first understand the nature of power. Second, nurses need to know how to use power as a resource for obtaining results. To this end we have spent considerable effort in designing a model of power so that power, as a complex concept, can be more easily understood. We have conceptualized and defined power as a pyramid having elements of *ability* based on *strength, willingness* based on *energy,* and *action* that yields *results.*

Our approach to power is a positive one. We believe that for too long nurses have viewed themselves as powerless, or have perceived power as a useless game, or have believed that power is not commensurate with humanistic values inherent in the profession of nursing. Perhaps these views reflect the misuse of power. One hardly needs to be reminded of what happens when high government officials abuse power and authority. Power needs to be viewed not as a tool to corrupt or destroy but as a resource to bring about planned change.

Another of our assumptions is that power resides in each of us. We have a variety of power bases that we need to use—personal power, organizational power, and social power. As nurse leaders develop an awareness of power and its potential for making human endeavors more productive, they can indeed translate power into influence through taking actions to meet both individual and organizational goals.

In light of these basic assumptions, a Power/Authority/Influence Model is presented in Part one and provides the reader with a framework for power and influence. The model conceptualizes procedures for setting goals, defining tasks, determining situational variables in both internal and external environments, using various power bases, using both formal and functional authority bases, and taking actions based on both a functional and a human relations approach to management. A human touch in the use of power is requisite if we are to humanize health care and educational systems, gain respect and trust, and make full use of the talent and potentials of health care providers.

Part two of the book addresses itself to the problem of how to help nurses develop power and translate power into influencing others. In essence, Part two reflects tools and techniques developed and used by us during the 5 years we have taught leadership courses to graduate students. It also reflects our experience as consultants to members of various health care and educational systems. Part two contains chapters by two guest contributors—Jocelyne Nielsen and Jacquelyne Gorton—who are faculty members of the University of California, San Francisco, School of Nursing, and who also serve the community as independent psychiatric practitioners.

We believe our book can be used as a basic text for leadership courses in nursing education programs and as a handbook for inservice training programs. It can also be used by nursing educators and nurse practitioners who are tired of playing the power game and who are motivated to use power as a positive force in bringing about desired change.

Our fervent hope is that student nurses, nurse practitioners, nursing service administrators, and nursing educators will be stimulated by the ideas in this book and indeed take action to exert influence—whether leadership is at the patient care level, at a top administrative level, or working with a multidisciplinary core of health professionals dedicated to the challenge of planned change in the delivery of health care.

The award of a nursing special project grant to the University of California, San Francisco, made this book possible. We gratefully acknowledge the Public Health Service and the University for the opportunity to develop and implement a Leadership Training Program.* We also acknowledge the many contributions of our students, who broadened our scope and gave us additional insights as we approached leadership from a new perspective.

Particular thanks are due to Carol Dolan and Jacquelyne Gorton, faculty members at the University of California, San Francisco, School of Nursing. They have diligently reviewed various drafts, shared valuable comments, and critiqued the final manuscripts.

---

*Graduate Training of Nurses for Decision Making in Health Care, Training Grant 09D 000394-05-01, Department of Health, Education, and Welfare, U.S. Public Health Service.

Our warmest appreciation is extended to Beth Graham, Wendy Whiteside, and Nancy Romer for their excellent performance in transcribing innumerable tapes, typing a multitude of drafts, and giving technical assistance in producing the manuscript.

Last but not least, we wish to express our indebtedness and gratitude to our families. We wish to give special thanks to Dr. R. James Claus for his ideas, expertise, counsel, and sustaining support.

Karen E. Claus
June T. Bailey

CONTENTS

xi

PART ONE

A framework for power and influence

The ultimate test of a leader is the wise use of power.
WARREN BENNIS

1 NEW PERSPECTIVE FOR NURSING LEADERSHIP: POWER/AUTHORITY/ INFLUENCE MODEL

THE TEST OF LEADERSHIP

If indeed the test of leadership is the "wise use of power," how can power be meaningfully defined—and how can nurse leaders learn to use power wisely? These were the questions that plagued us as we developed and taught leadership courses to graduate students enrolled in nursing on a large health science campus. The idea of power as a criterion measure for a leader stimulated new modes of thought about leadership and opened up for us a new approach to leadership.

The purpose of this chapter is to present a Power/Authority/Influence Model. We define power as the *ability* based on *strength, willingness* based on *energy,* and *action* that yields the results.

THE POWER/AUTHORITY/INFLUENCE MODEL FOR LEADERSHIP
An action model

The leadership model is designed so that nurses can take actions. It is also designed to give the nurse a conceptual framework to exercise leadership. The Power/Authority/Influence Model is not a theoretical discussion tool, although it is based in solid theory from social and behavioral sciences. Step-by-step procedures are presented to assist nurses to set realistic goals and to achieve desired results through action.

Developing the model

In developing an innovative approach to leadership, we surveyed literally hundreds of studies of leadership. We worked our way through the maze of leadership literature, not only to guide our own instructional strategy but also to help us develop a model. The Power/Authority/Influence Model is the culmination of our efforts and represents the synthesis of knowledge from a number of fields.

In the Leadership Development Program at the School of Nursing, University of California, San Francisco, our orientation was to be both theoretical and practical to provide ongoing experiences in leadership development within the

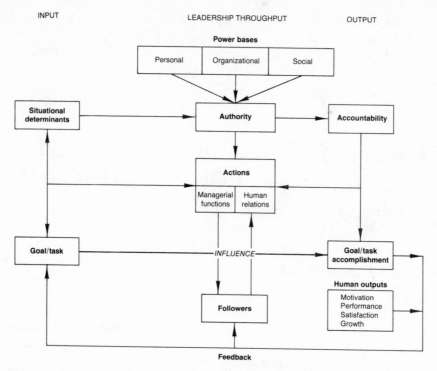

Fig. 1. Leadership throughput—the Power/Authority/Influence Leadership Model.

classroom setting, and when possible to assist students enrolled in practicums to relate classroom experiences to practice settings. In the classroom we used familiar and relatively risk free settings that were designed to assess leadership behavior of the students through simulation exercises. The model displayed in Fig. 1 is the result of these experiences. It is an active model—meant to be used.

Purposes of the model

The model provides nurse leaders with a systematic way to reach an organizational or individual goal. After defining the goal and determining what the tasks and human resources are to reach the goal, nurses can then assess their situation and ascertain sources of power, the authority base, their responsibilities, and sense of accountability. Nurses can then specify the managerial skills to be utilized and which human relations techniques should be used to influence the performance of others in order to reach organizational and individual goals.

The model highlights the fact that leadership is a relationship based on the willingness of others to follow. In addition to goal and task accomplishment, the leader must also be concerned with human outputs: motivation, performance, satisfaction, and growth. All outputs provide feedback that determines inputs into a different goal-task situation.

We view progression through the model as circular and cumulative. Nurse leaders who use appropriate power and authority bases can *act* to influence others to perform in the desired way, and thus be perceived as leaders. A leader becomes more powerful by practicing the art of influencing others in goal setting and goal accomplishment and by utilizing feedback from previous experiences. In the act of following, synergy occurs; that is, the combined efforts of leader and follower will yield greater results than the singular efforts of each individual. This knowledge and sense of synergy constitute one of the strongest bases for the appeal of accepting a leader's direction.

AN OPERATIONAL DEFINITION OF LEADERSHIP

Within the conceptual framework of the Power/Authority/Influence Model, we define leadership as a set of *actions* that influence members of a group to move toward goal setting and goal attainment. Inherent in the *actions* are situational variables; personal, organizational, and social power bases; formal and functional bases of authority; and accountability. Other elements in the spectrum of leadership actions are sound managerial and human relations behaviors and the use of influence strategies that will promote a willingness to follow so that individual and organizational goals can be achieved. Thus, leadership is viewed as multidimensional, encompassing the wise use of power, managerial functions, and human relations processes.

AN OVERVIEW OF LEADERSHIP THEORIES

Before we discuss each of the steps in the Power/Authority/Influence Model, we wish to present a summary of selected leadership theories that we believe have influenced our thinking and that have contributed to our approach to leadership.

The trait approach

Early theory and research on leadership focused on personality traits. Researchers identified leaders and followers and measured group members on personality traits. Differences between leaders and followers on these traits were then tested. Hundreds of studies have been conducted to identify special traits, but the search has been rather futile. Stogdill summarizes the difficulties inherent in the trait approach to leadership:

> The personality theorists do regard leadership as a one-way influence effect. While recognizing that the leader may possess qualities differentiating him from followers, they generally failed to acknowledge the reciprocal and interactive characteristics of the leadership situation (Stogdill, 1974, p. 9).

After World War II researchers began to look at behavior and leadership style. Several studies attempted to determine if groups were more effective under autocratic, laissez-faire, or democratic styles of leadership (Lewin, Lippitt, and White, 1939; Lippitt and White, 1943).

Leadership behavior studies

From the 1950s on, research on leadership focused on behavior. An impressive series of leadership studies were conducted by Shartle and Stogdill (1952).

Table 1. A sampling of researchers who have identified two basic dimensions of leadership behavior

Researchers	Names given to leadership behavior dimensions	
	Human relations	**Managerial**
Benne and Sheats (1948)	Group maintenance	Task
Shartle and Stogdill (1952)	Consideration	Initiating structure
Bales and Slater (1955)	Socio-emotional	Task
Bowers and Seashore (1966)	Peer leadership	Managerial leadership
Katz and Kahn (1966)	Employee-centered	Job-centered
Fiedler (1967)	Relationship-oriented	Task-oriented
House and Dessler (1974)	Supportive	Instrumental

Through observation, scaling, and factor analysis of the leader behavior observed in hundreds of groups an instrument was developed to measure several factors of leader behavior. This instrument was called the Leader Behavior Description Questionnaire (LBDQ) (Fleishman, 1973). Two important factors accounted for well over three fourths of the variance in leader behavior. These two factors were labeled *consideration* and *initiating structure*. Consideration was defined as the degree to which a leader or supervisor shows concern, understanding, and warmth toward group members or followers. Consideration also included the degree to which the leader is concerned with followers' needs and willing to explain his action. Initiating structure refered to task-related activities such as the assignment of roles and specific assignments of tasks within the group, defining goals, and setting and monitoring work procedures and standards.

These two functional dimensions of leadership are still prominent in most leadership theories. Table 1 samples some of the researchers who have studied leadership and who have determined the two basic dimensions.

Leadership as a relationship

An important contribution of leadership studies has been to show that leadership is not a property of the individual but rather is a complex relationship among a host of environmental, situational, personal and interpersonal, as well as organizational, variables. Leadership is the result of the interaction of a number of factors such as: (1) the leader, (2) the follower, (3) organizational characteristics, (4) characteristics of the external environment, (5) tasks and goals, (6) structural and authority variables, (7) work group variables, and (8) performance variables. Most recent research on leadership takes a contingency approach. Contingency approaches are those theories or models that postulate that leadership effectiveness is *contingent* upon the interaction of leader attributes with group, task, and environmental variables.

GOALS AND TASKS
Goals

Goal/task

Lateral movement through the model begins with goals and tasks that need to be accomplished. We have defined a goal as a statement of intent or outcome. We indicated that goals derive from purpose that in turn derive from basic needs (Bailey and Claus, 1975, pp. 34-35).

Functions of goals. Goals serve several functions: (1) they provide a source of identification and motivation for members of a group (Barnard, 1938; Clark and Wilson, 1961); (2) goals serve to orient and constrain the behavior of members of an organization (Simon, 1964); (3) goals may be employed to obtain support from the environment and to overcome opposition, particularly in a political sense (Parsons, 1960; Selznick, 1949); and (4) goals are an important basis for evaluation of performance (Dornbusch and Scott, 1975).

Goal setting as a motivator. Everyone has goals. Goals may be set by the person himself, in collaboration with other people, or exclusively by others. Most people actively pursue goals set by themselves and tend to rebel at goals set exclusively by others. Indeed, the negative reactions of avoidance and rebellion to goals set by others often become personal goals in themselves. Generally, the higher a person is in an organization, the more freedom he has to set goals and, consequently, the more satisfaction he derives from his job. Subordinates, however, must carry out the tasks that will accomplish the higher order goals. Using motivational forces *within* subordinates to move them toward accomplishing the tasks and attaining the goals is indeed the unique contribution of a leader. The skillful leader is a person who can move others to accomplish tasks that support goals that they may or may not have participated in setting. This is a particularly important contribution for a nurse leader because in nursing not only are many of the goals set by others, but the day-to-day tasks are also often determined by others.

Meyers (1970) has equated satisfaction with the relationship between achievements and goals:

$$\text{Satisfaction} = \frac{\text{Achievement}}{\text{Goals}}$$

The closer achievements approach goals, the greater the satisfaction. This relationship is circular, however, because as goals are attained, new goals are usually set. Energies then must be directed toward achieving new goals.

Meaningful goals. If goals are meaningful, tasks that may be boring, menial, or distasteful are more likely to be accomplished. This is why nurses who are committed to the goal of quality patient care will do a variety of routine, unpleasant tasks.

Factors that inspire people to achieve goals include characteristics of the goals themselves in addition to how well goal attainment satisfies their personal needs. Motivation or meaningful goals have five attributes:

1. They are usually influenced at least in part by the person attempting to reach them.

2. They are visible.
3. They are desirable.
4. They are challenging.
5. They are obtainable.

Meaningful goals, in other words, lead to the satisfaction of personal needs. The higher the need levels satisfied by a goal, the more important and meaningful the goal. The needs for security, affiliation, recognition, achievement, responsibility, growth, and self actualization are important personal motivators.

Evaluation. Goals also serve as the basis to set standards that are then used as tools for evaluation. This topic has been treated extensively in other places (see Chapter 13, Bailey and Claus, 1975).

Tasks

A task is an activity or set of activities carried out by a person or persons to attain a goal (Dornbusch and Scott, 1975). There are two basic types of actions associated with carrying out a task: decisions and implementations. Sociologists Dornbusch and Scott (1975) distinguish decisions from implementations by indicating that decisions are choices that affect future courses of action whereas implementations are those activities by which choices are executed. Although some choice is involved in any kind of behavior, those choices made in implementing decisions do not significantly alter the path already selected.

Task dimensions. Task dimensions determine how tasks are carried out in the work environment. The three task dimensions that determine whether a task can be handled in a routine fashion or requires discretion are: (1) predictability, (2) efficacy, and (3) clarity. Predictability is the extent to which it is possible to analyze the desired properties of performances or the outcome to be obtained. In studies of various professional groups in a number of organizational settings, Dornbusch and Scott (1975) found that task dimensions affected how tasks were allocated and how work groups were formed. When tasks are high on clarity, efficacy, and predictability, it is most efficient to direct individuals to perform specific, standardized activities.

In order to process tasks that are low on clarity, predictability, and efficacy, it is more effective to allow individuals to assess the amount of resistance to goal attainment and to adjust their actions accordingly. When there is a high risk of error, it is best to allow discretion in decision making since the specific tasks cannot be allocated in advance. Greater discretion usually means greater competence, training, and responsibility for acts.

Nurses' tasks. In a study of 124 hospital nurses, Marram (1971) listed five major task categories for nurses: carrying out physicians' orders, ward management, providing comfort and support, record-keeping, and observation and assessment. The nurses in Marram's study reported that the three most important tasks were carrying out physicians' orders, observation and assessment, and providing comfort and support. The task of carrying out physicians' orders had low delegated freedom and autonomy, whereas the task of observation and assessment had high freedom and autonomy. Nurses in Marram's study reported that record-keeping and carrying out doctors' orders were the highest in clarity, predictability, and efficacy. The characteristics of these tasks yielded less delegated autonomy and freedom for the nurse performers, but this tended to be preferred by the nurses themselves.

A study conducted by Bailey to identify behavioral criteria of professional nursing effectiveness identified seven major aspects of the professional, graduate staff nurses' job (Bailey, 1956). These aspects included: (1) demonstrating manipulative skill and technical competence, (2) demonstrating effective organization of work habits, (3) performing effectively in an emergency or stress situation, (4) providing the patient with emotional support, (5) demonstrating effective interpersonal relations with co-workers and visitors, (6) maintaining personal appearance and voice control, and (7) demonstrating professional ethical behavior. One hundred and eighty-seven interviews were conducted; nursing supervisors, patients, and physicians comprised the sample. Of the total of 419 behaviors reported by all three resource groups, the largest number of incidents was related to "providing the patient with emotional support" (Bailey, 1956).

Scott (1969) has suggested from studies of professional groups that when a substantial narrowing or distortion of original goals occurs, it is because professional workers or semiprofessional workers come to define what they can do as what they should be doing, since the true professional is allowed considerable latitude in making decisions. At this point it is useful to quote from Dornbusch and Scott with regard to the nursing profession:

> Semiprofessionals such as nurses, engineers and secondary school teachers, and full professionals, such as physicians and scientists, appear similar in being moderately high on efficacy and relatively low on predictability for many of their tasks. What may differentiate them is the level of goal clarity. The goals for semiprofessionals are relatively high in clarity, we argue, largely because the organizations by which they are employed assume the right to set goals to govern their task performance. This is one of the important senses in which these types of professionals are "heteronomous" or externally controlled (Scott, 1965). By contrast, full-fledged professionals, enjoying greater autonomy, conceive of their central tasks as relatively low on clarity, insisting on their right to participate in goal-setting and to adjust the desired end states according to changing views of the situation, new possibilities, and special circumstances (Dornbusch and Scott, 1975, p. 87).

POWER BASES

Personal	Organizational	Social

Vertical movement through the model starts with power bases and moves toward interaction between the leader and those who have elected to follow. In our model we discuss three power bases: the personal power base, the organizational power base, and the interpersonal and social power base.

The personal power base

A strong self-concept and heightened and growing self-esteem form the foundation of the personal power base. Personal power is also based on growth and development. It is particularly important that a leader take responsibility for personal growth and enhance the areas of strength that will provide for selection of various influence strategies.

Interpersonal-social power base

Interpersonal and social power bases are built on effective interactions with other people. Group cohesion depends on ability to share energy with others and to gain strength from others. The powerful person can cooperate and also allow others to participate and make decisions that are crucial to their well-being. Craig and Craig (1974) discuss the concept of synergic power, which is basically the growth of power that accrues to people who work together cooperatively. Synergy refers to the fact that the synergistic whole is greater than the sum of all the separate parts. Through synergy the satisfactions of all members of a group are improved and increased through interaction with others. Social power develops from interpersonal power and is based on the power of grouping, whether formal or informal, within organizational structures.

Organizational power base

Organizational power depends on a number of structural characteristics of an organization, and on the formal and functional authority bases discussed in Chapter 5. Nurse leaders must build on both the power and authority bases if they are to be successful in taking action to meet organizational and individual goals.

SITUATIONAL DETERMINANTS OF LEADERSHIP
Sources of situational variables

> Situational determinants

Most of the current leadership models tend to refer to at least four sources of situational variables that affect leadership performance: (1) the external environment, (2) the internal environment of the organization, (3) the nature of the groups operating within the system, and (4) the characteristics of the leader involved in the interaction (House and Dessler, 1974).

Contingency theory

Fiedler's research on contingency theory identified three major variables that contributed to the leader's influence and control. Fiedler called these variables situational favorableness in the contingency model. In order of importance, these three major determinants of situational favorableness are: (1) interpersonal relations between the leader and the follower; especially important here is the followers' acceptance of the leader; (2) the structure of the task and the degree to which the group's task is clear cut and unambiguous, with verifiable goals and specified procedures for reaching the goal; and (3) the leader's formal authority of his position, that is, his ability to reward or punish groups members (Fiedler, 1967).

Characteristics of subordinates and the environment

House and Dessler (1974) describe two broad classes of situational determinants of leadership behavior: characteristics of subordinates and environmental characteristics. With respect to subordinates' characteristics, leader behavior is acceptable to the extent that subordinates see such behavior as a source of personal satisfaction. Another mediating factor is the subordinates' own perceptions of their abilities to perform to the leader's standards. The higher the degree of perceived ability relative to the task that the leader demands, the less the subordinate will view the leader's directiveness and coaching behavior as acceptable. In these cases the leader who uses directive behavior is more likely to be seen as having excessive control. The environment of the subordinate is also an important factor in mediating leadership behavior. These factors consist of those things not controlled by subordinates but still important to their need satisfaction or their ability to perform effectively. House and Dessler (1974) classify three types of environmental moderators in this way: (1) the subordinate's task, (2) the formal authority system of the organization, and (3) the primary work group in which the subordinate must perform the task.

AUTHORITY

Authority

We are defining authority as the *right* to take actions (Hicks, 1972). We view authority as one of the most integral parts of individual and organizational behavior. We also view authority as complex and as a concept that has little consensus among scholars as to how it ought to be used (Simon, 1957). However, there appears to be some agreement on the major bases of authority.

Authority bases

The two major bases of authority are: (1) *formal or official authority* and (2) *functional or personal authority.* It is important to understand the bases of authority and their relationship to each other and to the power bases of our model. Through such an understanding, nurse leaders will be able to use both power and authority more effectively.

Formal authority

Formal authority is vested in the *position* that a nurse holds. It is sometimes called positional authority. For example, a director of nursing service, because of the role or position conferred by the organization, has implicit in the position a notion of legitimacy or social and ethical approval. The position carries with it the authority to take actions in order to carry out managerial functions. It involves making decisions and being held responsible and accountable for them. Formal authority defines which positions will be superior and which subordinate. In essence, formal or positional authority is a mechanism that enables nurse leaders to direct the work of others. The formal authority base involves both the *authority of legitimacy,* which accounts for subordinates deferring to authority, and the *authority of the position,* which derives from an acknowledged status inherent in the official role or position.

Formal or positional authority is constant. Incumbents may come and go, but positional authority remains. Formal authority carries with it a call of leadership. While a director of nursing service, because of positional authority, can direct and make decisions that affect subordinates, the director must recognize the dependency on the performance of others in order to get the job done. Without this recognition, subordinates can undermine *positional* authority and weaken the formal authority base.

Functional authority

Functional authority is sometimes known as *personal authority*. The sources of functional authority are derived from the *personal* qualifications of the nurse leader, particularly professional competence, experience, technical expertise, knowledge of managerial functions and human relations, and an understanding and use of *power*. Functional or personal authority can be a strong base of authority and can enable a person who may not have positional authority to wield a great deal of influence on others, as described in Chapters 4 and 7. If nurse leaders have professional, technical, and personal knowledge and skills, they will find that others will accept the authority and power. Nurse leaders who have a record of (1) being effective problem solvers and decision makers, (2) taking actions based on facts and relevant information, (3) using effective channels of communication, (4) having a high degree of creativity, (5) working with others through effective managerial and human relations processes, and (6) recognizing the need for personal and professional growth of all members in the organization will indeed have both *personal authority* and *personal power* (Bailey, 1974).

As pointed out earlier, individuals who operate from positional power only may come and go, but nurse leaders who may not have positional power but personal and professional competence of the highest order will remain in an organization because of a high level of performance and the value of the nurse leader to the organization.

A word about authority

Our final point is that both formal authority (positional) and functional authority (personal) are needed to meet the goals of the individual and the goals of the organization.

ACCOUNTABILITY AND RESPONSIBILITY

Accountability

We consider accountability and responsibility to be one of the most important components of the model. Without accountability and responsibility the person is not a *leader*, but is a *user* of people. A dean of a school of nursing or a director of nursing service must be accountable for reaching the goals of the school or patient care services. This means being personally responsible not only for task accomplishment but also for the growth and development of the subordinates who have been willing to perform the tasks. Subordinates need to feel satisfied and to be rewarded for attaining goals.

The public interest

The nurse leader is in a very central position in health care delivery systems. For this reason the nurse leader should be accountable for seeing that nursing functions are performed in the public interest. It is not enough to be accountable for performance of tasks that will benefit nursing as a profession. This indeed is important, but nurses are in a unique position to be consumer advocates and to see that health care delivery is in the interest of those who would seek it—that is, the public who needs it and pays for it. To date nurses have had the enviable position of being in the profession in order to benefit others. They have not been in the profession only for monetary rewards. Nurses have been self sacrificing and have accepted social responsibilities for the public welfare. This is one of their strongest bases of power and certainly the basis of their leadership in bringing about needed change.

A word about responsibility

Responsibility is not new to nurses. Indeed, nurses tend to take responsibility for tasks and to be accountable for them. Responsibility is an integral part of our model as it sensitizes nurses to the critical importance of maintaining professional accountability for their actions. If nurses are to be professional, they must be accountable for errors as well as for professional accomplishment. Accountability is a sense of overriding concern for the entire process. Responsibility is the sense of duty that comes with performing specific tasks. Taking responsibility is the first step in gaining authority, as we will discuss later. Responsibility is one of the most critical areas in the model in that true leadership cannot emerge unless the leader takes full and total responsibility and is accountable for any progress or regression.

LEADERSHIP ACTIONS
Managerial functions and human relations

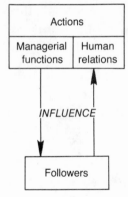

Leadership behavior consists of two major dimensions: managerial functions or task-oriented, formal behavior, and human relations or person-oriented behavior. Others have called the managerial functions of leader behavior the strategic functions of leadership (House and Dessler, 1974). Human relations dimensions of leadership behavior focus on using motivational forces within subordinates in order to get them to take actions. Part two deals with actions and how to develop leadership behavior. Human relations behaviors, taken without managerial functions, do not lead to task accomplishment; nor is the reverse true. In order to have leadership it is necessary to be concerned with both the managerial aspects, that is, the task-oriented types of things as well as the human relations variables. In other words, a leader must be both a manager and a concerned, considerate person. If both of these dimensions are found in a person's actions, along with the previously discussed factors such as strong power bases, favorable situational determinants, authority for action, and a sense of accountability for the process, then a group of subordinates or followers is likely to be willing to follow the desired directions of the leader.

The art of influence

Acceptance on the part of followers is known as influence. The degree of acceptability of a leader's behavior determines the degree of influence a person will have on followers and on a process. We cannot emphasize too strongly that we believe leadership is a relationship, a relationship not only between people, but between people and their environment.

OUTPUTS AS RESULTS
Goal/task accomplishment

| Goal/task accomplishment |

The model strongly points to the fact that actions should produce two kinds of results: (1) goal/task accomplishment, and (2) human outputs. In other words the goals of the individual should be met as well as the goals of the organization.

Task functions should be performed at a high level in order to reach organizational goals.

Human outputs

| Motivation Performance Satisfaction Growth |

The nurse leader must be concerned with human outputs, and indeed there must be positive human outputs if there is to be a continuance of leadership. People who have elected to follow must be positively motivated, maintain high performance, derive satisfaction from performance under the leader's direction, and continue to develop and grow both personally and professionally.

A word about leadership

A brief overview of the Power/Authority/Influence Model has been presented as a framework for nurse leaders who want to use nurse power effectively. The major keys to nursing leadership are: (1) *ability* of nurse leaders to know their *strengths* and develop them to the utmost, (2) *willingness* to use their *energy* in positive ways to enable them to maintain a high level of performance, and (3) *actions* taken by leaders that yield results and for which they are responsible and accountable. A turbulent, unstable world and changing environment mandate that nurse leaders must *lead*.

REFERENCES

Bailey, J. T.: The critical incident technique in identifying behavioral criteria of professional nursing effectiveness, Nursing Resarch **5**(5):52-64, 1956.

Bailey, J. T.: Leadership in nursing, Echo—Nursing Change and Challenge **4**(2):6, 1974.

Bailey, J. T., and Claus, K. E.: Decision making in nursing: Tools for change, St. Louis, 1975, The C. V. Mosby Co.

Bales, R. F., and Slater, P. E.: Role differentiation in small decision making groups. In Parsons, T., and Bales, R. F., editors: Family, socialization and the interaction process, New York, 1955, The Free Press.

Barnard, C. I.: The functions of the executive, Cambridge, Mass., 1938, Harvard University Press.

Benne, K. D., and Sheats, P.: Functional roles and group members, Journal of Social Issues **4**:41-49, 1948.

Bowers, D. G., and Seashore, S. E.: Predicting organizational effectiveness with a four-factor theory of leadership, Administrative Science Quarterly **11**:238-263, 1966.

Clark, P., and Wilson, J. Q.: Incentive systems, Administrative Science Quarterly **6**:129-166, 1961.

Craig, J. H., and Craig, M.: Synergic power: beyond domination and permissiveness, Berkeley, Calif., 1974, Proactive Press.

Dornbusch, S. M., and Scott, W. R.: Evaluation and the exercise of authority, San Francisco, 1975, Jossey-Bass.

Fiedler, F. E.: A theory of leadership effectiveness, New York, 1967, McGraw-Hill, Inc.

Fleishman, E. A.: Twenty years of consideration and structure. In Fleishman, E. A., and Hunt, J. G., editors: Current developments in the study of leadership, Carbondale, Ill., 1973, Southern Illinois University Press.

Hicks, H. G.: The management of organizations: A systems and human resources approach, ed. 2, New York, 1972, McGraw-Hill, Inc.

House, R. J., and Dessler, G.: The path-goal theory of leadership: Some post hoc and a priori tests. In Hunt, J. G., and Larson, L. L., editors: Contingency approaches to leadership, Carbondale, Ill., 1974, Southern Illinois University Press.

Katz, D., and Kahn, R. L.: The social psychology of organizations, New York, 1966, John Wiley & Sons, Inc.

Lewin, K., Lippitt, R., and White, R. K.: Patterns of aggressive behavior in experimentally created social climates, Journal of Social Psychology **10:**271-299, 1939.

Lippitt, R., and White, R. K.: The social climate of children's groups. In Baker, R. G., Kounin, J. S., and Wright, H. F., editors: Child behavior and development, New York, 1943, McGraw-Hill, Inc.

Marram, G. D.: Visibility of work and the evaluation process: Evaluation and authority for nurses in hospitals and teachers in open and closed schools, unpublished doctoral dissertation, Stanford, Calif., 1971, Stanford University School of Education.

Meyers, M. S.: Every employee a manager: More meaningful work through job enrichment, New York, 1970, McGraw-Hill, Inc.

Parsons, T.: Structure and process in modern societies, New York, 1960, The Free Press.

Scott, W. R.: Professional employees in a bureaucratic structure: Social work. In Etzioni, A., editor: The semi-professions and their organization, New York, 1969, The Free Press.

Scott, W. R.: Reactions to supervision in a heteronomous professional organization, Administrative Science Quarterly **10:**65-81, 1965.

Selznick, P.: TVA and the grass roots, Berkeley, 1949, University of California Press.

Simon, H. A.: Administrative behavior, New York, 1957, Macmillan, Inc.

Simon, H. A.: On the concept of organizational goal, Administrative Science Quarterly **9:**1-22, 1964.

Shartle, C. L., and Stogdill, R. M.: Studies in naval leadership, Columbus, 1952, Ohio State University Research Foundation.

Stogdill, R. M.: Handbook of leadership, New York, 1974, The Free Press.

The only limits of power are the bounds of belief.

H. WILSON

2 POWER

THE NATURE OF POWER

The purpose of this chapter is to present the reader with useful concepts of what power is all about. Although for too long nurses have appeared to feel powerless or have viewed power in negative ways, our goal is to dispel some of these beliefs. We view power and the effective uses of power as vital and positive forces in moving individuals toward the attainment of both individual and organizational goals in the delivery of health care services.

Definitions of power

Power as control over dependent persons. Traditional theorists define power as a relationship between two or more people in which one person is dependent on another. This dependency relationship allows the stronger person to exercise control over the dependent person. Theorists such as Weber (1947), Dahl (1957), and Emerson (1962) have a different view. They see power as an element of a social relationship and not as an attribute of a person. They do not subscribe to the idea that a given individual has power within himself. Rather, they view power in terms of the persons who are dependent and the situations in which the dependency relationship occurs.

Power as will to control. Power has also been defined as the ability and willingness of one person to sanction another by manipulating rewards and punishments that are important to the other (Dornbusch and Scott, 1975). Although this definition is in the line with traditional power theories, it does point out an aspect of power that is critical for nurse leaders. Power is seen as the capacity, ability, intention, or willingness to exercise some type of control over others. Power has been defined as: "any force that results in behavior that would not have occurred if the force had not been present" (Mechanic, 1962, p. 351). Power is more than a relationship or a dependency of one person on another and more than organizational authority. Power is derived from control—control over self first, then control over information, persons, and instrumentalities.

Power as collaboration. A newer conception of power is called *synergic power* (Craig and Craig, 1974). Synergy is the bringing together of dissimilar elements to create a new and effective agent for action. Synergism is cooperative action of independent persons in which the total effect of the collective action is greater than the sum of the effects of each action taken separately. A synergistic leader has a capacity to increase the satisfactions of all participants by purposefully generating increased energy and creativity to "co-create a more rewarding present and future" (Craig and Craig, 1974, p. 62).

Power as a continuum. Power is also seen as a continuum with two extreme types: synergic or group-oriented power on one side versus directive or traditional "carrot and stick" power on the other side. Craig and Craig (1974) defined power in general as "the capacity of an initiator to increase his satisfactions by intentionally affecting the behavior of one or more responders" (p. 45). In this view power is seen as an attempt to affect the behavior of others, no matter how indirectly or subtly the initiator exercises the power. The initiator is the power wielder; the responder, the object of power use. Craig and Craig maintain that directive power is primarily used by individuals to increase their own satisfaction and to advance their own satisfactions through attempts to shape the behavior of others. They imply that the power wielder seeks to control others and view directive power as a negative force.

Synergic power, on the other hand, is discussed in light of co-creation and collaboration and derives from "a general attitude of valuing and cherishing other people" (Craig and Craig, 1974, p. 60).

The dichotomy between synergic power and directive power appears to be too simplistic for the realities nurses face in the delivery of care. When life and death issues and the health and well being of others underlie decision making, there must be room for the use of positive directive power as well as collaborative effort. Some of the most effective "synergic leaders" of our times, such as Gandhi or Martin Luther King, have used directive power positively. These leaders decided what would be "good" for their followers and worked out strategies and tactics for using followers to attain shared goals (Craig and Craig, 1974, p. 66).

If nurse leaders are to be effective in improving health care delivery, they must see power as a positive force that can be used to benefit others. To effectively use power, they must know what it is and the various forms it might take.

POWER AS STRENGTH, ENERGY, AND ACTION

We define power as the ability and willingness to affect the behavior of others. The *ability* is based on strength: a powerful person is a strong person who has a self concept based on realistic awareness of his own strengths and weaknesses. The *willingness* is based on positive energy: a powerful person radiates energy, uses his own potential fully, and can see the strengths (and weaknesses) in others. Power is also based on *results,* on performance: a powerful person does indeed affect the behavior of others and the effects can be observed and felt.

The relationship of strength, energy, and action can be seen as a pyramidal force, with *strength* (the ability) as one of the elements supporting *energy* (the willingness to use the ability), which in turn supports the action itself (Fig. 2). Some years ago the hero of a well known television western series became famous with the slogan of his power: "Have gun, will travel." This phrase capsulizes the concept of power as a composite of strength, energy, and action.

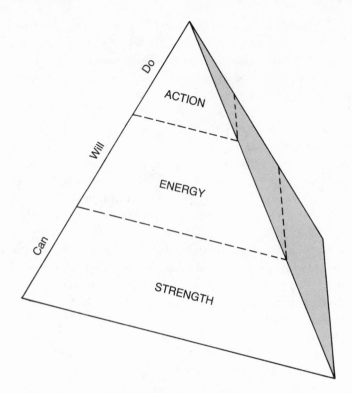

Fig. 2. The power pyramid.

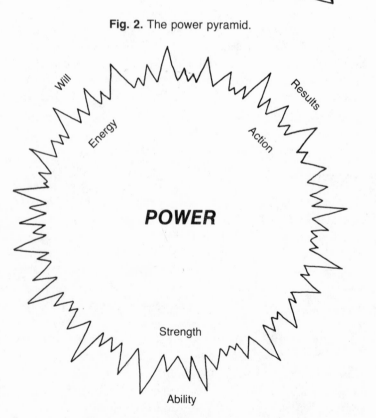

Fig. 3. The tripartite nature of power.

Our definition is neutral. It (1) allows for the positive or negative use of power; (2) provides for the use of different types of power; (3) enables power to be used by persons, groups, or organizations; (4) is not tied to dependency relationships; and (5) focuses on results and use. Fig. 3 shows the relation of the elements of power.

THE TRIPARTITE NATURE OF POWER

Power is composed of three basic elements that work in conjunction with one another. Without any one of these basic critical mass elements, true power is not possible. The three basic elements of power are *strength, energy,* and *action.* Ability and capacity derive from strength. Willingness derives from energy. The changes in performance of other people derive from both action and movement.

Strength. Strength is based on a strong self concept. A person who is strong has awareness of his skills and abilities that are useful to himself and to others. Strength is the basis for ability and the capacity for action, as noted in Fig. 2. Without strength a person is unable to be powerful.

Strength is also based on an awareness of reality. However, with strength there is also weakness. The strong person knows what his limitations are and seeks either to improve these weaknesses or to strategize so that the weaknesses do not become the primary focus of attention. Where there are peaks, there must be valleys. Strength needs to be balanced with weakness. But strength does not dwell on weakness; it dwells on the positive, the peaks of skills.

The strong person has the energy and the ability to spend an inordinate amount of time on difficult tasks and to benefit from long arduous work.

Energy. A strong person, a powerful person, has abundant energy. The person who uses power or strives to be a powerful person has "good vibrations" and others can detect the positive energy that he radiates. The positive energy of one person can be transmitted to others and can influence the state of their own energy level. For example, a head nurse who arrives in the morning and appears to be radiant and full of vitality can transmit this energy to the night nurse during report even though the night nurse might have felt exhausted. A powerful person transmits mental, physical, and even metaphysical or psychological energy. This person can not only direct his own activities but also influence the activities of others.

Energy indeed is the basis for *will.* In the delivery of health care we are concerned about the will to live, the will to get well. How many patients who do not have the energy for life have the will to live? We might also ask how many patients who have been diagnosed as terminal have defied the medical diagnosis and survived? There is ample evidence of the patients' will to live in the medical literature (Oyle, 1975).

Power should be used effectively, consistently, and constantly. The use of electrical energy is an example of the irregular use patterns that create difficulties for utility companies that must maintain a constant supply of energy. In order to keep power available, it is necessary to use it in a consistent manner. Otherwise, there is waste and loss of power.

Action. The powerful person acts. The powerful person acts to release motivational forces *within* others through involving them in goal setting procedures, through giving positive feedback, and through rewards. The powerful person takes action in problem solving and decision making. The powerful person acts in regard to his own personal development. He grows both personally and professionally. A powerful person grows in many dimensions: enhancing power, acquiring new authority, developing new skills, meeting new people, making new alliances, and striving for self control. The powerful person deals in results. Power can be measured by results. When people are motivated to use the positive forces of power within themselves, one may observe differences in their behavior. A powerful person uses energy and strength to get things done and encourages and rewards cooperation and collaboration. Others want to do things for a powerful person.

Power, or the movement of power, is shown in Fig. 4. Strength and energy allow *ability* and *will* to interact in such a way as to affect the performance of others. The tripartite nature of power is shown in Fig. 4 where the inner central critical mass or core of power is strength, energy, and action. The outer core or use of power is the result of ability, will, and observable results.

Historically, we can find evidence of leaders who capitalized on a person's strengths even though they may have presented weaknesses. For example, Lincoln used the strength of Grant as a general even though people complained about his weakness, which was imbibing liquor. When questioned about his selection of Grant as Union Commander, Lincoln commented that if he knew Grant's brand of liquor he would send a barrel of it to all the other generals. Lee, who was enraged because one of his generals had completely upset his own plans, evinced this same ability to look at the positive aspects of behavior. When asked why he did not replace the man, he turned in astonishment and said, "Why, that is an absurd question! The man performs." Drucker also confirms the importance of recognizing both strengths and weaknesses in his belief that for managers to get strength they have to put up with weakness (Drucker, 1974).

There have been few great commanders in history who were not self centered, conceited, and full of admiration for themselves. (The reverse does not, of course, hold: there have been many generals who were convinced of their own greatness, but who have not gone down in history as great commanders.) Similarly, the politician who does not want to be president is not likely to be remembered as a statesman. He or she will at best be a useful—perhaps a highly

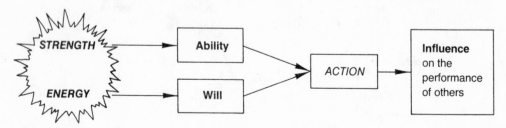

Fig. 4. Power: the ability and will to affect others' performance.

useful—journeyman. To be more requires a person who is self centered and confident enough to believe that the world—or at least the nation—really needs him and depends on his getting into power.

> If the need is for the ability to command in a perilous situation, one has to accept a Disraeli or Franklin D. Roosevelt and not worry too much about their lack of humility. There are indeed no great men to their valets. But the laugh is on the valet. He sees, inevitably, all the traits that are not relevant, all the traits that have nothing to do with the specific task for which a man has been called on the stage of history (Drucker, 1967, p. 87).

POWER VERSUS INFLUENCE

Power is the source of influence, whereas influence is the result of the proper use of power. Some scholars believe that getting people to behave in certain ways is equivalent to influence. Moreover, they contend that the degree of influence depends on the ability to control the rewards and punishments. This view of influence derives from the definition of power as the actual ability to control. Bennis and others (1958) have argued that control is based in part on a subordinate's acceptance of a leader's *right* to control rewards and punishments meted out to him.

Influence, then, is based on the reward systems that are controlled by the person who has power. Influence is therefore a result of manipulation of persons, information, and instrumentalities.*

We maintain that ascendancy is part of power and that influence indeed involves personal ascendancy or the ascendancy of certain values and viewpoints over others. This view is also suggested by Craig and Craig (1974).

POWER VERSUS AUTHORITY

Power has been defined as energy and strength and action. Authority, on the other hand, is an official or legitimatized right to use a given amount or type of power. Bennis and others (1958) have defined authority as the legitimatized right to means and control, whereas power is seen as the actual control of the means-end relationship. Authority is based on the right of a certain person to make people do things that they may not wish to do. Authority systems emerge out of power relations. Authority, which will be discussed in more depth later, can be either delegated or acquired. Most social scientists define authority as legitimate power.

THE CONCEPT OF LEGITIMACY

Legitimacy involves some kind of standard. It is a psychological concept that relates to a subordinate's internalized attitude toward a person's right to exercise power over him. As French and Raven (1959, p. 159) have stated: "In all cases, the notion of legitimacy involves some sort of code or standard, accepted by the individual by virtue of which the external agent can exercise his power." Legitimacy involves two basic questions: (1) whether or not the person has the *right* to

---

*Instrumentalities are defined as the physical plant of an organization, its resources, equipment, machines, money, humans, and materiel.

exercise the power over another person by virtue of his position, and (2) whether that person *should* have the right to exercise power over others. Legitimacy involves official authorization as well as the internalized values of the recipient of power use. It also involves the internalized value or acceptability of the use of power among peers or other observer groups. "Power is legitimate to the extent that there exist social norms which govern the exercise of power and the response to it" (Dornbusch and Scott, 1975, p. 56). Legitimate power is perceived as authority that can be regulated by social and cultural norms. However, power by itself is not subject to normative regulation. That is, with authority both the power wielder and the recipient are to some degree constrained and supported by the norm behavior expectations of the group. But this is not necessarily true with raw power.

Authorized power is equivalent to authority. Its base is the belief held by others that a certain person should have a certain type of power over another. The stabilized patterns on which the use of power is based can be either formal or informal. Formal authorized power usually resides in positions in organizations. These positions may have developed historically through custom or delegation. Informal authority is based on the personal characteristics or competencies of an individual. Informal authority is derived directly from one's personal power base. Power relations sometimes develop into authority because the power wielder makes use of positive reinforcement to encourage given behavior on the part of subordinates. When reinforcement is applied on a consistent basis, subordinates have expectations that make legitimate the use of that authority.

Endorsed power is based on colleagues' and subordinates' beliefs about a person's right to have power over others. Such power may or may not be authorized. By the same token authorized power may not be endorsed by the people who are subject to its use.

Social norms are necessary in order to support a distribution of power even in an informal group. Although power is usually not transformed into authority in an informal group, special structural arrangements may be necessary to enable the group to work together, rather than be torn apart by struggles for status and power. Social norms that distribute power enable leaders to lead and followers to accept leadership without disrupting group cohesion (Dornbusch and Scott, 1975). Formal organizations attempt to cultivate and establish belief in their legitimacy (Weber, 1947). Most organizations depend more on consent than on force to accomplish their objectives according to Caplow (1964). Authority then is sanctioned power that is institutionalized. Authority not only supports the power wielder but also constrains him. Authorized and endorsed power may be totally distinct. Authority that is endorsed but unauthorized is exemplified by what happened in prisoner of war concentration camps. When informal leaders in the POW camp emerged, they were immediately removed upon being detected, whereas authorized guards in the camp had endorsed authority but were not recognized by the norms of the captive groups.

In the nursing situation a head nurse may have the endorsed authority to manage a ward, but another nurse who is viewed as more competent may actually manage the unit through informal authority.

FACTORS AFFECTING POWER

There are several factors that affect the use and the character of power. Each of these will be discussed as they relate to nursing and the use of power in nursing situations.

Increased specialization and organizational growth

Increased specialization and new demands in the delivery of health care services have demanded a high level of expertise among nurse practitioners. Nurses with such expertise maintain power because patients, physicians, and other members of the health care team are dependent on them for these nursing skills. For example, intensive care nurses with a high level of expertise may have power over a new intern who does not possess the skill base in life saving measures that the nurse has acquired. The nurse should bear in mind, however, that power that stems from expertise is tenuous at best unless that expertise is difficult to replace.

One of the main sources of control and power emanates from information and research. Top managers in the organization depend on information and facts to guide them in the decision making process. This is especially true in health care delivery settings where legal and legislative constraints are critical. The nurse with a high level of expertise has the potential and power either to withhold or provide information to those in positions of authority.

Willingness to exert effort

The extent to which members of a group exercise power depends in large part on their willingness to expend effort in areas where persons of rank in the organization are reluctant to participate. Generally there is a direct relationship between the amount of effort a person is willing to exert in an area and the power he can command. For example, a secretary on a busy unit often makes decisions that are beyond the official power that resides in her position. Such practices can lead to sanctions against the head nurse. If the power to make these decisions is removed from the jurisdiction of the secretary, then it is done at a cost. That is, persons of high position in the organization will have to allocate more time and effort to decisions in these matters. If responsibilities are delegated, a certain amount of power must accompany the responsibility.

The acceptance of responsibility is the first step in acquiring authority. The need for flexibility in following rules with regard to delegation of authority and acceptance of responsibility necessitates a certain dependence on lower level staff. Unless higher ranking participants in an organization are willing to devote more time to a task, lower participants will likely obtain power relevant to that task.

In hospital settings physicians who are authorized to accomplish certain tasks often delegate certain tasks to nurses or indeed allow nurses to take the responsibility for doing these tasks even though they do not have the authority.

A word about work

In today's society there is a scarcity of people who really love the work they do. Artisans are no longer with us. Many of us work because of necessity. It would be interesting to know how many nurses arrive home from work and express feelings about how enjoyable their day has been. What is likely to happen if such a feeling of enjoyment is expressed? Usually people are more likely to listen and express sympathy to complaints about fatigue and all the things that went wrong. A person who enjoys the job is suspected of not working hard enough. Therefore most people find it more profitable to complain. But people who have a purpose beyond monetary gain, who enjoy the challenges of their work, and who are interested in power usually work hard, are productive, and enjoy what they are doing. This view is supported by Ringer who described his own experience in learning to be a powerful person:

> I learned that striving for a positive mental attitude will get you nowhere unless you have the ammunition to back it up. You develop a positive mental attitude by being prepared, by understanding the realities of what it takes to succeed, and by being good at the necessary techniques. It's a cycle: the more prepared a person is, the more positive his attitude, and, therefore, the better his chances of succeeding (Ringer, 1974, p. 6).

In order for power to grow and be useful, it must be used; it cannot be allowed to lie dormant.

A word about weakness

Friedenberg (1965) refers to Lord Acton's well known phrase: "Power tends to corrupt and absolute power corrupts absolutely." This might be paraphrased as "All weakness corrupts, and impotence corrupts absolutely." Not to reach for power is to limit potential, to limit one's potential for awareness and development of self-esteem. It limits one's consciousness, one's ability to use sources of energy and power and to obtain the abundant life. Often people tend to appear weak to avoid the responsibility for using power effectively.

USING POWER

"Unless power is used effectively, it is lost," is not an empty shibboleth. The overall purpose of power is to encourage cooperation and collaboration in accomplishing a certain task. Too often power is used for all the wrong reasons: (1) domination, in order to get other people to do things; (2) manipulation, which can often be ideological; and (3) aggressive persuasion.

Attractive personal attributes

It has been corroborated by research that people who are viewed as attractive are more likely to have access to persons and, therefore, are more likely to succeed in promoting various causes than persons who are viewed as unattractive. Dependence is the key to the power of this attractiveness or charisma, especially in an organization where several different levels of personnel depend on each other for services. Generally the more personable and attractive a person is, the more influence, control, and power that person will be able to exert over others.

Social space

Location and position in social space are important factors that influence the use of power. This has been studied in detail by Korda (1975) who suggests that the actual position and arrangement of desks and chairs may be used to gain authority and power. For example, if a person wishes to gain maximum power, he will position himself in a comfortable chair behind his desk leaving himself plenty of room and will position a visitor in a chair in front of him in a tightly closed arrangement so that the visitor has a minimum amount of psychological space or comfort.

The concept of centrality within an organization is also related to power. The more central a person is in an organization or a communication network, the greater is his access to persons, information, instrumentalities, and therefore the greater his potential power over others. A clear example is the dean's or director's secretary who has great centrality within an organization, access to information, and control in making appointments and scheduling events. She has no formal authority but considerable power.

Coalitions

Within complex systems such as hospitals or other health care systems there are a number of professional and paraprofessional groups who must work together—administrators, medical personnel, nurses, attendants of various levels, maintenance personnel, laboratory personnel, nutrition specialists, psychologists, social workers, and a cadre of other people who perform health care services. Often tasks within an organization become spheres of influence whereby a certain group will control activities related to the set of functions that they perform. Unions and trade associations have become an integral part of hospital life. Other coalitions also form such as ongoing special professional seminar groups that are somewhat formal. They can also be informal such as developing acquaintances and getting to know people who can help. For example, knowing the dispenser in the pharmacy or knowing the head of housekeeping services may mean, because of a personal power base and influence on a personal level, that the person will do special favors for the nurse.

Rules and regulations

In complex power structures or organizations with complex bureaucracies, such as government groupings, the norms of the organization can often be used to thwart attempted change. For example, in a study of control over organizational policy by staff, Scheff (1961) found that attempts of a large state mental hospital to change policies were frustrated by ward attendants and nurses. Ward physicians were the focal point of staff control over the administration. Physicians were generally unprepared for administrative tasks, held their positions for short periods of time, and were overassigned to duties. Staff, on the other hand, were more familiar with established rules and regulations and had been on the job for many years. In addition, nurses frequently assumed responsibilities legally assigned to ward physicians in order to help the physicians accomplish their tasks. As a result, physicians were dependent upon nursing staff and subject to considerable social control. By using four major control techniques (withholding information, manipulation of patients, disobedience, and withholding cooperation), nurses were able to control not only the ward physicians but also major policies of the entire organization. Similarly, elected officials often depend on the bureaucrat who knows the rules and regulations of the organization and has a vested interest in seeing that certain things continue as they are. A newly elected president of an organization may have the best intentions of making changes, but may need years to dislodge the inertia that has developed prior to his arrival. Position power can be gained by persons with tenure who can be neither fired nor moved to other positions.

POWER AS A MOTIVATOR

In studies of managers over several years McClelland discovered that an effective manager is a person who needs power and likes to use it (McClelland and Burnham, 1976). The need for power was found to be a more important variable than the need for achievement. The need for power and influencing others, however, must be disciplined, controlled, and directed toward the benefit of the institution as a whole and not toward the manager's personal aggrandizement. Other findings indicated that a manager's need for power must be greater than his need to be liked by other people, that the manager needs to help subordinates feel strong and responsible, and that he reward subordinates for good performance.

SUMMARY

Power is presented as a positive force, encompassing an individual's strength, energy, and action. Strength provides nurses with ability. But more is needed in this pyramid of power. There must be *willingness* and *energy* to take *actions* if one is to influence others. In order to develop a positive mental set toward using power effectively, nurses need to say, "I *can* do it" and "I *will* do it" and then *do* it!

REFERENCES

Bennis, W. G., and others: Authority, power and the ability to influence, Human Relations **11**:143-155, 1958.

Caplow, T.: Principles of organization, New York, 1964, Harcourt Brace Jovanovich, Inc.

Craig, J. H., and Craig, M.: Synergic power: Beyond domination and permissiveness, Berkeley, Calif., 1974, Proactive Press.

Dahl, R. A.: The concept of power, Behavioral Science **2**:201-215, 1957.

Dornbusch, S. M., and Scott, W. R.: Evaluation and the exercise of authority, San Francisco, 1975, Jossey-Bass, Inc., Publishers.

Drucker, P. F.: The effective executive, New York, 1967, Harper & Row, Publishers.

Drucker, P. F.: Management, New York, 1974, Harper & Row, Publishers.

Emerson, R. M.: Power-dependence relations, American Sociological Review **27**:31-41, 1962.

French, J. P. R., Jr., and Raven, B.: The bases of social power. In Cartwright, D., editor: Studies in social power, Ann Arbor, 1959, The University of Michigan Press.

Friedenberg, E. Z.: Coming of age in America, New York, 1965, Random House, Inc.

Korda, M.: Power: How to get, how to use it! New York, 1975 Random House, Inc.

McClelland, D., and Burnham, D.: Power is the great motivator, Harvard Business Review **54**(2):100-110, 1976.

Mechanic, D.: Sources of power of lower participants in complex organizations, Administrative Science Quarterly **7**:349-362, 1962.

Oyle, I.: The healing mind, Millbrae, Calif., 1974, Celestial Arts.

Ringer, R. J.: Winning through intimidation, Los Angeles, 1974, Los Angeles Book Publishers.

Weber, M.: The theory of social and economic organization, Henderson, A. M., and Parsons, T., translators, Parsons, T., editor, New York, 1947, The Free Press.

SUGGESTED READINGS

Bickman, L.: The social power of a uniform, Journal of Applied Social Psychology 4(1):47-61, 1974.

Castenada, C.: Tales of power, New York, 1974, Simon & Schuster, Inc.

Clark, K. B.: Pathos of power, New York, 1974, Harper & Row, Inc.

de Bono, E.: PO: A device for successful thinking, New York, 1972, Simon & Schuster, Inc.

de Bono, E.: Lateral thinking for management: A handbook for creativity, New York, 1971, American Management Association.

Galloway, B. T.: The nurse as a professional manager, Hospitals 48:89, 1974.

Heimann, C. G.: Four theories of leadership, Journal of Nursing Administration 6(5):18-28, 1976.

Kalisch, B. J., and Kalisch, P. A.: Is the history of nursing alive and well? Nursing Outlook 24:362-366, 1976.

Mahoney, M. J., and Thoresen, C. E.: Self-control:

Power to the person, Monterey, Calif., 1974, Brooks/Cole Publishing Co.

Miller, J. P., and Fry, L. J.: Social relations in organizations: Further evidence for the Weberian model, Social Forces 51:305-19, 1973.

Mulder, M.: Power equalization through participation? Administrative Science Quarterly 16(1):31-39, 1971.

Peter, L. J., and Hull, R.: The Peter principle, New York, 1970, Bantam Books, Inc.

Polk, B. B.: Male power and the women's movement, Journal of Applied Behavioral Science 10:415-431, 1974.

Reiff, R.: The control of knowledge: The power of the helping professions, Journal of Applied Behavioral Science 10:451-461, 1974.

Sampson, R. V.: The psychology of power, New York, 1965, Pantheon Books, Inc.

Scheff, T. J.: Control over policy by attendants in a mental hospital, Journal of Health and Human Behavior 2(2): 93-105, 1961.

Stevens, B. J.: ANA's standards for nursing services: How do they measure up? Journal of Nursing Administration 6(4):29-31, 1976.

Teulings, A. W. M., Jansen, L. O. O., and Verhoeven, W. G.: Growth, power structure and leadership functions in the hospital organization, British Journal of Sociology 24:490-505, 1973.

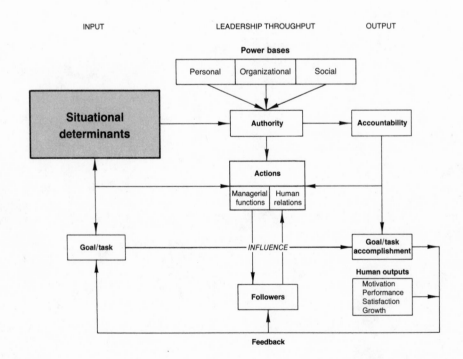

INPUT   LEADERSHIP THROUGHPUT   OUTPUT

Power bases

Personal	Organizational	Social

Situational determinants

Authority

Accountability

Actions

Managerial functions	Human relations

Goal/task

INFLUENCE

Goal/task accomplishment

Human outputs

Motivation
Performance
Satisfaction
Growth

Followers

Feedback

You gotta know the territory.
MUSIC MAN

3 SITUATIONAL DETERMINANTS OF NURSING LEADERSHIP

THE NATURE OF SITUATIONAL DETERMINANTS

A closer examination of the Power/Authority/Influence Leadership Model indicates that the nature of the situation determines to a large extent the sources of *power* available to the nurse leader, and thus the leader's actions.

Determinants of the situation are: (1) the external environment—the social milieu; (2) the nature and behavioral characteristics of the leader and the group members—the *people;* and (3) the internal environment—the purposes, goals, tasks, structure, policies, and procedures of the organization.

THE EXTERNAL ENVIRONMENT

Nurse leaders should become aware of environmental factors and problems beyond their own health care organizations. They must broaden their perspective and develop an awareness of the larger social environment in which they find themselves and understand how external forces have impact on health organizations, health members, and health consumers. A wide variety of external forces exert influence, both directly and indirectly: (1) economic, (2) sociocultural, (3) ecological, (4) technical-scientific, (5) religious-philosophical, and (6) legal-political. It is beyond the scope of this book to discuss each of these forces in detail. Rather, it is our intent to bring to the attention of nurse leaders forces in the larger society that may serve as either constraints or resources in influencing the delivery of health care. For example, organizations in the space industry might be heavily oriented toward technical-scientific factors in the external environment, whereas in health care systems, the economic factors, particularly inflation, are having a tremendous impact. This is not to say that other factors in the external environment are unimportant, but to point out that situations vary and that one must be knowledgeable about factors that seem to dominate a situation at a particular time.

FIEDLER'S CONCEPT OF "FAVORABLENESS"

A basic question for nurse leaders relative to understanding the relationship between situational factors and their effect on leadership behavior might be, "To what extent do situational variables determine the *actions* of the leader?" One of the most widely known scholars in the field of leadership contends that the

29

response and actions of leaders to various situations depend primarily on what he has labeled the "favorableness" of the situation (Fiedler, 1967). Three basic elements inherent in Fiedler's concept of favorableness include the following: (1) the degree to which the task to be performed is structured, (2) the amount of power available to the leader through his position, and (3) the quality of the interpersonal relationships between the leader and the subordinates.* It is these factors, more than the personality of the leader or the particular nature of the task, that describe the extent to which situational factors determine the actions of a leader.

PEOPLE AS SITUATIONAL DETERMINANTS

Leadership operates with people and through people. The dependency on people for meeting the goals of an organization is a well-known fact. Indeed people are the foundation of an enterprise and are a precious resource.

Since gaining favorable responses from people in the organization is a major task of leadership, the leader must relate to group members in such a way as to receive positive responses from the membership (Fiedler, 1967). Both leader and followers must be viewed as having: tasks and functions to perform, abilities and capacities to understand each other, determination to grow and work together, and a strong resolve to deal constructively with conflict.

Conflict as a people problem

In an organizational setting people who occupy varied and specialized roles have to interact and depend on each other as mediators of rewards to facilitate the accomplishment of their goals. Evidence suggests that people do derive satisfaction from the exercise of power or control over others (Watson, 1965; Watson and Bromberg, 1965). Despite the use of effective controls, wherever there are people working in proximity, there is bound to be conflict.

Scarcity of resources. A primary reason for conflict in health care organizations is related to the financial constraints and the availability of human resources. In reviewing related research, one notes that the degree of conflict has been operationally defined as the scarcity of resources available to subjects in a situation that involves bargaining (Fischer, 1969). In their work as practitioners or administrators nurses can easily recognize that their time is indeed a resource for which many individuals compete. On a nursing unit where there are often thirty patients and three registered nurses, the nurses' time may be thought sufficient for the maintenance of a satisfactory level of patient care. And in many situations this will be true. It is the *emergency* nature of direct patient care services and the many contingencies that arise that often cause conflict. For example, several interns and physicians may appear on a unit at the same time and require the assistance of a nurse to carry out a patient's treatment; an orderly or aid may request the nurse to help with a difficult patient; and a postoperative patient may go into shock.

In the situations described, the decisions and actions of the nurse will affect the patient, relationships with physicians, and relationship with other members

---

*These three elements are discussed in Chapters 7 and 10.

of the health organization. In other words the goals and needs of the organization, its client population, the work group, and the nurse leader will be profoundly affected by the way in which nurses respond to the demands of conflict and stress.

The situation in health care organizations is made more complex by the transient nature of the patient population. Patients with particular needs and acuity levels are admitted, treated, transferred, and released; residents and interns rotate, and there is a high attrition rate of nurses. Because health care organizations are complex, it may be helpful for nurses to look at decisions they make in relation to satisfying the competing needs of various groups' behavior. Nurses must make agreements to allocate their time according to expected outcomes, and for the support and help they believe they can realistically expect from the competing various groups.

The importance of managerial skills. It must be pointed out that one of the goals of planning and the developing of organizational power is to minimize conflict situations insofar as this is possible. One reason that nurse leaders may need to develop policies is to reduce conflict and to strength their organizational power. When interpersonal conflict comes about in an organization, it is usually because people at some level have failed to coordinate their goals and objectives. The result of this failure is that one person often perceives that what was considered to be a gain has somehow turned out to be gainful for another individual. The hospital situation in particular gives rise to some conflicts of relatively minor importance (disagreements about equitable scheduling) compared to other serious conflicts (the inability to contact a physician when a patient is in cardiac arrest).

Minimizing conflict. Nurse leaders should try to minimize conflicts. They should try to utilize all the power bases—personal, organizational, and interpersonal. When conflict is intense, nurses may find the legitimacy of their status appears less firm and, consequently, this will not encourage positive behaviors.

As Parsons (1963) has observed, all modes of influence require the presence of trust. This trust seems to be related to belief in the credibility of the communication that flows from the power wielder to the person being influenced. Usually under conditions of intense conflict, those involved are inclined to believe that the threats of the other person will indeed be carried out, rather than to believe that the positive promises will be kept. Kite (1964) also reports that people being influenced consider coercion to express more pressure, to be more controlling than the offer of rewards.

Intensity of conflict. A number of other research studies indicate that when conflict is intense, people prefer to use coercion as a form of influence (Goodstadt and Kipnis, 1970; Lindskold and Tedeschi, 1970; MacLean and Tedeschi, 1970; Rothbart, 1968). The level of the intensity of conflict is also a factor in the frequency with which coercion and threats are used. Keeping in mind that the nurses often have to allot their time in what resembles a bargaining situation, we recall the definition of the level of conflict as the degree of scarcity of resources for which bargaining transpires (Fischer, 1969). In practice, the more demands being made on a nurse to be in two places at one time (as so commonly happens in night shifts), the higher the level of conflict. In such situations nurses should expect more attempts at coercion from the people attempting to strike bargains for their time.

Use of coercion. We have explained that it is a goal in most organizations to avoid conflict by anticipating where it might occur but that when conflict is intense the use of coercion may be necessary. However, caution is important regarding the use of coercion in conflict situations. When coercive influence strategies are used, the people involved tend to perceive the conflict as greater because of the use of coercion. A series of classic studies involving bargaining behavior found that when both sides were offering threats, the results hurt the outcome of bargaining (Deutsch and Krauss, 1960). These findings were interpreted as showing that when both sides used threats, the conflict tended to spiral—that is, the conflict became more intense, mutual hostility grew, and the outcomes suffered.

Similar interests. When a relationship or an interaction between two people involves interests that are similar, influence can be expressed in forms that would be impossible when interests are divergent or at odds with each other. For example, a nurse on the evening shift of a small hospital may understand that it is important to follow the physician's order for laboratory service on a blood sample from a newly admitted diabetic. Both the physician and the nurse have the same basic interest. But the nurse may know that, given the hospital's laboratory procedures, it is impossible to have such work done at night. Her personal power may be insufficient to influence the laboratory to change its policy. In this case the nurse could attempt at a later time to use her organizational power to have procedures changed. If she were to succeed, she would improve the level of services available to patients and also enhance her own power both in the eyes of other nurses and other professionals with whom she works. But given the pressures of the situation and the need for a short-term solution, it is more likely that the nurse would (if the physician persisted) telephone the laboratory technician, explain the acute need, and request that the technician help her out of a tight spot and also meet the patient's need. This tactic could solve the immediate problem and would also serve to enhance the physician's respect for the nurse and her *ability* to gain cooperation from other members of the team. In this situation the nurse would be using personal power as stopgap measure. She could also take the next step and exert enough influence on the organization so that laboratory technicians would take their turns and officially be "on call."

Conflicting interests. When conflicting interests occur, a different influence strategy and a different power base may be needed. Consider the case of the patient who needs a gastric lavage. Suppose an intern has never done this procedure. The nurse, experienced in this practice, tells the intern that if he wishes her help she will stand by and assist in any way she can. She may act as the patient's advocate in this situation, holding his hand and instructing him how to breathe to make the procedure less traumatic.

Use of rewards. When the level of conflict is low, it appears that social interactions, including bargaining behavior, are based on rewards. An advantage in the use of rewards as opposed to coercion is the reaction that they inspire. The offer of a reward in a conflict situation or of a promise from a trustworthy source invites the person being influenced to respond by also offering a reward or a promise of positive behavior or cooperation. It has been suggested that the tendency in people to help those who offer to help them is universal (Gouldner, 1960). For the nurse leader bargaining with groups and individuals who are competing for her time and her attention, this may be useful information. If she is known within the unit, department, or the organization to be honest and trustworthy in her communication, then the offer of reward or the promise of help will be the most effective way to deal with conflict situations. Research suggests that when the person with influence offers a reward in a conflict situation, the offer will be effective in getting cooperation. Sometimes, neither the size of the promised reward nor the credibility of the reward is as important as the gesture of reward that invites a return of help (Lindskold and others, 1970; Lindskold and Tedeschi, 1971).

It is apparent, therefore, that social conflicts will be reduced in some way when reward gestures are made and cooperation is offered in return. In a bargaining situation it is minimally fair for both sides to expect to gain something. The nurse should realize that her offer to help others who infringe on her time might inspire them to reciprocate by offering some of their skills or time in cooperation. In fact, there is reason to believe that this may be a positive counterpart of the "conflict spiral" that we referred to earlier. That is, a promise of help will invite immediate cooperation and improve or increase other potential sources of influence. The tactic of threats, on the other hand, typically results in a decrease in cooperation or the desire to accommodate the other party in the bargaining situation. In one series of studies it was noted that given certain conditions, the person in a position of influence would indeed prefer reward power over other influence strategies (Butler and Miller, 1965; Miller and Butler, 1969; Miller, Butler, and McMartin, 1969). When a choice of using strategies of reward or coercive power was available and the element of cooperation in a situation was emphasized, the person with influence preferred to use reward power.

Use of persuasion. In most situations where social influence is to be used, the person with influence probably prefers to use persuasion over any other mode of influence. When influence in the form of persuasion is used, the person who is being persuaded often perceives his compliance as having been caused by factors other than himself (Bem, 1967). But it is also possible, when persuasion is used, for the target person to be convinced that he accommodated for personal or other reasons whether or not it was actually true (Fotheringham, 1966). By logical analysis, the target person can see his choice of action as the rational outcome of some communication from the person in power. The process of rationalization may cause a person to overlook or not admit the importance of some factor other than communication that influenced him to comply.

When the level of conflict is extremely high, persuasion will not be effective. Given the emotional pressure of intense interpersonal conflict, the target person is more likely to interpret attempts at persuasion with suspicion. Any warnings will be seen as extremely threatening. Promises of rewards may be indistinguishable from bribes and false promises. Therefore, the nurse leader must know the degree of conflict that is invested by each side in the bargaining situation before attempting to deal with it by either persuasion or coercive power.

Communication as an action tool

When we discuss influence strategies in Chapter 7, the reader will note that influence is viewed as a result of power and that influence strategies serve to promote effective leader-follower interactions. When leaders share information with groups and communicate the information effectively, the leader is more likely to be perceived by other persons in the groups as a leader or as a person who exerts influence. The same principle holds true for the use of influence in a situation that requires the accommodation of competing interests—the bargaining situation that we have been describing.

A bargaining tool. In terms of the negotiation framework, the nurse leader should remember that communication is a key to the settling of misunderstanding and that it is part of an influence strategy in developing organizational power. Three particularly facilitative functions of communication have been pointed out as applicable in reconciling competing interests in conflict situations (Smith, 1968):

1. To make known one's limits and to discover those of others. This task involves the framing of questions for discovering relevant information and minimizing antagonism. The person doing the probing for information will want to discover the least that the other person is willing to give in as part of the bargain and will want to keep to himself the least concession that he is willing to make.

2. To exercise influence through either reward or coercive power and to be subject to influence from the other person. Since we are describing communication, the process will involve messages coming from both sides. As we should discuss later, two-way communication is preferred because it allows for greater accuracy and satisfaction in developing relationships and in building power bases.

3. To make offers for arrangements to end conflict through solutions that were proposed earlier and not accepted. It is the communication process that allows both parties to express reasons for being unable to make accommodations. In the process of working out these reasons together, both sides reach a new understanding of the obstacles. In this way communication may result in an offer of help, which may in turn provoke a reciprocal response.

Obviously, communication is closely related to the settlement of conflict. As a situational factor the availability of communication will determine the kinds of settlements that can be reached. If opportunities for communication are restricted, it follows that the means of influence available will likewise be limited. In such conditions people tend to depend more on the use of communication than they need to. In an organizational setting this may mean more dependence on memos when face to face contact is impossible or reliance on actions to express attitudes. The problem with tacit communication is that it is susceptible to wide interpretation. Smith (1968) found that limits on communication ultimately affect the settlements reached in conflict situations because settlements had to come from within a narrower range. The fact that a wide range of communication allows for a broader range of settlements indicates that some people have better skills than others in the art of influence and persuasion.

Modes of communicating. The frequency with which a leader influences others is thought to be related to the number of different ways in which that person influences others. The range of modes of influence is related to the leader's applied power. When a leader is limited in modes of influence, the usefulness of any single mode seems to decrease. In other words it appears that more forms of communication assure the leader a better chance at being successful than if the leader uses only one mode—for example, short memos.

Studies show that when leaders attempt to deal with problems with subordinates they do indeed depend on many different types of power bases (Goodstadt and Kipnis, 1970; Kipnis and Cosentino, 1969; Kipnis and Lane, 1962; Kipnis and Vanderveer, 1971). The nurse leader may find many channels of influence available: meetings with the staff and with the hospital administration and hospital board, interactions with physicians and other members of the health care team, informal contacts with other nurses, memberships on committees and in professional organizations, and participation in seminars, community councils, and other public service groups. It is the leader's responsibility to realize that these are not disparate channels but have the potential for reinforcing each other once she knows her own strengths and attempts to seek out opportunities for developing organizational power. A nurse leader may find that she has difficulty getting support from her administrative staff but that she does have the support of nurses at the unit level. For example, a director of nursing service may have complaints from families who have a loved one in an intensive care unit with whom they wish to spend a few minutes. The director may try to do something about the complaint but the head nurse on the unit resists even though the staff nurses are aware of the needs of both the patient and his family. The director should use the channel of communication to discover reasons for the head nurse's resistance. For the director to complain to other staff nurses would in effect only limit her channels of communication and would not resolve the conflict.

Channels of communication are also distinguished by the form in which the communication takes place. Nurses can depend on face to face contact and spoken communication when they want the mutual involvement and immediate feedback available from such an interpersonal exchange. But in some situations the goals of the communicator may be to minimize emotional overtones and personal exchange. Whereas spoken language is free, casual, elliptical, and fluent, written communication is comparatively precise and formal. Some situations require the precision of written forms. Physicians are often criticized by nurses and others for relying on spoken communication when a written directive, with its heightened authority and permanence would be more useful. An order to a laboratory to make an exception to its usual practice to accommodate a pressing need would be extremely effective if it were sent in writing from a physician. The exact nature of the request would be clear and the reasons for the demand would be understood. Instead, a physician will often tell a nurse to tell a person in the laboratory that he wants work done immediately. In this way the burden is on the nurse to make a forceful communication for which she may not have the authority. Nurses might use their organizational power to institute procedures that would require physicians to make such directions more explicit.

Structure of the system. Within formal settings such as organizations the structure of the communication system will also affect the frequency with which influence is attempted. Nurses derive a tremendous advantage from their central location in a complex communication network. Through contact with patients, physicians, colleagues, and a multitude of others, nurses have access to an inordinate amount of information. It is the use of this information that enables nurses to develop organizational power. It has also been suggested that the advantages of centrality encourage self confidence in the person with the information, confidence that attempts at influence will succeed (Tedeschi, Schlenker, and Lindskold, 1972). This sense of confidence reinforces the advantage of the availability of information and enhances the likelihood of the central person's success at using influence.

In an earlier study it was noted that the central position in information networks permits the person to have interaction with the people he chooses and, moreover, increases the feeling of independence and autonomy of that person as he perceives it (Leavitt, 1951). Indeed, the degree of the centrality of a person's position was found to be positively related to another important influence ability: the willingness of that person to work at an optimal level when participating in groups tasks (Shaw, 1964). It is well established that the personal satisfaction of members of a group is directly related to their centrality (Leavitt, 1951; Mulder, 1959; Watson, 1965; Watson and Bromberg, 1965). When people are in a central position, they also perceive themselves as being in favorable position for exercising influence.

Within an organization the control of information is an important source of power. The relation of the central place in a communication network to the opportunity for high status should be clearly understood by nurses because they have a great deal of access to information from many sources. Ultimately, this relation produces an important cycle:

1. Persons in a central position in a communication system are permitted to receive more messages then do peripheral persons and, consequently, send more messages to others than do people without the advantage of centrality (Watson and Bromberg, 1965).
2. The control of varied information, based on centrality in the network, gives a person high status.
3. Persons with high status influence people more than others, partly because they have more opportunities to communicate more widely within the organization.
4. Through influence, persons with high status enhance their own status more than do people with lower status.

INTERNAL ENVIRONMENTAL INFLUENCES
Physical and social arrangements

The physical setting in which interaction takes place determines to a large extent the nature and degree of social influence. These factors may involve problems that limit opportunities for influence. In the university setting, for example, a teacher unable to have a classroom large enough to accommodate all the students who sign up for a course will be able to influence fewer students; the faculty member who must share a small office with three other people will be limited in ability to have satisfactory conferences with students.

In the clinical setting physical factors may include the condition of equipment and whether or not its allocated space makes for maximum efficiency. Other important physical factors in a hospital are cleanliness, the efficiency of architectural design, adequate social space for patients assigned to wards, adequate space in the nurses' station, availability of a lounge for nurses, a quiet room for patients and families, and a conference room for multiple purposes. All these influence the atmosphere of the work group and indirectly at least may limit the influence that a nurse leader may exert. If nurses must compete with physicians for the use of the nursing station, it is difficult for a head nurse to direct ward activities. Physicians sometimes choose the nurses' station as a place for conferences, without realizing what this does to the efficiency of the nursing staff.

In another study several chairs at a round table were kept empty (Ward, 1968). In this seating arrangement, it was found that people who sat opposite the greatest number of other people tended to be the ones who did most talking and, when measures were taken, they were also perceived by others as leaders. The advantages of facing people is another aspect of the advantages of centrality, which has been confirmed by other studies (Howells and Becker, 1962). The flow of information to a central place, in terms of messages and the arrangement of desks in relation to each other, influences the style of language that people use in communicating (Moscovi, 1967). When people sat at desks facing each other, they tended to use normal, colloquial language, even if a screen kept them from seeing each other directly. But people who were at desks that were side by side or back to back showed a tendency to use language that was more in the style of written messages.

Seating arrangements at meetings may influence the tone of discussion. It has been found that when people talk to each other over the corner of a table, a feeling of cooperation prevails. But when two people face each other across a table, they are far more inclined to see each other as competitors (Argyle and Kendon, 1967). Nurses can observe these effects in informal interactions as well as at formal negotiating sessions and may want to engineer seating to facilitate ease of communication.

In formalized communication channels some participants may be insulated from others by organizational "distance." That is, a person in a position of great influence may have the option of minimizing his contact with subordinates except through written messages. The communication may flow downward from the leader much more frequently than from subordinates to the high authority.

For the nurse leader the use of distance to avoid contact with subordinates will probably be self defeating. Interpersonal power cannot be expected to grow under such conditions. It has been found that people would more readily exploit another if they did not expect to meet the individual, than they would if some personal interaction in the future were expected (Marlowe, Gergen, and Doob, 1966).

Finally, the leader's influence strategies may be influenced by the size of the group. When a group is large, a leader has to respond to more demands, to participate more, and will probably become more autocratic (Bales, 1953; Hemphill, 1950). The group will also show changes as its size increases. The cohesiveness within the group, the degree of satisfaction of participants, and the social pressures toward conformity have all been found to decrease when group size increases (Cartwright and Zander, 1968). It is reasonable to expect that a leader of a large group has less time for attention to each group member. Given these conditions, he may be more likely to change his means of working for group goals. Instead of interpersonal power and communication and feedback, he may use coercive measures. Studies show that as group size increased, leaders used persuasion less and depended more on threats (Kipnis and Consentino, 1969; Kipnis and Lane, 1962).

Humanizing the internal environment

A review of the literature suggests that a number of questions are being raised by investigators as to how to maximize human functioning in the world of work (Friedlander and Greenberg, 1971; Likert, 1967; Moos and Insel, 1974; Walton, 1973). These questions seem to be primarily three kinds: (1) How should the quality of working life be conceptualized? (2) What are the criteria or guidelines for improving the quality of work life? (3) How can man's perceptions of his work environment be assessed?

In answer to the first question Walton (1973) suggests that the "quality of working life" and the work environment should be conceptualized comprehensively. He further contends that the concept should embrace legislative acts such as child labor laws, the Fair Labor Standards Act, and workman's compensation laws. The concept should also include the unionization movement, the findings of psychologists in the 1950s that demonstrated a positive relationship between morale and productivity, the reforms in the 1960s for equal employment opportunity and job enrichment, and concepts of the 1970s based on values that emphasize human needs and goals.

With these concepts in mind, Walton (1973) developed eight major conceptual categories that appear to be basic criteria measures for analyzing the quality of the work environment. These criteria measures include the following: (1) adequate and fair compensation, (2) safe and healthy working conditions, (3) immediate opportunity to use and develop human capacities, (4) future opportunity for continued growth and security, (5) social integration in the work organization, (6) constitutionalism in the work organization (privacy, free speech, equity, due process), (7) work and the Total Life Space (time for family, hobbies, civic activities), and (8) social relevance of work life. These guidelines could be further developed and made into checklists for nurse managers and employees to use.

Another approach in humanizing the work environment, meeting the needs of the worker and the needs and goals of the organization, has been described by Dyer (1972) who proposed that conditions in three interrelated systems affect both the worker and the organization. These systems include the social system, the operation system, and the administrative system. Guidelines have been developed by Dyer (1972) for each of the systems.

From the guidelines it appears that both the role and the needs of the worker are made explicit. Should these guidelines be adopted by health care organizations, an important first step would be taken in humanizing the work environment, meeting the needs and goals of the worker, and increasing productivity.

In an attempt to answer the third question, "How can man's perceptions of his work environment be assessed?" Moos (1974) and his associates at the Social Ecology Laboratory at Stanford University have developed an instrument to measure the work environment. Subscales on the Work Environment Scale include: (1) order and organization, (2) control, (3) clarity of the task, (4) innovation, and (5) physical comfort. Although findings on the Work Environment Scale are limited because of its recent development, the scale appears to hold promise for gathering data on worker's perceptions of their own work locale. Using such a tool, sharing the findings with group members, and taking action on those dimensions that appear to account for nurses' dissatisfaction are ways in which nurse leaders can humanize the health care environment and assist nurses in deriving more satisfaction from their work.

REFERENCES

Argyle, M., and Kendon, A.: The experimental analysis of social performance, In Berkowitz, L., editor: Advances in experimental social psychology, vol. 3, New York, 1967, Academic Press, Inc.

Bales, R. F.: The equilibrium problem in small groups. In Parsons, T., Bales, R. F., and Shils, E. A., editors: Working papers in the theory of action, Glencoe, Ill., 1953, The Free Press.

Bem, D. J.: Self-perception: An alternative interpretation of cognitive dissonance phenomena, Psychological Review **74:**183-200, 1967.

Butler, D. C., and Miller, N.: Power to reward and punish in social interactions, Journal of Experimental Social Psychology **1:**311-322, 1965.

Cartwright, D., and Zander, A.: The structural properties of groups: Introduction. In Cartwright, D., and Zander, A., editors: Group dynamics: Research and theory, ed. 3, New York, 1968, Harper & Row, Publishers.

Deutsch, M., and Krauss, R. M.: The effect of threat upon interpersonal bargaining, Journal of Abnormal and Social Psychology **61:**181-89, 1960.

Dyer, W. G.: The sensitive manipulator, Provo, Utah, 1972, Brigham Young University Press.

Fiedler, F. E.: A theory of leadership effectiveness, New York, 1967, McGraw-Hill, Inc.

Fischer, C. S.: The effect of threats in an incomplete information game, Sociometry **32:**301-314, 1969.

Fotheringham, W. C.: Perspectives on persuasion, Boston, 1966, Allyn & Bacon, Inc.

Friedlander, F., and Greenberg, S.: Effects of job attitudes, training, and organization climate on performance of hard-core unemployed, Journal of Applied Psychology **55:**287-295, 1971.

Goodstadt, B., and Kipnis, D.: Situational influences on the use of power, Journal of Applied Psychology **54:**201-207, 1970.

Gouldner, A. W.: The norm of reciprocity: A preliminary statement, American Sociological Review **25:**161-79, 1960.

Hemphill, J. K.: Relations between the size of the group and the behavior of "superior" leaders, Journal of Social Psychology **32:**11-22, 1950.

Howells, L. T., and Becker, S. W.: Seating arrangement and leadership emergence, Journal of Abnormal and Social Psychology **64:**148-150, 1962.

Kipnis, D., and Cosentino, J.: Use of leadership powers in industry, Journal of Applied Psychology **53:**460-466, 1969.

Kipnis, D., and Lane, W. P.: Self confidence and leadership, Journal of Applied Psychology **46**:291-295, 1962.

Kipnis, D., and Vanderveer, R.: Ingratiation and the use of power, Journal of Personality and Social Psychology **17**:280-286, 1971.

Kite, W. R.: Attributions of causality as a function of the use of reward and punishment, unpublished doctoral dissertation, Stanford, Calif., 1964, Stanford University.

Leavitt, H. J.: Some effects of certain communication patterns on group performance, Journal of Abnormal and Social Psychology **46**:38-50, 1951.

Likert, R.: The human organization, New York, 1967, McGraw-Hill, Inc.

Lindskold, S., and others: Factors affecting the effectiveness of reward power, Psychonomic Science **26**:68-70, 1972.

Lindskold, S., and Tedeschi, J. T.: Reward power and attraction in interpersonal conflict, Psychonomic Science **22**:211-213, 1971.

Lindskold, S., and Tedeschi, J. T.: Threatening and conciliatory influence attempts as a function of source's perception of own competence in a conflict situation, mimeographed manuscript, Albany, 1970, State University of New York at Albany.

MacLean, G., and Tedeschi, J. T.: The use of social influence by children of entrepreneurial and bureaucratic parents, mimeographed manuscript, Albany, 1970, State University of New York at Albany.

Marlowe, D., Gergen, K. J., and Doob, A. N.: Opponent's personality, expectation, and interpersonal bargaining, Journal of Personality and Social Psychology **3**:206-213, 1966.

Miller, N., and Butler, D.: Social power and communication in small groups, Behavioral Science **14**:11-18, 1969.

Miller, N., Butler, D., and McMartin, J. A.: The ineffectiveness of punishment power in group interaction, Sociometry **32**:24-42, 1969.

Moos, R., and Insel, P., editors: Issues in social ecology: Human milieus, Palo Alto, Calif., 1974, National Press.

Moscovi, S.: Communication processes and the properties of language. In Berkowitz, L., editor: Advances in experimental social psychology, vol. 3, New York, 1967, Academic Press, Inc.

Mulder, M.: Power and satisfaction in task-oriented groups, Acta Psychologica **16**:178-225, 1959.

Parsons, T.: On the concept of influence, Public Opinion Quarterly **27**:37-62, 1963.

Rothbart, M.: Effects of motivation, equity and compliance on the use of reward and punishment, Journal of Personality and Social Psychology **9**:353-362, 1968.

Shaw, M. E.: Communication networks. In Berkowitz, L., editor: Advances in experimental social psychology, vol. 1, New York, 1964, Academic Press, Inc.

Smith, D. H.: The classification of communication: Problems and a proposal, Pacific Speech **2**:15-24, 1968.

Tedeschi, J. T., Schlenker, B. R., and Lindskold, S.: The exercise of power and influence: The source of influence. In Tedeschi, J. T., editor: The social influence process, Chicago, 1972, Aldine Publishing Co.

Walton, R.: Quality of working life: What is it? Sloan Management Review **15**:11-23, 1973.

Ward, C. D.: Seating arrangement and leadership emergence in small discussion groups, Journal of Social Psychology **74**:83-90, 1968.

Watson, D. L.: Effects of certain social power structures on communication in task-oriented groups, Sociometry **28**:322-336, 1965.

Watson, D., and Bromberg, B.: Power, communication, and position satisfaction in task-oriented groups, Journal of Personality and Social Psychology **2**:859-864, 1965.

SUGGESTED READINGS

Deutsch, M.: Studies of interpersonal bargaining, Journal of Conflict Resolution **6**:52-76, 1962.

Fiedler, F. E.: The contingency model—a reply to Ashour, Organizational Behavior and Human Performance **9**:356-368, 1973.

Fiedler, F. E.: Personality and situational determinants of leader behavior. In Fleishman, E. A., and Hunt, J. G., editors: Current developments in the study of leadership, Carbondale, Ill., 1973, Southern Illinois University Press.

Fiedler, F. E., and Chemers, M.: Leadership and effective management, Glenview, Ill., 1974, Scott, Foresman and Co.

Froman, L. A., and Cohen, M. D.: Threats and bargaining efficiency, Behavioral Science **14**:147-153, 1969.

Gahagan, J. P., and Tedeschi, J. T.: Effects of promise credibility, outside options and social contact on interpersonal conflict, mimeographed manuscript, Albany, 1970, State University of New York at Albany.

Harford, T., Solomon, L., and Cheney, J.: Effects of proliferating punitive power upon cooperation and competition in the triad, Psychological Reports **24**:355-360, 1969.

Hollander, E.: Leaders, groups, and influence, New York, 1964, Oxford University Press, Inc.

Insel, P., and Moos, R.: The work environment scale, Palo Alto, Calif., 1972, Stanford University, Social Ecology Laboratory, Department of Psychiatry.

Insel, P., and Moos, R.: Psychological environments, Expanding the scope of human ecology, American Psychologist **29**:179-88, 1974.

Kramer, M.: Reality shock: Why nurses leave nursing, St. Louis, 1974, The C. V. Mosby Co.

Smith, D. H.: Communication and negotiation. In Thayer, L. O., editor: Communication spectrum,

Flint, Mich., 1968, National Society for the Study of Communications.

Tedeschi, J. T., Bonoma, T., and Novinson, N.: Behavior of a threatener: retaliation vs. fixed opportunity costs, Journal of Conflict Resolution 14:69-76, 1970.

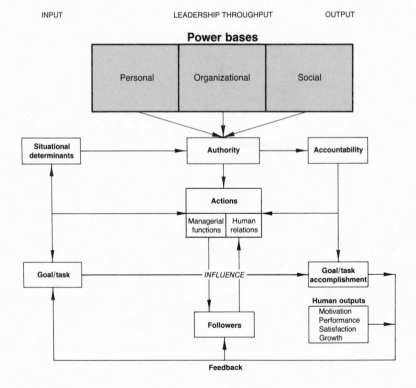

INPUT   LEADERSHIP THROUGHPUT   OUTPUT

Power bases

Personal   Organizational   Social

Situational determinants → Authority → Accountability

Actions

Managerial functions | Human relations

Goal/task — *INFLUENCE* → Goal/task accomplishment

Human outputs
Motivation
Performance
Satisfaction
Growth

Followers

Feedback

*To be successful in using power, you have to have
a sense of power.*

                    W. MICHAEL BLUMENTHAL

4 POWER BASES FOR LEADERSHIP

Effective leadership is built on a pyramid of power—strength, energy, and action—as pointed out in Chapter 2. Nurse leaders must develop each of these power elements if they are to effect change in health care delivery. In our definition of power as the *ability* and *will* to act, we note that all three elements of power relate to the pyramid of power, each element being a side of this pyramid. That is, there is a necessity to attend to: (1) the *strength,* which yields the *ability;* (2) *energy,* which vitalizes the *will;* and (3) the *action* itself, which provides the *results.* In addition to the elements of power there are three *bases* of power— personal power, organizational power, and interpersonal or social power. Inherent in each of these power bases is the tripartite nature of power: strength, energy, and action. Fig. 5 shows the relationship of these three major power bases as they unite in forming a strong power source.

PERSONAL POWER
Strength

A key element of power is strength. Most modern scholars of power believe that personal strength is the most important element in the personal power base (Brouwer, 1976; Heider, 1958; Korda, 1975; McClelland and Burnham, 1976; Ringer, 1974; Tedeschi, 1972). Personal strength is derived from a strong and realistic self concept, which involves awareness of strength as well as weaknesses.

A new theory of clinical psychology, transactional analysis, is based on the building of strong self concepts (Berne, 1964; Harris, 1967; Meininger, 1973). Transactional analysis theory is based on the premise that a personality is made up of three parts: the *Parent,* the collection of memories and orientations that are learned in the first 5 years of life; the *Child,* the feelings associated with the facts stored in the past; and the *Adult,* the computerlike part of the personality whose function it is to process data, compute probability, and make decisions on fact. The Adult part of the personality takes data from three sources: the Parent, the Child, and its own observations of reality. One of the prime foci of transactional analysis is to assist a person to face present realities by getting in touch with his feelings and surroundings and to determine if projections and descriptions of feelings offered by the person are indeed the real feelings. Such analysis requires learning to see oneself and to look at oneself in a clear perspective.

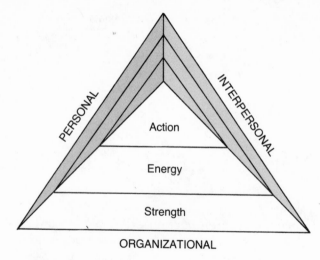

Fig. 5. The three dimensions of the power pyramid.

Developing a strong self concept

Personal strength is based on growth. The concept of growth, underlying personal strength, assures the individual that he is not only "OK" but that he is also getting better through growth. Disclosure, feedback, and reinforcing behaviors are techniques for growing in personal strength and for enhancing personal effectiveness in working with others.

There are certain steps that can be taken to promote growth in personal strength. First, the person must examine himself. Self examination serves to lay the groundwork for insight. Without insight, personal growth will not occur. Insight is often painful and reached with difficulty because it causes one to look at himself. Insight is the first step in changing behavior.

The next step is to raise one's sights; that is, to determine the direction and to set expectations for performance and goal achievement. Self examination promotes the notion that if one has a problem the next logical step is to search for a solution. Personal growth begins with new self expectations regarding one's capabilities and resources. Concepts of management and complex technological tools in health care systems are demanding different expectations of the health care team. To meet the expectations of others, one must develop and change his own self expectations. A critical step is to get perceptions of one's behavior from other people. This type of feedback is essential for personal growth. Colleagues, superiors, subordinates, and patients can all provide valuable feedback to nurses, providing they are willing to listen and do not react defensively. The next steps are to make a personal commitment to grow and then accept responsibility for one's own personal and professional growth. Nurses will grow in strength and power only if they are willing to set goals and to make a commitment and to accept the responsibility for achieving these goals.

Exposure to experience or people will not in itself produce growth. Growth occurs only if leaders internalize the experiences. For example, knowledge should become a vital part of the leader's cognitive and information bases so that these baselines can be used in the problem solving and decision making process.

To broaden perceptions, nurse leaders need a strong, positive image of themselves in both the home and work environments if they are indeed to use power effectively.

As nurses become more powerful and take on increasingly higher leadership positions, it is important that they analyze the roles of other health care professionals and examine facts in the external environment that affect health care services as we discussed earlier. It is not enough to view nursing and health care delivery from an exclusively nurse-oriented perspective.

One of the basic strengths and power bases of nurses is their ability to look at the health care needs of people from a consumer's point of view. But more than *ability* is required. Nurses must take *actions* that will provide consumers with *preventive* and health *maintenance* care rather than only *sick* care. Such a broad perspective on health care coupled with initiating and providing these dimensions in meeting *health* care needs can indeed move the nursing profession forward.

Self realization

Maslow (1970) maintained that we could not be totally human if we did not reach a stage of self realization, which he defines as becoming what we are capable of becoming. This level is characterized by creative experience. Historically, we find evidence of strong, powerful people overcoming incredible odds to accomplish their goals: Michelangelo fought against artistic and political opposition in order to sculpt; Beethoven composed after deafness; Milton wrote poetry after blindness.

The strong person fulfills himself through living. As a person grows he achieves more power—more power within himself. In the growing process the self concept is evolving: (1) self direction and self expectations change; (2) perceptions become clearer and broader, and personal and professional goals evolve. This process is often known as maturing. We refer to the process as personal growth, which we maintain is essential to the development of strength needed for personal power.

Health as a source of strength

Nurses, as health professionals, ought to be particularly sensitive to the potential power derived from health. Nurses, who give so much of their energy to heal others, should be acutely aware of the source of power that their own health provides. One cannot easily perceive a person as being powerful if that person constantly faces serious health problems. Because power comes from within a person, it is important that all sources of strength and energy are known and used.

Control is an aspect of health. A powerful person can control his own health status to a large extent. Health rules advocated by Dr. C. M. Lindsay, a National Fellow at the Hoover Institute, proved that the best health insurance readily available to almost everyone at relatively low cost is "good" health habits. Health rules include the following: (1) don't smoke, (2) get adequate sleep, (3) eat nourishing foods, (4) drink moderately, and (5) exercise daily. Most nurses do indeed know these rules, but many of them do not incorporate them into their daily living. When such simple guidelines for maintenance of health become part of the nurse's life style, not only will nurses minimize their own need for "sick care" services but they will more likely serve as role models for their patients and incorporate aspects of preventive medicine into patient care activities.

Strength and resiliency

A powerful person is able to survive failure, humiliation, and a variety of crises. John F. Kennedy called this deepened wisdom "grace under pressure." Power is not based only on winning. By setting standards and self expectations that require winning all the time, a person is doomed to failure. Unattainable goals lead to a joylessness—an endless struggle for control or a compulsive need to be on top, which can never be satisfied. Charles Colson has said of the Watergate situation, "Everybody thinks the people surrounding the President were drunk with power . . . but it wasn't arrogance at all. It was insecurity. That insecurity began to breed a form of paranoia. We overreacted to the attacks against us and to a lot of things" (Lipset, 1973). In other words, self pity does not correspond to a sense of power. Truly powerful people can accept defeat as well as victory.

Mental strength

A person's mental strength derives from expertise, thinking capabilities, and realistic self appraisals. Mental strength is tied closely to one's physical strength. "The surest way to become sloppy in your technique, and thus make costly errors, is to allow yourself to become mentally and physically fatigued" (Ringer, 1974).

Emotional, psychological, and psychic strength

Emotional, psychological, and psychic strength depend on one's own value system and respect for the value systems of others. Acceptance of others begins with a positive attitude toward oneself. It involves the ability to solve problems and to deal with a crisis. Psychological strength is based on warmth and true concern for others and for humankind in general. Many of the situations in which nurse leaders perform are extremely stressful. Part of the emotional strength of a leader comes from the ability to manage anxiety and to act under pressure. Personal strength grows as the leader experiences success. Every problem is a challenge for the leader, which can provide insights into her own abilities and those of her associates.

Personal energy

Treasury Secretary Blumenthal, former President and Chairman of Bendix Corporation, once stated that "Energy is the basic requirement of power" (Korda, 1975, p. 38). Energy is based on a sense or a feeling of power, or to paraphrase Blumenthal, the gall to think that one is powerful. Power is a feeling. The energy that yields power is a feeling that one counts for something. *Energy* aligned with *strength* will yield *action*—the *will* and *ability* to get *results*. Energy provides the sustenance that can uplift the individual and thus make a positive impact on others. Being tuned into one's inner self and to others will provide the energy to be powerful.

Will and one's own motivational forces to be powerful can yield the energy necessary to exercise power. Another way of encouraging energy from which to derive power is to surround oneself with personal power sources. For example, one can choose the colors that make him feel powerful. By surrounding himself with these colors and with things that serve as symbols of power, the individual can derive energy and expand power. It has been suggested that dark blue is a symbol of power for many people (Korda, 1975).

One's energy source is much like that of a utility company and must follow the principle of constancy of flow. That is, utilities must regulate the usage of energy or electricity in order to use the generating capacity with maximum efficiency. Nurses likewise should strive to use their energy in such a way as not to overload it. Not using one's energy through positive control is as bad as an overload. Start up time, when one generates the energy needed for power, is too expensive. Nurses should know how to regenerate themselves through appropriate use of leisure time; even leisure time should count for something.

Action

Using one's strength and energy to generate power is not enough—one must take *action*. Power is based on actions to control oneself, to control others, to control events, and to control the environment. Personal power does not mean being passive and letting things happen. Rather it implies being forthright and assertive in terms of controlling one's own behavior. There is no way to escape the doing, the action that is critical to the use and possession of power.

Powerful people move assuredly and slowly, being careful not to upset the status quo without careful planning. "Powerful people have the ability to dramatize themselves and their actions so that even the most unimportant events acquire meaning" (Korda, 1975, p. 257). Nurses who are unable to understand that they have power through possessing unique abilities will be unable to dramatize their actions.

Political and social consciousness has not reached the nursing profession to the extent found in other professions. To date there is no television program entitled "The Nurses." Physicians and paramedics, firefighters, police, and lawyers are represented on television. But nowhere is there a dramatization of the many challenges of nursing as a profession. Personal power of nurses must be enhanced not only through nurses dramatizing their own actions but also through TV dramatization.

INTERPERSONAL-SOCIAL POWER

Interpersonal power and social power are derived from relationships with other people.

Interpersonal strength

In developing interpersonal power one often discovers that two heads are better than one, that intelligence can be multiplied, and that groups have more strength than individuals. Nurses have become acutely aware of this through strong professional nursing organizations. The strength of a group depends on the cohesion and unification of the group members as they relate to goal setting and attainment. Indeed the very existence of a group is dependent on maintaining effective relationships among members. This often causes difficulties among members of the health care team, particularly between nurses and physicians where females dominate the nursing profession and males dominate the medical profession. Men have traditionally played the aggressive power games, and women have been considered outsiders in the game. But all this seems to be changing. More men are entering nursing; more women are entering medicine; and male-female roles are becoming less distinct.

Nurses and physicians can become more cooperative and collaborative if they will find ways to more effectively work together in solving patient care problems and in the promotion of health. They should learn to capitalize on each other's strength rather than to be fearful. It is necessary for members of both professions to feel strong and responsible and to recognize that just as physicians do not want to practice nursing, nurses do not want to practice medicine. Both need to be powerful in their own way, to have mutual respect, to reward each other, and to recognize that there are dependent, interdependent, and intradependent functions in the delivery of health care services. A team spirit and a feeling of pride are important sources of interpersonal power. Performance in the delivery of health care can reach a high level if members of the health care team can work together more effectively in the attainment of quality health care to all at a reasonable cost.

Interpersonal energy

Just as strength can be enhanced by numbers, so can energy; just as nurses give support to patients and their families, they must give *moral support* to each other. Moral support really implies that there has been an exchange of positive energy that bolsters a person and assists him to reach his goals more easily. A nurse who sees a person floundering should offer help and support. A surge of energy will result from such an interaction. This phenomenon has been called "synergic power" and is defined as the whole of the cooperative effort, which is greater than the sum of the individual parts (Craig and Craig, 1974). It is the positive energy that takes the best parts from those involved and creates something greater.

Interpersonal power can grow out of social activities that provide opportunities for exchange of energy. For example, social gatherings allow for an opportunity to develop alliances and to make decisions in an informal way. Such alliances and collaborative effort enhance the development of the will to act.

Interpersonal action

Professions have long used jargon and rituals to bind a group together. Professions also use legislation as a tool in furthering their interests. The nurse leader can enhance perceptive interpersonal power by direct action in leading groups toward mutually established goals. The use of systematic problem solving techniques and decision making can also enhance interpersonal action (Bailey and Claus, 1975) and serve as a tool to strengthen the social power base, particularly when problem solving and decision making are approached through the use of the group process.

ORGANIZATIONAL POWER

Organizational power is power derived from position and authority within a formal organizational structure. Organizational power is largely based on controls.

Organizational strength

Like a person an organization must base its strength on its ability to sanction (Tedeschi, 1972). Strength is also based on locational and environmental factors that have been described in terms of geographical locations of offices, furniture arrangement in offices, color, window arrangements, and social space (Korda, 1975).

Organizational power is also based on authority either delegated or acquired. Authority, or the use of power derived from it, implies responsibility. The strength of organizational power based on authority comes from its control mechanisms—primarily its control over people and over information. A person who controls information is indeed powerful, since this implies the ability to analyze the information, to process it, and to assume responsibility for it.

Strength in an organization is also derived from position power in both the formal and informal structures. In some situations the informal structure exerts a great deal of power. Strong leaders may de-emphasize authority, provided they have developed sufficient strength and energy in informal alliances within the organization to accomplish their goals.

Organizational energy

Consistency of leadership behavior is an important quality in organizational energy. The willingness to sanction has important effects on a leader's credibility and power. Like a utilities company the person who uses organizational power must be consistent in the use of that energy or some of the power will be lost. Subordinates deserve to know what to expect from the leader.

Organizational energy as well as strength is derived from locational factors: where one is situated is important in the way one's energy is perceived and applied. In meetings the most energy is perceived to generate from the person who sits at the head of the table, preferably near a window with the next most energizing person sitting to the right. This has been described as organizational power through "locational advantage" (Korda, 1975). Organizational energy is also derived from organizational growth. Organizations cannot be static. They

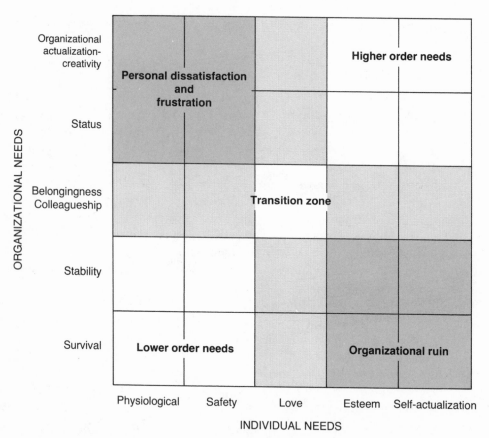

Fig. 6. Organizational-Individual Needs Matrix. Unshaded boxes indicate areas where personal needs and organizational needs correspond. These are the areas of greatest potential power.

must grow, expand, and change if they are to meet the changing needs of the society they serve.

Nurse leaders have many opportunities to expand their organizational power bases into areas that are not claimed directly by others. There is an urgent need for nurses to share health care information with patients and their families and to view health *teaching* as an integral part of their responsibility. They must teach patients and their families the importance of good health habits. They also need to remind patients that they have a *responsibility* for their own health status and that maintaining daily health is equally as important as seeking care when they are ill.

Organizational action

Nursing leaders must be willing to use position power in an organization, and the organization must sanction the power inherent in the position. An important aspect of organizational action is the control of information flow. This involves controlling not only formal information but also the control of "leaks," gossip, conjectures, and other kinds of information that flows from the organization's informal information network.

Matching individual and organizational needs

Organizational power is enhanced by matching individual needs with organizational needs. Organizational needs, like personal needs, can be classified according to level. Lower order needs include economic survival, stability, and membership in a group of similar organizations with similar interests. Higher order needs are status and creative growth.

An individual within an organization who realizes that the organization's primary needs are lower order and who sympathizes with these needs will be better able to direct his efforts toward meeting these needs. Nurse leaders who are concerned about their employment status and professional association are operating on need levels that enable them to more easily tune into the problems of a hospital's tight operating budget, high turnover rate, and concern with delivering high quality care than those who are striving for individual status or prestige.

Organizational-Individual Needs Matrix

A matrix for matching individual and organizational needs is helpful in assessing the "fit" of an individual's needs and consequent drives with the need pattern of the organization for which he works (Fig. 6). By placing a dot on the matrix at the points where individual and organizational need levels intersect, it is possible to determine whether an individual can gain personal power and satisfaction while attempting to meet organizational needs and gain organizational power. An ideal match is when individual and organizational needs are similar (as shown in the white boxes). Intersection in the shaded boxes produces various degrees of power loss. The dark areas indicate mismatches and places where serious problems might occur. Personal dissatisfaction, anger, and frustration derive from an organization's insensitivity to the survival needs of its personnel while it exercises power primarily to gain status. Nurses will have more power when they feel there is a match between their own needs with those of the organization.

REFERENCES

Bailey, J. T., and Claus, K. E.: Decision making in nursing: Tools for change, St. Louis, 1975, The C. V. Mosby Co.

Berne, E.: Games people play, New York, 1964, Grove Press, Inc.

Brouwer, P. J.: The power to see ourselves, Harvard Business Review 54(1):66-73, 1976.

Craig, J. H., and Craig, M.: Synergic power: Beyond domination and permissiveness, Berkeley, Calif., 1974, ProActive Press.

Harris, T. A.: I'm ok, you're ok, New York, 1967, Harper & Row, Publishers.

Heider, F.: The psychology of interpersonal relations, New York, 1958, John Wiley & Sons, Inc.

Korda, M.: Power: How to get it, how to use it! New York, 1975, Random House, Inc.

Lipset, S. M., and Raab, E.: Watergate: The vacillation of the President, Psychology Today 7(6):77-84, 1973.

Maslow, A.: Motivation and personality, rev. ed., New York, 1970, Harper & Row, Publishers.

Meininger, J.: Success through transactional analysis, New York, 1973, New American Library, Inc. (Signet Books).

Ringer, R. J.: Winning through intimidation, Los Angeles, 1974, Los Angeles Book Publishers Co.

Tedeschi, J. T., editor: The social influence processes, Chicago, 1972, Aldine Publishing Co.

SUGGESTED READINGS

Altman, I.: The environment and social behavior, Monterey, Calif., 1975, Brooks/Cole Publishing Co.

Bass, B. M., and Franke, R. H.: Societal influences on student perceptions of how to succeed in organizations: A cross-national analysis, Journal of Applied Psychology 56:312-318, 1972.

Dowling, W. F., and Wayles, L. R.: How managers motivate: The imperatives of supervision, New York, 1971, McGraw-Hill, Inc.

Foster, C.: Developing self control, Kalamazoo, Mich., 1974, Behaviordelia, Inc.

Franklin, J. L.: Down the organization: Influence processes across levels of hierarchy, Administrative Science Quarterly 20:153-164, 1975.

Gray, L. N., and Mayhew, B. H., Jr.: Proactive differentiation, sequence restraint, and the asymmetry of power: A multidimensional analysis, Human Relations 25:199-214, 1972.

Greene, C. N.: The reciprocal nature of influence between leader and subordinate, Journal of Applied Psychology 60:187-193, 1975.

Griesinger, D. W., and Livingston, J. W., Jr.: Toward a model of interpersonal motivation in experimental games, Behavioral Science 18(3):173-188, 1973.

Heimann, C. G.: Four theories of leadership, Journal of Nursing Administration 6(5):18-28, 1976.

Herzog, A.: The B. S. factor, New York, 1974, Penguin Books.

Hollander, E. P.: Style, structure and setting in organizational leadership, Administrative Science Quarterly 16(1):1-9, 1971.

Kaye, D.: The woman boss: Getting there is only half the problem, Mainliner 20(6):34-37, 1976.

Lassey, W. R., editor: Leadership and social change, Iowa City, Iowa, 1971, University Associates.

Loring, R., and Wells, T.: Breakthrough: Women into management, New York, 1972, Van Nostrand Reinhold Co.

McClelland, D.: The two faces of power. In Kolb, D. A., Rubin, I. M., and McIntyre, J. M., editors: Organizational psychology: A book of readings, Englewood Cliffs, N. J., 1974, Prentice-Hall, Inc.

McClelland, D., and Burnham, D.: Power is the great motivator, Harvard Business Review 54(2):100-110, 1976.

Misumi, J., and Seki, F.: Effects of achievement motivation on the effectiveness of leadership patterns, Administrative Science Quarterly 16(1):51-59, 1971.

Moustakas, C. E.: Finding yourself, and finding others, Englewood Cliffs, N. J., 1974, Prentice-Hall, Inc.

Nolan, M. G.: Wanted: Colleagueship in nursing, Journal of Nursing Administration 6(3):41-43, 1976.

O'Reilly, C. A., III, and Roberts, K. H.: Information filtration in organizations: Three experiments, Organizational Behavior and Human Performance 11(2):253-265, 1974.

Patchen, M.: The locus and basis of influence on organizational decisions, Organizational Behavior and Human Performance 11(2):195-221, 1974.

Pollard, W. E., and Mitchell, T. R.: Decision theory analysis of social power, Psychological Bulletin 78(6):433-446, 1972.

Rogers, C. R.: On becoming a person, ed. 2, Boston, 1961, Houghton-Mifflin Co.

Schmalenberg, C. E., and Kramer, M.: Dreams and reality: Where do they meet? Journal of Nursing Administration 6(5):35-43, 1976.

Shiflett, S. C., and Nealey, S. M.: The effects of changing leader power: A test of "situational engineering," Organizational Behavior and Human Performance 7(3):371-382, 1972.

Smith, R. J., and Cook, P. E.: Leadership in dyadic groups as a function of dominance and incentives, Sociometry 36(4):561-568, 1973.

Stevens, B. J.: The nurse as executive, Wakefield, Mass., 1975, Contemporary Publishing, Inc.

Teulings, A. W. M., Jansen, L. O. O., and Verhoeven, W. G.: Growth, power structure and leadership functions in the hospital organization, British Journal of Sociology 24:490-505, 1973.

Wood, M. T.: Participation, influence, and satisfaction in group decision making, Journal of Vocational Behavior 2(4):389-399, 1972.

INPUT   LEADERSHIP THROUGHPUT   OUTPUT

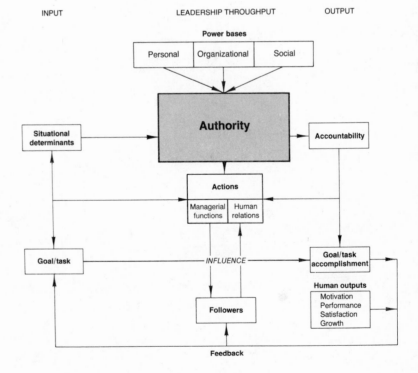

*We can confer authority; but power or capacity
no man can give or take.*

MARY PARKER FOLLETT

5 AUTHORITY

DEFINING AUTHORITY

Authority is an integral component of both individual and organizational behavior. It has been defined as the *right* to act (Hicks, 1972) and also as the *right* to command (Tannenbaum, Wechsler, and Massarik, 1961).

Despite the importance of authority there is confusion among management scholars about its real meaning. Simon concluded that "there is no real consensus today as to how the term 'authority' ought to be used" (Simon, 1957, pp. xxxiv-xxxv). For our discussion we are using authority to mean the right to act (Hicks, 1972).

A FRAMEWORK FOR UNDERSTANDING AUTHORITY

We believe our model can serve to clarify a complex and often misunderstood concept. The Power/Authority/Influence Leadership Model alerts nurse leaders that to understand authority a multidimensional approach is necessary. Authority as shown in the model indicates a *fusion* of situational variables, power bases, accountability, and responsibility, which in large measure give nurse leaders additional insights into making the most of their authority as they take action. Thus authority is perceived as a dyadic relationship. Authority makes itself felt through leadership *actions,* is determined to a large extent by the situation, and is always associated with responsibility and accountability. It is illogical to make nurses responsible and accountable for actions without giving them the authority to complete the task. Yet this is one of the most critical errors committed by nurse leaders.

SOURCES OF AUTHORITY

Although there appears to be some confusion as to how authority should be used, there seems to be considerable agreement on the bases of authority (Peabody, 1960). Behavioral and social scientists (Bennis, 1959; Presthus, 1960; Simon, 1957) and others classify authority as deriving primarily from two sources: (1) formal or positional authority and (2) functional or personal authority. We believe that nurse leaders should familarize themselves with both types of authority and understand that both types are needed for leadership action.

FORMAL AUTHORITY

Formal or positional authority is tied to the person's formal role, position, or office. Formal authority determines which positions are superior and which are subordinate. It is considered formal because the authority is conferred by the organization. Within the formal authority base, two distinct kinds of authority emerge.

Authority of legitimacy

This type of authority is sometimes perceived as legal or hierarchical authority. Authority of legitimacy implies social approval or deference of group members toward authority. For example, the position of director of nursing, because of the sanctions inherent in the professional role, may be perceived as having the *right* to make decisions and take actions, and therefore nurses will accept the authority.

Authority of position

Positional authority is tied to a person's job or position. The authority resides in the position or office and not in the *person*. Positional authority, sometimes knows as official authority, is conferred by the organization and determines superior-subordinate relationships and the need for delegation. Incumbents may come and go, but the authority of the position remains. Nurses frequently believe that this is the only type of authority and that if they are not directors or deans they have minimal authority in an organization. This is not necessarily so as we shall discuss subsequently.

FUNCTIONAL AUTHORITY

Functional authority is sometimes known as informal authority or personal authority (Dornbusch and Scott, 1975). The sources of functional authority are derived from: (1) professional-technical knowledge, expertise, and experience; and (2) the knowledge of management techniques and human relations.

Authority of competence

A new graduate staff nurse may have difficulty with certain technical procedures such as catheterization or suctioning a tracheotomy. An older, experienced staff nurse may be perceived by the new graduate as having technical expertise, and the new graduate may seek her help. This kind of technical knowledge based on experience and expertise is known as the *authority of competence,* which is based on information or functional authority.

Authority of person

Authority vested in the person is somewhat different from the authority of competence. Rather than the technical expertise, the authority of person is vested more in leader-follower relations. It is grounded in both human relations and functional aspects of management, and is often perceived as a fusion of leadership skills.

Personal or functional authority is needed as well as formal authority to achieve goals. This we would like to highlight because nurses have tended to view themselves as being powerless. Unless they are in top management positions, they fail to use their technical expertise or human relations skills to move an organization forward. Personal authority relies heavily on the initiative of nurses to go beyond the bounds of their positional authority. It represents an area of authority in which nurses can move out to increase a substantial portion of their power in all three power bases—personal, social, and organizational.

For example, a staff nurse on an inpatient psychiatric unit saw the need for staff to meet with the physicians to share approaches for patient care. At her suggestion these meetings were held on a bimonthly basis. As a result of these meetings the staff felt more appreciated by the physicians and patient care was better coordinated. This change was brought about by this nurse's use of personal power to solicit the physicians' and staff's cooperation. This staff nurse had no position or formal authority to call these meetings but used her own initiative and her human relations skills to acquire personal authority.

Normally personal authority is present in a very random manner in an organization. Few organizations seriously and systematically set out to encourage the acquisition of authority by those in the organization who have the initiative, sense of responsibility, and creativity to expand their power base.

Personal authority is in evidence in all areas of nursing practice. Nurses commonly develop procedures that are used by personnel over whom they have no authority. By developing a specialized procedure, the nurse becomes an expert in its use and acquires personal authority on the basis of that expertise, such as the authority of the IV nurse.

Nurse leaders can achieve personal or functional authority through using their personal power base. They can use their *ability* based on strength, willingness based on *energy,* and take actions to produce *results.*

A TYPOLOGY OF AUTHORITY

The two basic sources of authority, formal and functional, are presented in a matrix form in Fig. 7. There are also three types of authority presented in the matrix: (1) supervisory, (2) operational, and (3) commitment. *Supervisory authority* is basically power over people; *operational authority* is the power over action and

Authority source	Type of authority		
	Supervisory (over people)	Operational (over actions/things)	Commitment (over agreements)
Formal (positional)			
Functional (personal)			

Fig. 7. Authority Matrix used to determine types of authority held by a nurse leader.

things—the power to manage affairs in order to get things done; and *commitment authority* is the power to enter into agreements with others for joint actions.

This matrix can be used by nurses as a checklist to determine what types of authority they have at their disposal.

THE NATURE OF AUTHORITY

The effectiveness of the activities of an organization and its growth depend largely on how effectively the authority vested in the organization is used. Without authority there is no real power. Yet authority is only one dimension of power. Those who have authority and wield power must also be accountable for its proper use.

Authority is meaningful only when it is used to move individuals toward personal and organizational goals. In order to move people, it is necessary for the person who has authority to make decisions. To be powerful, the person with authority must know how to manage people, how to set goals, and how to move others toward accomplishing these goals.

Negative attitudes toward authority

In recent years the word "authority" has had negative connotations in our society. This is easily seen by the attempts to mask the strength and dominance of the power structure in health care delivery. Nurses are often caught in a situation where they are encouraged to participate in management decisions while the underlying hierarchy of the hospital maintains the real authority. However, hospital administrators and physicians are having to relinquish complete authority or control over the health care delivery systems. The civil rights acts, the women's movement, the Nurse Practice Act, expanded roles for nurses, the rise of consumerism, a more humanistic approach to management, the complexity of organizational structures, and better prepared nurses are a few of the factors that account for the shift. Indeed, nurses are the central personnel in the delivery of care for they are the ones who must translate physicians' orders into actions and relay critical data to physicians for evaluation. Nurses control the feedback system and derive tremendous power from this position and from their personal competence and expertise.

Untapped personal authority

Nurse leaders should be sensitive to the three major reasons that there is so much unused functional or personal authority in organizational settings. First, most organizations do not see that they can positively encourage the acquisition of functional authority; they relay heavily on the formal authority vested in position, roles, or offices that are perceived as legitimate. Secondly, some nurses in managerial positions tend to be fearful of using functional or personal power because nurses in general are not risk takers (Bailey, McDonald, and Claus, 1972). Third, traditional line organizational concepts support the underlying feeling that it is dangerous to permit power to be distributed informally throughout an organization. In the case of health care delivery systems the people in management often believe in strict lines of formal authority because of legal liability problems. However, this makes it very difficult for them to see the advantages of functional or personal authority as a resource within the organization that can be acquired by people with initiative, technical and professional expertise, and knowledge and skills in human relations.

The organizational structure is an acceptable and useful means for distributing responsibility within an organization, but it is certainly not the only means that can be used. Some provision is needed for flexibility in order to cope with constantly changing situations. This is particularly critical in health care delivery where new techniques and new knowledge are constantly being introduced. Formal authority through the organizational structure is generally exercised authority. Concomitant with this attitude is the overestimation of the risks involved in possible errors in judgments by less experienced persons. This leads to rigid control and the absence of a climate that encourages vigorous use of delegated authority.

Nurses and authority

Few organizations stimulate an employee's acquisition and use of authority. Acquisition and use of authority must be cultivated at the top management level and encouraged throughout the structure. In health care delivery, particularly where the nursing profession is concerned, there is a distressingly large reservoir of underutilized authority, an untapped power source that can change the entire form of health care delivery and, indeed, the entire quality of life. A critical reason for the existence of this underutilized authority in the nursing profession is that nursing management and other health care systems fail to encourage nurses' use of formal authority or their acquisition of additional authority through personal initiative. Few health care delivery systems utilize the nurses' personal authority creatively or treat it as a productive resource. Consequently, nurses must find ways to use their own personal authority and power.

Job descriptions commonly state the responsibilities for functions, tasks, and results but rarely tell a nurse what authority exists to manage people. The missing ingredient in most job descriptions is a explanation of the authority that can be exercised over others. It is much easier to describe responsibilities than to discuss authority. Responsibility can be discussed in terms of definite functions and tasks. Authority cannot. The nurse's authority is commonly defined as that which is necessary to carry out the responsibilities of the job. But this merely creates confusion between the words responsibility and authority. Description of the responsibilities of a position does not suffice to define the authority vested in that positon to do those jobs.

DELEGATION OF AUTHORITY

Knowing the bases or sources of authority is fundamental to nurse leaders. Of equal importance is the effective delegation of authority. The complexity and growth of organizations make it imperative that each person in the organization be given an opportunity to operate at the highest level of performance.

Decentralization

Although formal authority is still largely centralized in some institutions, decentralization of authority has been gaining considerable impetus in health care and educational systems. A decentralized organization is subdivided into a number of separate subgroups that are virtually independent in terms of their daily management operations. All of these groups, however, are under strong control of a central administrative unit when it comes to major policy decisions. A large university school of nursing is a prime example of a decentralized organizational structure. Decentalization is a response to the problems that arise as the size of an enterprise increases. Decentralization involves the massive delegation of authority to major subordinate groupings or subdivisions within a large organization, often known as departments. Each decentalized division may act almost like a separate or independent operating unit. When decentralization occurs in a large hospital, a great deal of authority is delegated at the unit level. For example, nurse leaders may be delegated the authority to hire and fire; to plan, implement, and control their own budget; and they are judged on the performance of these delegated tasks.

Decentralization has the following advantages: (1) it places decision making authority at the lowest managerial level and spreads the decision making capabilities over a wider number of people; (2) it decreases the potential for conflict among various managers in an organization; (3) it satisfies the need of persons with leadership potential to act independently in their area of competence; and (4) it provides opportunities for utilizing the ever-increasing number of specialists who are needed to deal with the increasing complexity of day to day operations.

The art of delegating

Delegation is the act of entrusting authority to someone who then performs as the representative of the person who gave authority. Control is utilized when authority is delegated.

It is said that it is impossible to delegate all of one's authority; that is, the higher level manager always maintains a part of authority for the actions of subordinates and a part of responsibility. Therefore, the person who has authority is obliged to *account* for how he uses it. This is the basis of accountability.

The person who has a responsibility for doing a task should have the authority to control whatever resources are needed to carry out that task. It is blatantly unfair to require a person to accomplish an objective and limit that person's right to use the tools needed to do the job. Delegation of authority cannot be effective unless responsibility is tied to authority. Although authority can be delegated, there is some question of whether responsibility can be delegated; that is , nurses who are in high level management positions are answerable for the results produced by the authority of the position they hold. Nurse managers are responsible for the output of subordinates. When a director of nursing service delegates some of her authority to an assistant director, she cannot divest herself of any of the responsibility for accomplishing those tasks properly. The director of nursing service remains fully and actively responsible for seeing that delegated authority is exercised properly.

Reasons for delegating

There are several reasons for delegating authority. Usually the persons at the top of an organization cannot personally attend to all aspects of the operations of an organization. Delegation of authority to others to accomplish tasks makes it easier to exercise overall control over the ongoing activities of an organization.

In a health care delivery system the size of the work force is a basic reason for delegation of authority. Imagine dealing with all aspects of the delivery of patient care services in a large, complex, bureaucratic system without intermediate levels of management. The increasing use of nursing and medical specialists within a health care organization also mandates that authority be delegated.

The act of delegating authority to another person creates a need for adequate knowledge of management in order to control the use of authority by subordinates. Job descriptions should reflect the authority base.

Experiences of nurses often hinder the successful delegation of authority. Nurses who work their way up through a health care system often have a hard time letting go and allowing others to take responsibility. This is a critical problem in nursing. It is common to hear nurses comment that it is easier for them to do it themselves than to have someone else do it.

AUTHORITY RELATIONSHIPS
Line and staff defined

Authority relationships are centered around the problems of *line* and *staff* authority. *Line* functions are those that have direct responsibility for achieving the goals of an organization, whereas staff functions are those elements that help the line to work more effectively. Both line and staff authority are concerned with relationships.

Line authority

Line authority is authority delegated by an organization's top management personnel to immediate subordinates who are charged with carrying out operations. This first tier of managerial personnel then redelegates some of the power down the line to the next level. Line authority is possessed by individual supervisors as a result of distribution throughout an organization. Line authority is the power to direct subordinates in everyday performance of their assigned tasks. It gives a manger the right to make decisions in a particular operational area. Line authority is also used for passing information and directives down the organizational channels. Fig. 8 illustrates how power is distributed in a line structure. Persons at the succeeding levels have less authority than those at high levels. For example the hospital administrator controls the largest number of units within the hospital system. Each succeeding level keeps a certain number of units for its own and passes down a certain number of authority units.

It can be seen from the relationships in Fig. 8 that units of authority are often

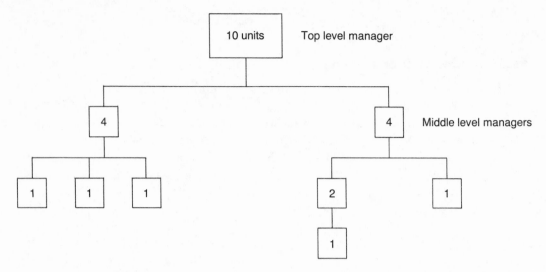

Fig. 8. Hypothetical distribution of line authority units in an organization.

associated with the number of people; that is, middle level managers have more persons working under them. This is not always the case, but in certain specialty areas of health care delivery, such as coronary and intensive care units, the number of high level professionals in ratio to patients and subordinate personnel means a high level of personal authority is vested in each of the nurses because of their technical expertise and experience.

Staff authority*

Staff authority is a form of authority delegated to specialized staff personnel in an organization. Staff authority is usually associated with the higher level management in an organization and revolves around specialized functions that may be applicable to the entire organization. Staff personnel are usually answerable only to a person having line authority, such as an advisory committee to a dean of a school of nursing. Staff functions are sometimes thought of as those of "thinking" or "counseling," whereas line functions are more action oriented (Koontz and O'Donnell, 1972).

GUIDELINES FOR DEVELOPING PERSONAL AUTHORITY AND POWER BASES

If the health care system will encourage the use of functional or personal authority, especially by nursing staff, it can do a great deal to alleviate dissatisfaction among professionals who feel that they lack opportunity to exercise authority but are held responsible for the accomplishment of certain tasks. A number of personal needs can be met, encouraging nurses to use their personal authority

---

*See Arndt, C., and Huckabay, L.: Nursing administration, St. Louis, 1975, The C. V. Mosby Co., pp. 74-79 for a more complete discussion.

and power. Nurses have both technical and professional knowledge and expertise. The use of personal power and authority will: (1) provide an increased sense of contribution, (2) enhance prestige, and (3) provide opportunities to control factors that make it possible for people to meet goals and live up to assigned responsibilities. In general it is assumed that if nurses use the personal authority inherent in their jobs, they will perform at a significantly higher level.

Acquiring personal authority

Since personal authority is authority nurses can gain through their own efforts, there are certain procedures that can be utilized in expanding their power and authority within an organization. We have all heard the word machiavellian used to characterize behavior or principles suggesting cunning and duplicity. Machiavelli was a fifteenth century Italian statesman or politician who advised kings how they might gain more power during the time when many Italian city-states were vying for more power. Machiavelli wrote a book called *The Prince* in which he exorted double dealing and deceitful and crafty methods for gaining power in a court situation. As a result the word machiavellian has come to characterize a hypocritical, self serving modus operandi.

In today's health care delivery environment machiavellian techniques are unnecessary and unwise. Nurses start from the very strong personal power base of wanting to improve the welfare of others. This positive orientation should not be damaged by machiavellian methods of increasing administrative power and authority. When acquiring authority through personal power bases, one must remember that the acquisition of authority is not an end in itself. Also the attempt to acquire authority should not be made unless a person is willing to be held responsible for the actions taken based on that authority. There are some basic techniques that can help a nurse acquire personal authority in an organizational setting. First, nurses should acquire a broad view of the entire health care delivery operation. A limited perspective of the entire operation produces limited understanding of the constructive measures that can be taken to improve health care delivery and patient care. The nurse interested in acquiring leadership within an organization and improving patient care should look at key documents such as policies, procedures, short- and long-term goals, and plans to become familiar with the mission of the system.

The nurse should also be aware of the formal authority in the organization. It is helpful to look at job descriptions, functional statements, and organizational charts.

Phasing in personal authority

A relatively safe method for using personal authority is by operating almost entirely within the framework of a function presently delegated. For example, the nurse who discovers a better way of carrying out a responsibility, but a method that departs from previous practice, is using personal authority. Nurses do this quite often when they think of new patient care practices that relate initially to their area of expertise or assignment but require additional initiative in order to effect.

Preparing for action

One method to acquire authority is to carefully prepare an action intended to influence decisions that are actually outside one's formal or positional authority. Often this is done by means of a confrontation at a meeting. One must research the necessary facts and figures and even practice how to make the pitch for his own point of view. Facts and information are powerful tools.

Gaining peer support

Authority can be acquired by influencing not only decision makers but also colleagues. A basic tactic here is to gain support and cooperation from colleagues in accomplishing some activities that might meet with resistance if one were to seek authority and approval through conventional authority channels. By convincing peers and aligning the support of others who would be involved in the same level of operation, the nurse develops a strong interpersonal power base. A way to do this is to arrange to get together informally with other persons at the same level who agree on a joint course of action. Nurses might even try out the action on a pilot basis in parallel with an existing system. If the results are successful, they can move for acquisition of authority from a higher place in the organization.

Dealing with clients and patients

A parallel technique to gaining support of one's peers is that of gaining support of persons outside the organization but in health care delivery. The patients or clients are really the base to the system and perhaps the most potent source of power for the nurse. There are many transactions that nurses make with patients and their families that enhance acquisition of authority. On these occasions nurses commonly make a decision and work with the patient in a way that they know will be of special benefit to the institution.

Developing pilot projects

Nurses are sometimes strong in this particular area. If a new procedure is being considered, a pilot project is appropriate, such as "rooming in," which has been initiated by nurses. With pilot operations one must keep in mind that if good results are produced there must be documented evidence of the success. This is one of the critical problems in nursing. Nurses need to document their successes with hard data.

SUMMARY

The importance of having a strong personal authority base cannot be overemphasized in acquiring authority. The use of personal authority is critical in expanding power and influence in an organization. Personal authority, indeed, is the power that encourages a nurse to use technical and professional expertise, management techniques, and human relations in creative ways. One cannot expand power without using personal initiative and authority or relying heavily on the personal power bases of a strong self concept and self esteem.

The nurse who seeks to use initiative and gain organizational power must be willing to be not only responsible for putting the ideas into effect but also acccountable. This means the nurse must live with the results and be able to determine where those results were successful or where they need modification. Successful nurse leaders know when to use formal authority and how to develop their personal authority base. There must be a sense of commitment to the interests of nursing, to patient care, to the organization in which one works, and to the nursing profession. The desire to become involved in the affairs of the profession and the organization is the essence of true professional nursing. Nurse leaders who exercise both formal and personal authority and use their power bases can indeed move toward meeting the "ultimate test of leadership which is the wise use of power" (Bennis, 1976, p. 176).

REFERENCES

Arndt, C., and Huckabay, L.: Nursing administration: Theory for practice with a systems approach, St. Louis, 1975, The C. V. Mosby Co.

Bailey, J., McDonald, F., and Claus, K. E.: An experiment in nursing curriculums at a university, Belmont, Calif., 1972, Wadsworth Publishing Co. Inc.

Bennis, W. G.: The unconscious conspiracy, New York, 1976, AMACOM.

Bennis, W. G.: Leadership theory and administrative behavior: The problem of authority, Administrative Science Quarterly 4:259-301, 1959.

Dornbusch, S. M., and Scott, W. R.: Evaluation and the exercise of authority, San Francisco, 1975, Jossey-Bass, Inc., Publishers.

Hicks, H. G.: The management of organizations: A systems and human resources approach, ed. 2, New York, 1972, McGraw-Hill, Inc.

Koontz, H., and O'Donnell, C.: Principles of management: An analysis of managerial functions, New York, 1972, McGraw-Hill, Inc.

Peabody, R.: Authority in organizations: A comparative study, doctoral dissertation, Stanford, Calif., 1960, Stanford University.

Presthus, R.: Authority in organizations, Public Administration Review 20:88-91, 1960.

Simon, H.: Administrative behavior, New York, 1957, Macmillan, Inc.

Tannenbaum, R., Wechsler, I., and Massarik, F.: Leadership and organization: A behavioral approach, New York, 1961, McGraw-Hill, Inc.

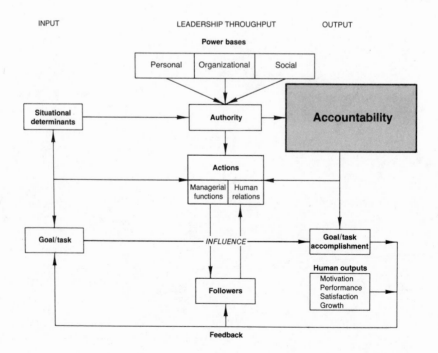

INPUT   LEADERSHIP THROUGHPUT   OUTPUT

Power bases

| Personal | Organizational | Social |

| Situational determinants | | Authority | | **Accountability** |

Actions

| Managerial functions | Human relations |

| Goal/task | *INFLUENCE* | Goal/task accomplishment |

Human outputs
Motivation
Performance
Satisfaction
Growth

Followers

Feedback

Only as we determine how we can direct our
services to where they are needed and can accomplish
the greatest good do we translate the morality
of accountability into responsible action.

EDITH P. LEWIS

6 ACCOUNTABILITY AND RESPONSIBILITY

RESPONSIBILITY AND ACCOUNTABILITY IN NURSING

The crisis in the health care system has made new demands on providers of health care. Not only is society demanding that health care services be provided at a reasonable cost to all segments of society, but it is also asking for accountability and responsibility from health professionals.

Responsibility and accountability have become critical issues in nursing. To some extent factors in the social milieu have contributed to this concern. The rise of the consumer movement to improve the quality of goods and services in general and health care in particular has been a major factor. A more enlightened public has also been important. Nurses themselves have recognized the need to involve patients in the process of their own care and in assuming responsibility for the choices about their own life style. The Patient's Bill of Rights also addresses the issue (Annas and Healey, 1974).

The effects of these factors on the nursing profession should indeed be viewed as a challenge and as a vehicle for moving the profession forward. But because of the other attitudes that accompany requests for accountability, and because of the connotations of being "called to account," nurses may shudder at the prospect. Like other health professionals, professional nurses are being led to defensive practice. The tendency to be overly cautious, to take few risks, to shun creativity and innovation is one of the negative responses of being "called to account." This reaction no doubt comes from the high stakes in the delivery of health care. A nurse supervisor who makes an error of judgment may, in some situations, be charged with negligence.

We prefer to look at accountability and responsibility as opportunities for nurses in leadership positions to introduce planned change. To a great extent accountability and responsibility come from an attitude within a person. The person who feels responsibility for doing a good job and welcomes accountability will, with adequate skills, be an effective leader.

Survey research shows that nurses are motivated by a desire for taking on more responsibility (MacDonald, 1975). Moreover, the attitudes of a nursing supervisor toward responsibility, as toward many other concepts, will filter down to the staff nurses (White, 1971). Therefore, nurse leaders must channel accountability and responsibility into productive avenues for personal and staff development, as we shall explain. Because responsibility is in part a philosophical and ethical consideration, different nurse leaders will articulate its meaning in different terms. However, its fundamental place remains among the professional values of the nurse leader.

As professionals, nurses are charged with a certain amount of accountability and responsibility of various kinds. Inherent in the role of nurse leaders are special functions and activities that involve both human and material resources. Practically and legally the dean or director is responsible for the competence of those who participate in information gathering, fact finding, problem solving, and many other team activities.

There is evidence that nurses want responsibility (Godfrey, 1975). Some health care settings, however, which are physician-dominated, seem to nurses to be inimical to personal accountability of an individual health care practitioner (Gortner, 1974). The courage required to seek and take responsibility is obvious, especially in light of the changing public expectations concerning health care. Courage can be rewarded through careful use of newly acquired responsibility.

THE NATURE OF ACCOUNTABILITY AND RESPONSIBILITY
Definitions

The term *accountability* implies liability for one's actions and is *process-oriented*. An accountable person is one who is answerable for the use of his authority. Accountability also involves others' expectations of one's behavior. Registered nurses are accountable because their expertise and training provides bases for expectations of what their behavior *should* be in given circumstances. Accountability is tied closely to value systems and cultural expectations.

The term *responsibility,* on the other hand, is much more specific and is *task-oriented*. A responsible person has been delegated authority to do a task and has a *duty* to perform adequately.

In sum a leader is accountable for the performance of followers, who in turn are responsible for carrying out certain tasks.

DIFFERENCES BETWEEN ACCOUNTABILITY AND RESPONSIBILITY

Responsibility expresses one's obligations of performance; accountability implies that one's actual performance *will* be judged against performance expectations. Another important difference between accountability and responsibility exists in terms of scope. Responsibility may be assigned for specific tasks on a regular basis, such as being assigned as a treatment nurse if the functional approach is used as a modality of patient care. The tasks and responsibilities of a primary care nurse or a nurse practitioner will be quite different in scope than that of the nurse assigned functional modality of nursing care.

Accountability supercedes responsibility. Nursing directors are accountable for the delivery of nursing services, whereas staff nurses are responsible for the various tasks and activities that comprise direct patient care.

The type of health care services provided influences the nature of responsibility involved. For example, cutbacks in mental health care facilities may require nurses to make decisions about who is or is not ready for discharge. The great number of "walking wounded" who leave the facilities may reflect attitudes about this responsibility (Cant, 1976). A psychiatric nurse reports that a critical point in the therapeutic relationship, the impact of commitment, comes with the therapist's recognition of the patient's illness and from this commitment follows the responsibility of entering the healing relationship (Finkleman, 1975). For psychiatric nurses this responsibility is part of their contract and commitment to alleviate those problems. Another facet of mental health care has been considered in terms of the unusual problems that may require staff accountability (Freed, 1975).

Although staff nurses are responsible for the care of patients, consider what happens when a psychiatric patient is discovered to have left the hospital without staff permission. In all probability nursing care activities will be subordinated to the concrete action of laying blame with the question, "Who was with him last?" Nurses in such a situation know that it is usually the team member with lowest status who is held responsible. As Freed speculates in describing this hypothetical situation: "This kind of accountability will stultify initiative and innovation, and it can result in staff behavior which is rigid, narrow and nonproductive—but safe" (Freed, 1975, p. 36). Accountability, as it is practiced, will influence the entire milieu of the institution. If nurses would assume 100% responsibility in their professional roles, not only would the results improve patient care services, but their energy could be used to bring about needed changes.

Accountability is a management function, an executive activity. Nurse leaders must recognize their role in accountability and in overseeing the responsibilities of subordinates. Responsibility might be viewed as having two phases: (1) carrying out assigned activities to achieve results, and (2) accounting to a supervisor for the degree of success in completing prescribed tasks (Terry, 1972). In considering these two phases of responsibility one sees that they will appear in the health care setting as they are carried out by staff nurses at the direction of the nurse leader.

The accountability of the nursing supervisor or nursing dean precedes in importance and time the responsibility of all subordinates. This precedence of accountability is of critical importance. Directors of nursing service are accountable for the delivery of quality patient care. They must plan for the delivery of care within the constraints of human and material resources. Within this framework one can think of accountability as an insurance policy. The effective director of nursing service does not have to wait for a crisis to be held accountable. Through careful planning, clarity of goals, well-defined job descriptions, role clarity, and carefully developed policies and procedures, nurses in top management can take positive steps toward accountability.

Changes in responsibility

Current changes in the nursing profession include not only new roles for nurses but expanding nurses' role in a variety of dimensions. Political participation of nurses at the local, state, and national levels to improve the delivery of care as well as their own professional practice exemplifies some of the added responsibilities of nurses. Changes in nurse practice acts and requirements of continuing education for renewal of the license exemplify changes that have come about through nurses assuming responsibility. In addition nurses are beginning to assume more responsibility for the care of the elderly, particularly the elderly with chronic diseases who are confined to nursing homes and who until recently had inadequate nursing care (Mullane, 1975).

TYPES OF RESPONSIBILITY AND ACCOUNTABILITY

To whom are nurses accountable? In answering this question, one appreciates the complexity of the changing demands on nursing service and the requirements of the nursing education system in its response to social needs and the vagaries of legislation.

Personal responsibility

Before nurse leaders can expect subordinates to cultivate an attitude of responsibility for their performance, accountability and responsibility must be demonstrated by top management. Nurse leaders must indeed serve as effective role models. In some situations it is only when nurse leaders accept responsibility for their own actions that they can appreciate their effect on others (Binderman, 1974; Whitehead, 1972). Developing a sense of personal accountability and responsibility can indeed enhance the nature of influence.

Nurse leaders are largely responsible for their own continued learning and growth. Working in a clinical or an academic setting does not imply that one's knowledge stays up to date. Rather, special effort is required to stay abreast of the knowledge and technical advances. Building on one's knowledge base has a high payoff for nurse leaders in terms of power. In a team situation, for example, the nurse leader who is up to date on professional matters enhances her power bases and influence strategies. Continued learning goes beyond reading professional journals. There is an obligation to share knowledge and ideas through publishing, conducting as well as attending conferences, and engaging in studies to extend or validate knowledge.

Interpersonal responsibility to one's staff

Part of being accountable to one's staff involves the need for sharing responsibility with them. In a paradoxical way responsibility is like love: the more one gives away, the more one has. Nurses as a group are known to be motivated by the need for achievement, which implies a desire for responsibility (MacDonald, 1975). Through assuming responsibility, nurse leaders will be upgrading efficiency and productivity in two ways. First, nurses will become more effective leaders as they develop their skills in directing subordinates and communicating effectively with them. Second, through encouraging and expecting staff to be responsible, nurse leaders are building a nursing team who can function more effectively and efficiently in meeting goals. Likewise, the dean of a school of nursing is not only responsible and accountable to the chief campus officer for planning and administering a nursing curriculum to meet the goals of the school of nursing, the health care needs of consumers, and the educational needs of students, but is also responsible and accountable to faculty members.

Team accountability, a product of the multidisciplinary approach, may be a mixed blessing. If the team's accountability is substituted for personal accountability, the team needs direction. In a nursing team situation it is often the responsibility of the team leader to allocate tasks so that accountability is maximized. For example, if a new graduate nurse is weak in some skill, it is the responsibility of both the new graduate nurse and the team leader to augment these skills.

The prudent head nurse may have to guard against the social consequences of teamwork. Some preliminary research indicates that in decision making tasks, groups tend to take greater risks than individuals (Yinon and Bizman, 1974).

Organizational responsibility

Nurses in leadership positions are accountable for developing and maintaining standards and for achieving organizational goals. A significant dimension of this accountability relationship revolves around changing the licensure procedures so that institutions rather than individual practitioners would be licensed (Passos, 1973). The fact that approximately 67% of all nurses are employed in hospitals and related institutions appears often in pro–institution licensure arguments. In the opinion of some nurse leaders this change would seriously erode the excellence of nursing (Driscoll, 1972).

Changes in types of health agencies in which nurses provide patient care brings changes in the requirements of accountability. Consider, for example, the innovative approaches to meet the needs of consumers who require minor surgery. Surgical centers have been developed where minor surgery is performed on an outpatient basis (Cooper, 1976). The head nurse, working with a small staff, would be accountable to some extent for instructing patients in postoperative care in these settings. Institutions should obtain more input from nurses in budgetary planning and control. Cutting operating costs in a growing concern for nonprofit hospitals (Forbes, 1976).

Part of the nurse leader's accountability to an institution extends to the patients in the institution. Some nurses maintain that policies at many institutions that require the rotation of nursing personnel result in a lack of continual contact and thus the nurses are not accountable to patients (Passos, 1973). In some settings this problem may be the product of complicated communication channels. Nurse leaders who are responsible for scheduling staffing of a unit should be sensitive to the needs of both patients and staff members. In the broader sense nurse leaders are accountable for the work environment of health care delivery. Part of their responsibility is to see that the work environment meets the needs of staff. In its totality this environment includes physical surroundings, supply distribution arrangements, and equipment, as well as scheduling and the human elements that make up the psychological milieu. Nurse leaders must meet the environmental needs of staff members. For example, during one of our consultation visits it was found in one large, complex acute care setting that no provisions had been made to furnish personnel with a warm meal, not to mention a quiet place to eat. Such insensitivity to environmental conditions leads to counterproductivity.

Accountability to the nursing profession

The nursing education system provides the source for changes in the nursing profession through its educational programs. Deans of schools of nursing, faculty members, and directors of inservice health care agencies have a special challenge and opportunity to teach student nurses and nurses their role in the area of responsibility and accountability.

A basic task of nursing educators is to prepare students for the performance standards to which they will be held accountable as professionals. These standards are dynamic; as standards change, the requirements of nursing education are modified. In recent years the trend toward team nursing has created a need for nurses with leadership skills and effective communication skills. Curricula of many schools of nursing are beginning to meet these needs. However, a perusal of nursing school bulletins across the country indicates a dearth of courses specifically designed to train nurses in leadership or management.

The growing emphasis on the economical use of professional personnel continues to be of immediate concern. Nevertheless, as a nurse educator observes, educational programs are not emphasizing the professional nurse's accountability for learning to assess patient care in terms of using professional skills economically and delegating some tasks to less highly trained personnel (Lio, 1976).

The clinical experience that nurses receive in their education tends to concentrate on the performance of specific patient care activities that may involve some nurse-patient communication and some nurse-instructor communication. But the environments in which students find themselves as practitioners demand much more. For example, the nurse needs skills in translating professional language into terms that can be understood by nonprofessional work associates as well as by the patient and his family (Lio, 1976). Even more basic is the negligence of many curricula to prepare nurses to function in settings where patient care is a shared activity requiring cooperative effort. Because this is alien to most new graduate nurses' expectations, they may find themselves reluctant to take responsibility for the work of nonprofessional workers or for the standards of performance of nurses with relatively less experience (Kramer, 1974). The failure of educational institutions to be accountable to their students may result in graduates who do not understand how to deal with opportunities for accountability in their own practice.

Quality. In being accountable to students, one of nursing educators' primary concerns is ensuring high quality instruction. Deans and other nursing school administrators are often pressured to stress the need for diversity in educational programs and for nontraditional approaches or alternatives. Given the changing nature of the profession, such considerations have value indeed. But diversity cannot be cultivated at the expense of quality. Only those alternatives should be adopted that safeguard quality and that are at least of equal educational value if the educational institution is truly accountable to its students.

Three areas that have been noted for their special importance to high quality education and accountability are: facilities, course offerings, and qualified faculty (McMullan, 1975). In addition, admission policies must also be considered. The dean or director of a school of nursing must be accountable to the students who are admitted to nursing programs. Is it ethical, for example, for an institution to admit students who are not likely to succeed in the program? Questions of this sort will become more common as the fruits of consumerism applied to education continue to grow (Millard, 1975). Regulations to protect education consumers are being developed. Judicious administrators and faculty of nursing education programs will probably want to become familiar with various regulations. These regulations do not confine themselves to the student loan program but treat many problems related to consumer protection and educational malpractice.

Curricula in nursing education are expected to demonstrate responsiveness and accountability to social forces. At the present time there are clear indications that the need exists to prepare nurses as primary health care providers. Prior to the Nurse Training Act of 1971 and the publication of the HEW report *Extending the Scope of Nursing Practice* (November 1971), there was an urgent unmet need to prepare nurses for primary nursing roles.

Many schools of nursing across the country are designing nursing curricula to train nurses for new and extended roles; others have yet to meet this need. If, for example, a dean or director of a school of nursing allows faculty to design and implement a curriculum solely to indulge their own interests and expertise, nurses in these top management positions are failing to meet the needs of not only the students but also the health agencies in which the students will eventually practice, and they should be held accountable for this dilemma.

The social accountability of professional nurses

"Evaluation of one's performance by peers is a hallmark of professionalism, and it is through this mechanism that the profession is held accountable to society" (Passos, 1973, p. 18). In general terms there are three dimensions of nursing's accountability to society: (1) the responsibility to provide service, (2) the responsibility to provide education to the public about health matters, and (3) the responsibility to educate the public about the nursing profession and its social contribution.

Nurses possess a level of education and expertise in health care that has high value for society. The level of the nurses' professional knowledge and society's level of knowledge about health are, however, in a dynamic relationship. People are becoming increasingly well-educated about ways to maintain their own level of health. To an increasing extent they are assuming new responsibilities for preventive medicine through incorporating simple health rules into their life styles such as attention to nutrition, exercise, and rest and eliminating smoking and excessive use of alcohol and drugs. By implication, this trend requires that the knowledge of practicing nurses should be more advanced, technical, and sophisticated than the information generally accessible to the well-informed lay person. Nurses, in turn, have a responsibility to share information that can help in the well-being of the patient.

The delivery of health care is a responsibility of some 800,000 registered nurses in the United States. The nature of that care is determined in part by expressed needs and in part by the capabilities of professional nurses and nurse leaders. Five areas have been stressed as particularly important in terms of meeting long-range consumer health care needs (McMullan, 1975):

1. Participation of health care providers and consumers is needed to plan for comprehensive delivery of health care services.
2. Institutional facilities and communities need a health team system that includes the consumer and concentrates on consumer needs to offset attention to the strictly defined practitioner's roles.
3. A nursing care team should include nurses from all types of training programs and there should be consumer participation.
4. Health professionals are needed to assist consumers in becoming informed and effective participants in promoting and maintaining their own health.
5. There is a growing need for health care practitioners to provide primary health care.

NURSING'S TRADITION OF ACCOUNTABILITY

The development of a scientific base for the practice of nursing is a new dimension of accountability in nursing. By tradition the practice of accountability in nursing has been based on its association with humanitarianism (Gortner, 1974). No one is suggesting that this humanitarian dimension of accountability is inappropriate, but it is not sufficient by itself. Nurses are also charged with accommodating scientific values in accounting for practice.

To some extent the development of the scientific-based accountability depends on the development of philosophies of practice. Most institutions have an expressed philosophy of practice that permeates the milieu. But individual practitioners ought to think about their rationale for the many activities of patient care and apply this rationale to their observations and to the data they gather in investigating practice.

Indications of interest in philosophies of practice are increasing: over 50% of all current federally funded nursing projects are concerned with investigations into nursing practice. Some service settings, outstanding in their clear demonstration of a philosophy of practice, are attracting highly trained professional nurses who are sympathetic to these philosophies. The Loeb Center for Nursing in New York, which is run entirely by nurses, characterizes such a setting. Nursing practice at the Loeb Center reflects the philosophy of care of the leaders of the institution. The success of a humanistic, concerned approach in the delivery of nursing care to the elderly who are suffering from a variety of chronic diseases is well documented (Strauss, 1975).

The basis for nursing's sense of accountability

A nationally prominent nurse leader has speculated that characteristics of outstanding settings such as the Loeb Center include a tradition of not only the humanistic values of caring but also accountability in practice (Gortner, 1974). Accountability for nursing practice in such settings, as Gortner observes, shows marked similarity to the commitment of a scientist in choosing a problem for investigation and planning for its resolution. These similarities include:

1. *A predisposition to scientific activity.* Many nurses are exposed to the scientific method early in their training. Although only a relatively small number of nurses may devote their skills primarily to research, all nurses and particularly nurse leaders can apply the methods of observation and evaluation to their daily organizational activities.

2. *A deep interest in the subject matter.* For nursing leaders, this interest may enhance interaction with other professionals. Physicians, for example, often do not understand the domain of nurses' practice but can be made aware through the expressed interest of nurse leaders in improving their knowledge. This same interest can help nurse leaders to analyze their environment to determine the forces and factors in the organization, which are potential accelerators or inhibitors of productivity.

3. *A continually questioning mind.* This element of accountability prompts nurse leaders to read extensively in professional journals and to seek out and confer with fellow professionals who have expertise in given areas of interest. A sense of incompleteness of one's knowledge compels many accountable nursing investigators to return to their clinical or experimental laboratories to try to find new explanations to account for what they observe.

4. *A consideration and reconsideration of each emerging set of findings.* Outstanding nurse researchers sometimes spend years studying problems that first drew their interests when they were students. The scientific activity of reassessment is critical to the improvement of nursing practice. One solution to a problem is only one answer to one question; there may be new ways of asking the question that lead to even more significant answers. As methodical investigators, nurse leaders may need help in reconsidering important problems. One of the purposes of publication is exactly this: to expose one's ideas to constructive criticism and analysis by other trained professionals.

5. *Objectivity to avoid the prophecy of self fulfillment or self interest.* In educational, service, and research settings, nurse leaders have many opportunities to control events or to manipulate them. Acting from self interest, a director of nursing service may be included to appoint a fellow professional beyond the person's level of competence. Such actions not only are unfair to the employee and other members of the staff but also seriously affect the patient and the quality of care in the institution.

6. *Intellectual and personal honesty.* Nurse leaders may feel that the many demands on their time do not allow them to devote their skills to research as much as they would like. But this does not excuse failure to give credit to students or younger faculty members who have indeed been deeply involved and made a major contribution to a research project. Faculty should reward students for such endeavors by co-authority or having students contribute under their own names.

PUBLIC AWARENESS OF NURSING

Through efforts in the delivery of primary health care, nurse practitioners will help improve the public's understanding of the valuable contributions of nursing and will also appreciate lower health care costs. Raising consumer consciousness is a responsibility of every nurse. Nursing education has a special role in this task. Baccalaureate nursing programs must provide educational and clinical experiences that will enable nurses to practice as primary health care providers. Skills needed for this professional nursing role include skills and knowledge in health education of clients and families, intellectual and interpersonal skills necessary to serve as a nursing team leader or as a member of a health care team in a variety of health care settings; and the political know-how for initiating involvement in community health affairs.

SUMMARY

We have explored the accountability and responsibility of nurse leaders in service and educational settings and the societal trends that require changes in the dimensions of accountability. Requirements of accountability include competence to meet performance standards, an ethical sense to guide one's actions, and a sense of commitment to the delivery of quality health care services.

The primary difference between accountability and responsibility is that responsibility should be delegated to subordinates, whereas accountability rests with the leader in health care settings. Responsibility and accountability have been shown to be related to power. Nurse leaders can enhance their use of expertise and legitimate power bases by accepting responsibility and welcoming opportunities for accountability.

Several types of responsibility incumbent on most nurses at some times have been identified. They include: (1) personal responsibility; (2) interpersonal responsibility to one's staff; (3) institutional responsibility; (4) professional responsibility, particularly in reference to education; and (5) social responsibility, both in terms of providing care and providing information.

The results of responsibility and accountability have been examined in reference to the personal development and growth of nurse leaders, the enrichment of staff or faculty members, the improvement of the work environment, and the impact of quality health care on the attitudes of the consumers and on their perceptions of the nursing profession.

REFERENCES

Annas, G. J., and Healey, J.: The patient rights advocate, Journal of Nursing Administration 4(3):25-31, 1974.

Binderman, R. M.: The issue of responsibility in gestalt therapy, Psychotherapy: Theory, Research and Practice 11(3):287-288, 1974.

Cant, G.: Valiumania, New York Times Magazine, February 1, 1976, pp. 34-44.

Cooper, R.: Day-surgery centers snip away red tape, put clamps on costs, The Wall Street Journal, January 23, 1976, p. 1.

Driscoll, V. M.: Independence in nursing: Challenge

or burden? Can we exist without it? Michigan Nurse 45:12-15, 1972.

Extending the scope of nursing practice, Washington, D.C., November 1971, Department of Health, Education and Welfare.

Finkleman, A.: Commitment and responsibility in the therapeutic relationship, Journal of Psychiatric Nursing and Mental Health Services 13(1):10-14, 1975.

Free-enterprise the answer? Forbes Magazine, January 15, 1976, p. 40.

Freed, E. X.: Accountability in mental health care,

Journal of Nursing Administration 5(7):36-37, 1975.

Godfrey, M. A.: Your fringe benefits—How much are they really worth? Nursing 5(1):73-75, 1975.

Gortner, S. R.: Scientific accountability in nursing, Nursing Outlook 22(12):764-768, 1974.

Kramer, M.: Reality shock: Why nurses leave nursing, St. Louis, 1974, The C. V. Mosby Co.

Lio, A.: Leadership and responsibility in team nursing, Nursing Clinics of North America 8(6):267-280, 1976.

MacDonald, M. R.: Matching personalities with position: A study of job satisfaction, Supervisor Nurse 6(4):43-50, 1975.

McMullan, D.: Accountability and nursing education, Nursing Outlook 23(8):501-503, 1975.

Millard, R. M.: The new accountability, Nursing Outlook 23(8):496-500, 1975.

Mullane, M. K.: Nursing care and the political arena, Nursing Outlook 23(11):699-701, 1975.

Passos, J. Y.: Accountability: Myth or mandate? Journal of Nursing Administration 3(3):17-22, 1973.

Strauss, A.: Chronic illness and the quality of life, St. Louis, 1975, The C. V. Mosby Co.

Terry, G. R.: Principles of management, ed. 6, Homewood, Ill., 1972, Richard D. Irwin, Inc.

White, H. C.: Some perceived behavior and attitudes of hospital employees under effective and ineffective supervision, Journal of Nursing Administration 1(1):49-54, 1971.

Whitehead, J. A.: Clinical responsibility and its proper reward, Nursing Mirror 13(4):42-43, 1972.

Yinon, G., and Bizman, A.: The nature of effective bonds and the degree of personal responsibility as determinants of risk taking for self and others, Bulletin of the Psychonomic Society 4(2-A):80-82, 1974.

SUGGESTED READINGS

Coulton, M. R.: Labor disputes: A challenge to nurse staffing, Journal of Nursing Administration 6(4):15-20, 1976.

Incident reporting—nurses' responsibility, The Regan Report on Nursing Law 13(8):1, 1972.

Lewis, E. P.: Accountability: How, for what, and to whom? Nursing Outlook 20(5):315, 1972.

McClure, M. L.: Entry into professional practice: The New York proposal, Journal of Nursing Administration 6(5):12-17, 1976.

Modlin, H. C.: Science and technology vs. ethics and morals, Bulletin of the Menninger Clinic 37(2): 149-59, 1973.

Parker, W. S.: Realities of responsibility, Nursing Times 67(3):1053-1054, 1971.

Stevens, B. J.: Accountability of the clinical specialist: The administrator's viewpoint, Journal of Nursing Administration 6(2):30-32, 1976.

Visitor's safety: Nurses share responsibility, The Regan Report on Nursing Law 13(9):2, 1972.

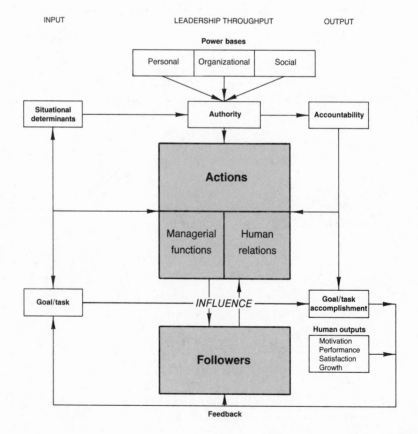

INPUT   LEADERSHIP THROUGHPUT   OUTPUT

Power bases

| Personal | Organizational | Social |

Situational
determinants → Authority → Accountability

Actions

| Managerial functions | Human relations |

Goal/task — *INFLUENCE* — Goal/task accomplishment

Human outputs
Motivation
Performance
Satisfaction
Growth

Followers

Feedback

*Nurses can have a profound impact on health
care if—and only if—they will work and speak
out. . . . The name of the game is power.*

DOROTHY J. NOVELLO

7 TRANSLATING POWER INTO INFLUENCE

THE NATURE OF INFLUENCE

If indeed the name of the game in nursing is power and nurses are admonished to "use it or lose it," a critical question becomes, "How can nurses exercise power in productive ways?"

We believe that to exercise power in productive ways nurses must understand that influence is the *result* of power. There is considerable support in the literature for our position. Parsons (1963) describes influence as ways of getting results and promoting interactions. Influence has also been defined by other scholars as a *"causal* relationship between the application of power and another's behavior" (Schlenker and Tedeschi, 1971, p. 291). The leadership-influence-power relationship has been described by Hollander and Julian (1970) as one in which the nature of leadership implies a particular influence relationship between two or more persons through the application of power.

INFLUENCE STRATEGIES

In reviewing the literature on influence and power relations, particularly the works of French and Raven (1959), it appeared to us that there are a number of strategies that a nurse leader can use to influence individuals and groups. These influence strategies can indeed serve as ways to effectively channel the elements of the leader's power (strength, energy, and action) into productive results. Strategies of the leader for promoting influence include the following: (1) obtaining and sharing accurate information, (2) demonstrating a high level of expertise, (3) using legitimate authority in effective ways, (4) promoting ways in which subordinates can identify with the leader, (5) effectively using rewards and punishments, (6) understanding manipulative behavior, and (7) effectively controlling the work environment. A closer look at each of these influence strategies and how they can be used by nurse leaders follows.

Information

It has been said that an element of personal power is not simply information and knowledge but the control of information (Reiff, 1974). In many activities a leader is able to influence others, primarily because of access to accurate information and the ability to communicate it effectively to followers. For example, an important component of effective decision making is accurate information. It follows that the person who has accurate information has a powerful tool; thus the relationship of power to decision making is obvious. Its implications in an organizational setting have been studied with particular interest (Wood, 1973). Information is related to decision making and hence to power and influence to such a great extent that control of information is a way of controlling decisions. Nurse leaders thus need to share information with nurses on the unit level so that if the decision making process has been decentralized, nurses at the unit level can take *actions* based on *facts*.

Expertise

The degree to which a nurse leader is perceived by others as having special knowledge or skill is an important factor in influencing others. Luchins and Luchins (1961) demonstrated that an expert's opinion is more influential than the majority of a group. It is to be expected that the expertise of the person with the influence will be evaluated on two scales: (1) the extent to which the expertise is perceived to surpass that of the person being influenced and (2) the extent to which the knowledge is perceived to be in relation to some external standard or value. In a situation in which a strategy of expertise is perceived, it is essential that the person being influenced believe in both the ability and the integrity of the expert.

As a professional group, nurses must grow and develop their expertise so it can be used as an influence strategy. Sometimes nurses fail to make known to patients, other professional groups, or society that they are indeed experts in the area of providing nursing and health care services. In communicating with patients, nurses often present themselves as the physician's handmaidens rather than as professionals with unique knowledge and skills who serve as *members* of the health care team to augment the role of other health professionals. A summary of the handmaiden phenomenon has been offered by a nurse leader in a recent study: "It is more rewarding or less threatening for her (the nurse) to please the physician than it is to meet the needs of the patient" (Kalisch, 1975, p. 24). This explanation may or may not be justified. But the fact remains that nurses have opportunities for communicating their own expertise but often do not maximize these opportunities.

In using expertise as an effective strategy to influence others, nursing administrators and supervisors have the task of: (1) communicating their expertise as professionals through expert performance (actions speak louder than words), (2) setting high standards of performance for subordinates and effectively measuring the performance, (3) providing opportunities for subordinates to grow personally and professionally, and (4) assuming responsibility for their own professional and personal growth.

Legitimacy

Authority or the right to do something serves as a basis for an influence strategy based on legitimacy. The legitimacy of a leader's role is based on norms and expectations held by group members. The meaning of what is or is not legitimate is difficult to understand because of the complexity and number of sources of legitimacy. Like other relationships in an organization it has a subjective element: if subordinates perceive that the benefits and rewards that they derive from their work under the direction of their leader meet their expectations and appear to be fair, the power of the leader may be perceived as legitimate (Blau, 1964).

In an organizational setting, legitimacy is often a result of relationships between positions rather than between people. But in the health care delivery setting, in which clients are a transient part of the organization, legitimacy as a means to exert influence is necessary. If, for example, patients do not perceive that what physicians do is legitimate, they may not comply with their orders. Much to the surprise of physicians, noncompliance has been studied and found to be as high as 33 to 50% (Davis, 1968). Since nurse leaders need to be able to assess a situation and determine which influence strategy will be most effective in bringing about a desired change, it is important to realize that the stronger the rationale for selecting a particular influence strategy, the greater its potential effectiveness.

Identifying with the leader

The strategy of identifying with the leader is based on the subordinates' identification with the leader. In simple terms, it means that the subordinate either has or wants a feeling of oneness with the leader. Such a relationship in which persons being influenced "identify with" the leader comes from a feeling on the part of the subordinates that they know the leader, share common goals and values, and can communicate effectively.

Such a referential strategy rests heavily on communication skills. Setting a climate for effective interaction and knowing how to listen carefully and sympathetically are important elements of the communication process. Another important communication skill is knowing how to ask relevant questions that might help another person express thoughts. Communication skills are indeed an integral part of "the human side of leadership."

Effectively using rewards and coercion

An influence strategy that depends on rewards recognizes the ability of the leader to shape and limit the relationship of the individual to the organization. A basic concept of coercion relates to the perception held by one or more persons that another person is able to mediate rewards for them. The social aspect of the relationship is critical. If both persons do not agree about what constitutes a reward, the strategy is weak. In other words, if nursing service administrators or deans of a school of nursing perceive themselves as dispensing rewards but the recipients of these rewards do not perceive them as such, then the nurses in the leadership roles will not be effective in influencing subordinates through the use of reward.

Coercion reflects how the subordinates perceive the leader's use of punishment. Coercion may be confused with reward power in several ways: when a leader withholds a reward, is this perceived as coercion or punishment? Or, from a different perspective, does the person who takes away a punishment give a reward in doing so? The answer, of course, rests with the person being influenced. If the action looks or feels like a reward, then it is indeed a reward. The difference between the bonus and the onus is simply one of the perception of the person being influenced.

Manipulation

Manipulation of cues affecting a decision is a basic technique in the strategies of manipulation. The need to apply this technique is determined somewhat by the prediction of someone's behavior. That is, knowing in advance what someone is likely to do, one can apply some kind of preliminary influence. Studies show that risk takers can affect the decision of a whole group by making risks appear relatively unimportant compared to the reward anticipated (Kelley and Thibaut, 1969). Another influence strategy involves the indirect control of decision alternatives as an aspect of manipulation. Alternatives are controlled through secrecy and manipulation of information to promote ignorance. This technique restricts the number and the range of perceived alternatives, affects the values and abilities of the decision maker, and ultimately affects the quality of a decision.

Environmental controls

The work environment. The importance of the work environment to productivity was discovered in a now classic series of management studies that are probably familiar to many nurse managers. The Hawthorne studies, conducted in the 1920s at the Hawthorne Works of the Western Electric Company, were scientific studies of human behavior in an industrial setting (Roethlisberger and Dickson, 1939). These studies mark the beginning of the behavioral approach to management. The initial study attempted to determine experimentally how worker productivity was affected by varying degrees of illumination. The researchers attempted to control all variables in the experiment while manipulating changes in lighting. But the results were most unsatisfactory. It appeared that some variable other than lighting was influencing workers. This finding led the researchers to design and execute a number of other studies related to the human elements of worker productivity. Scholarly discussion of these studies in modern management literature testifies to their impact for the behavioral approach to management (Miles, 1974).

Basically, one may draw two conclusions. First, the Hawthorne studies represent a pioneering effort at indepth, systematic, and analytical study of the human factor in management, an extremely complex element. Second, the studies showed that the climate of supervision profoundly affects the behavior of work groups. No conclusion is possible concerning how one type of supervision helps a group attain goals more effectively than another kind. But one may conclude that it is indeed the work climate that influences a group to respond either positively or negatively toward attaining its goals and those of the organization.

These findings have far reaching implications for the nurse manager. They can serve as the basis for understanding the importance of human relations in creating a climate that will improve productivity. Therefore, it is within the power of the nurse managers to influence the group's effectiveness in the attainment of goals. The effect, as one can see, is cyclical or self renewing. Success in attaining goals comes from a positive work environment. Each successful experience in goal attainment encourages subordinates to work toward new goals, having experinced success and satisfaction.

Other environmental controls. Agendas are an important type of environmental control. The agenda for a meeting or a listing of decision priorities sets the stage for the types of influence strategies that can be used and provides an important means of control on the activities of others. The person who determines what will be discussed, who will be heard, and in what order has considerable power. This person has a "gatekeeping" function. The gatekeeper determines who will get through at any given time and often prescribes what types of communication are permissible. Executive secretaries often have this type of power in their ability to determine who will and who will not see the director of nursing service or the dean, and whose memos get read and whose do not.

Another dimension of environmental control operates in terms of the number of people available for different behavioral settings. Limiting the number of people in a given setting has been observed to have profound social influence (Barker, 1968). When too few people participate in a given group, each member must then perform more activities and contribute more time to the group's work. The planning committee of an organization such as a health care institution could conceivably make inordinate demands on the time of group members if the committee were insufficiently constituted. In health care delivery settings the dimension of environmental control is relevant because nurses work in many settings.

INFLUENCE THROUGH LEADER/FOLLOWER RELATIONS

It is our thinking that if leaders are to exert influence in the achievement of both organizational and individual goals ways must be developed to maximize leader/follower relations. The findings of a leadership theorist support our position in his discovery that leader-member relations are the most important factor for leadership effectiveness (Fiedler, 1967).

People in health care environments tend to know a great deal about procedures, techniques, and life saving measures; they also tend to assume that it is important to understand the bio-psycho-social needs of patients. But what they seem to ignore is the importance of establishing effective human relations between the leader and the led, whether it be head nurses and their relationships to members of the unit or deans of a school of nursing and their relationships to faculty, students, and staff. To assist nurse leaders to bridge the gap, the following guidelines are suggested as a way to develop more effective leader/follower relations.

1. *Developing a climate of mutual respect.* Respect between leader and followers means recognition of feelings as well as of ideas. Both leader and followers need

to respect themselves as a first step toward mutual respect. As leaders develop their self confidence and self esteem, they will have greater understanding and acceptance of others who are different from themselves. This same principle holds for followers.

"Nothing succeeds like success" is indeed a truism directly related to the result of power. Successful nurse leaders attain a high level of performance in a multitude of activities and responsibilities: they set goals that are challenging and attainable, exercise reasonable controls in achieving goals, and believe that when goals are achieved, positive feedback should be employed.* They feel confident in their role and exude positive energy. A number of studies have shown that leaders who are confident do indeed influence others (Bass, 1961; Higbee, 1969).

Self esteem is closely related to self confidence. Self esteem gives one self accorded status irrespective of the position one might hold. Persons with high esteem have been found to be more sensitive to meeting needs of others and are more prone to *act* rather than to *react*. Nurse leaders should take actions that are both remedial and preventative (Higbee, 1969).

It has been demonstrated that children with high self esteem are compliant to both threats and punishments; hence they avoid punishment but attain more rewards than children with low self esteem (Lindskold and Tedeschi, 1970). A strong sense of self esteem makes people feel personally powerful (Guetzkow, 1968). There is also evidence that high self esteem can be induced. Bavelas and others (1965) demonstrated in their leadership training program that individuals can be trained to become more self confident and that their self esteem can be increased. These findings have implications for nurse leaders. Guidelines and instructional tools for developing self esteem are found in Chapter 8.

2. *Keeping the channels of communication open.* By being open and honest, nonjudgmental leaders and followers can minimize misunderstandings, exchange ideas, and engage in problem solving and decision making processes in a more productive way.

3. *Providing meaningful, productive work.* For too long the knowledge and skills of professional nurses have not been utilized. Kramer (1974) has addressed her research endeavors to demonstrate that nurses do indeed leave nursing because of the disparity between what they were educated to do as professional nurses and what they were *permitted* to do in the work world. With decentralization of nursing care and the resultant increase of decision making activities at the unit level, it appears that nurses are being given an opportunity to deliver better patient care and that in doing so their work has taken on new and challenging dimensions.

4. *Providing opportunities for continuous learning and for personal and professional growth.* This has been a weak link in some health care settings. Mandatory continuing education courses for relicensure of nurses in California and other states have provided the impetus for continuous learning of nurses. Nurses need op-

---

*Although these attributes are discussed in Chapter 8, a brief overview is included in this chapter because of the relationship of self esteem to the personal power base.

portunities to gain new knowledge and skills in the practice of their profession; they also need to be helped in the process of "becoming" (Maslow, 1965).

BASIC SKILLS FOR INFLUENCING

Although early studies of leadership focused on a trait approach, these studies have failed to significantly differentiate characteristics of the effective leader from the ineffective leader (Bennis, Benne, and Chin, 1969). However, it is important for nurse leaders to look at their own strengths and weaknesses in an effort to grow and to increase their effectiveness in influencing others. A descriptive approach using behavioral patterns may be more helpful.

Mintzberg (1973) as a result of his study categorized behavioral patterns of leaders into eight categories that have implications for the nurse leader.

1. *Peer skills.* The ability to establish and maintain a network of contacts with equals.
2. *Leadership skills.* The ability to deal with subordinates and the kinds of complications that are created by power, authority, and dependence.
3. *Conflict-resolution skills.* The ability to mediate conflict, to handle disturbances under psychological stress.
4. *Information-processing skills.* The ability to build networks, extract and validate information, and disseminate information effectively.
5. *Skills in unstructured decision making.* The ability to find problems and solutions when alternatives, information, and objectives are ambiguous.
6. *Resource allocation skills.* The ability to decide among alternative uses of time and other scarce organizational resources.
7. *Entrepreneurial skills.* The ability to take sensible risks and implement innovations.
8. *Skills of introspection.* The ability to understand the position of a leader and his impact on the organization.

These guidelines are indeed extensive and demanding. They can, however, provide nurse leaders with worthy goals as they attempt to exert influence in health care organizations and to meet the ultimate test of influence, which is power.

REFERENCES

Barker, R. G.: Ecological psychology, Stanford, Calif., 1968, Stanford University Press.

Bass, B. M.: Some observations about a general theory of leadership and interpersonal behavior. In Petrullo, L., and Bass, B. M., editors: Leadership and interpersonal behavior, New York, 1961, Holt, Rinehart & Winston.

Bavelas, A., and others: Experiments on the alteration of group structure, Journal of Experimental Social Psychology 1:55-71, 1965.

Bennis, W. G., Benne, K. D., and Chin, R.: The planning of change, ed. 2, New York, 1969, Holt, Rinehart & Winston.

Blau, P. M.: Exchange and power in social life, New York, 1964, John Wiley & Sons, Inc.

Davis, M. S.: Variations in patients' compliance for doctor's advice, American Journal of Public Health 58:274-288, 1968.

Fiedler, F.: A theory of leadership effectiveness, New York, 1967, McGraw-Hill, Inc.

French, J. R. P., Jr., and Raven, B.: The bases of social power. In Cartwright, D., editor: Studies in social power, Ann Arbor, 1959, The University of Michigan Press.

Guetzkow, H.: Differentiation of roles in task-oriented groups. In Cartwright, D., and Zander, A., editors: Group dynamics: Research and theory, ed. 3, New York, 1968, Harper & Row, Publishers.

Higbee, K. L.: Fifteen years of fear arousal: Research on threat appeals: 1953-1968, Psychological Bulletin 72:426-444, 1969.

Hollander, E. P., and Julian, J. W.: Studies in leader legitimacy, influence and innovation. In Berkowitz, L., editor: Advances in experimental social psychology, vol. 5, New York, 1970, Academic Press, Inc.

Kalisch, B. J.: Of half gods and mortals: Aesculapian authority, Nursing Outlook **23**(1):22-28, 1975.

Kelley, H. H., and Thibaut, J. W.: Group problem solving. In Lindzey, G., and Aronson, E., editors: The handbook of social psychology, vol. 4, ed. 2, Reading, Mass., 1969, Addison-Wesley Publishing Co., Inc.

Kramer, M.: Reality shock: Why nurses leave nursing, St. Louis, 1974, The C. V. Mosby Co.

Lindskold, S., and Tedeschi, J. T.: Threatening and conciliatory influence attempts as a function of source's perception of own competence in conflict situation, mimeographed manuscript, Albany, N.Y., 1970, State University of New York at Albany.

Luchins, A. S., and Luchins, E. H.: On conformity with judgments of a majority or an authority, Journal of Social Psychology **53**:303-316, 1961.

Miles, R. E.: Human relations or human resources? In Kolb, D. A., Rubin, I. M., and McIntyre, J. M., editors: Organizational psychology: A book of readings, Englewood Cliffs, N.J., 1974, Prentice-Hall, Inc.

Mintzberg, H.: The nature of managerial work, New York, 1973, Harper & Row, Publishers.

Parsons, T.: On the concept of influence, Public Opinion Quarterly **27**:37-62, 1963.

Reiff, R.: The control of knowledge: The power of the helping professions, The Journal of Applied Behavioral Science **10**(3):451-461, 1974.

Roethlisberger, F. J., and Dickson, W. J.: Management and the worker, Cambridge, Mass., 1939, Harvard University Press.

Schlenker, B. R., and Tedeschi, J. T.: The exercise of social influence, Paper presented at the Seventeenth International Congress of Applied Psychology, Liege, Belgium, July, 1971.

Wood, M. T.: Power relationships and group decision making in organizations, Psychological Bulletin **79**(5):280-293, 1973.

SUGGESTED READINGS

Appelbaum, A., and others: Dependency versus autonomy: The group conference method applied to an organizational problem, Bulletin of the Menninger Clinic **39**(1):47-66, 1975.

Ashley, J.: About power in nursing, Nursing Outlook **21**:637-641, 1973.

Berlew, D. E.: Leadership and organizational excitement. In Rubin, I. M., and McIntyre, J. M., editors: Organizational psychology: A book of readings, Englewood Cliffs, N.J., 1974, Prentice-Hall, Inc.

Bernal, H.: Power and interorganizational health care projects, Nursing Outlook **24**:419-421, 1976.

Deloughery, G. L., and Gebbie, K. M.: Political dynamics: Impact on nurses and nursing, St. Louis, 1975, The C. V. Mosby Co.

Dunnette, M. E., editor: Handbook of industrial and organizational psychology, Chicago, 1976, Rand McNally College Publishing Co.

Eisenhower, L. A., and others: Building a faculty team, Nursing Outlook **24**:437-440, 1976.

Elsberry, N. L.: Power relations in hospital nursing, Journal of Nursing Administration **2**(5):75-77, 1972.

Fenn, M., Mungovan, R., and Towell, D.: Developing the role of the unit nursing officer, Nursing Times **71**(7):262-264, 1975.

Franklin, J. L.: Down the organization: Influence processes across levels of hierarchy, Administrative Science Quarterly **20**(2):153-164, 1975.

Gardner, J. W.: Self-renewal: The individual and the innovative society, New York, 1971, Harper & Row, Publishers.

Gazda, G. M.: Human relations development: A manual for educators, Boston, 1973, Allyn & Bacon, Inc.

Gore, W. J.: Administrative decision making: A heuristic model, New York, 1964, John Wiley & Sons, Inc.

Hersey, P., Blanchard, K. H., and LaMonica, E. L.: A situational approach to supervision: Leadership theory and the supervising nurse, Supervisor Nurse **7**(5):17-22, 1976.

Hughes, C. L.: Goal setting: Key to individual and organizational effectiveness, New York, 1965, American Management Association.

Hunt, J. G., and Larson, L. L.: Contingency approaches to leadership, Carbondale, Ill., 1974, Southern Illinois University Press.

Kalisch, B. J.: Of half gods and mortals: Aesculapian authority, Nursing Outlook **23**(1):22-28, 1975.

Kinsella, C.: Consultant's role must be clearly defined, American Nurse **7**(12):12, 1975.

Kipnis, D.: Does power corrupt? Journal of Personality and Social Psychology **24**(1):33-41, 1972.

Lassey, W. R., editor: Leadership and social change, Iowa City, 1971, University Associates.

Leininger, M.: The leadership crisis in nursing: A critical problem and challenge, Journal of Nursing Administration **4**(2):28-34, 1974.

Make the most of your authority, Hospital Supervision **8**(24):1975.

McClelland, D., and Burnham, D.: Good guys make bum bosses, Psychology Today **9**(7):69-70, 1975.

Miller, S.: Dialogue with the higher self, Synthesis **1**(2):122-139, 1975.

Mullane, M. K.: Nursing care and the political arena, Nursing Outlook **23**(11):699-701, 1975.

Nolan, M. G.: Wanted: Colleagueship in nursing, Journal of Nursing Administration **6**(3):41-43, 1976.

Novello, D. J.: The national health planning and resources development act, Nursing Outlook **24**(6): 354-358, 1976.

Pierce, S. F., and Thompson, D.: Changing practice: By choice rather than chance, Journal of Nursing Administration **6**(2):33-39, 1976.

Riggs, J. L., and Kalbaugh, A. J.: The art of management: Principles and practices, New York, 1974, McGraw-Hill, Inc.

Rubin, I., and Beckhard, R.: Factors influencing the effectiveness of health teams, Milbank Quarterly **50**(3):317-335, 1972.

Schmalenberg, C. E., and Kramer, M.: Dreams and reality: Where do they meet? Journal of Nursing Administration **6**(5):35-43, 1976.

Sims, H. P., Jr., and Szilagyi, A. D.: Leader structure and subordinate satisfaction for two hospital administrative levels: A path analysis approach, Journal of Applied Psychology **60**(2):194-197, 1975.

Steers, R. M., and Porter, L. W.: Motivation and work behavior, New York, 1975, McGraw-Hill, Inc.

Stevens, B., Management tools needed, American Nurse **7**(9):9, 1975.

Stogdill, R. M.: Handbook of leadership: A survey of theory and research, New York, 1974, The Free Press.

Tannenbaum, A. S.: Social psychology of the work organization, Belmont, Calif., 1967, Wadsworth Publishing Co. Inc.

Tedeschi, J. T., editor: The social influence processes, Chicago, 1972, Aldine Publishing Co.

Tobin, H. M., and others: The process of staff development: Components for change, St. Louis, 1974, The C. V. Mosby Co.

Van Dersal, W. R.: How to be a good communicator—and a better nurse, **4**(12):58-64, 1974.

Wergin, J. F.: The evaluation of organizational policy making: A political model, Review of Educational Research **46**(1):75-116, 1976.

PART TWO

Developing power and influence

Self awareness is the responsibility of knowing and using what one is.

FRITZ PERLS

8 DEVELOPING PERSONAL POWER THROUGH SELF AWARENESS AND SELF ESTEEM

JACQUELYNE GORTON, R.N., M.S.

How many nurses remember the sense of pride they felt when they first selected the nursing profession as a career? How many of these same nurses are aware of the satisfactions that can be derived from their nursing role today? How often do we hear nurses express contentment or share feelings of professional fulfillment with their chosen career?

Unfortunately, it is far more common to hear nurses express dissatisfaction with their work environment and their low esteem of themselves as people and as professionals (Benner and Kramer, 1972; Kramer and Baker, 1971; McCloskey, 1974; Menzies, 1960). Nurses often claim that they are powerless, they lack professional status, and their knowledge and skills are not being utilized. Statements such as, "I can't do what I want to do to improve patient care," "The doctors and administration control what goes on here," "No one appreciates what I do; I only hear about my mistakes," reflect nurses' feelings of powerlessness and uselessness.

If nurses view themselves in negative ways, a critical question becomes, "How can nurses be helped to value themselves, to get in touch with themselves, and to derive more satisfaction in both their professional and personal lives?"

The overall purposes of this chapter are: (1) to help nurses understand the process of self awareness and (2) to describe how developing self awareness improves one's self concept and self esteem (and thus enables a nurse to be a more powerful, positive force).

WHAT IS SELF AWARENESS?

Self awareness has been defined as how well one knows and understands himself and how he thinks he comes across to others. When nurses begin to attend to their own thoughts, feelings, or behaviors, they are experiencing self awareness (Barksdale, 1972). Nurses are using their self awareness if when they feel their legs aching they decide to wear support hose.

91

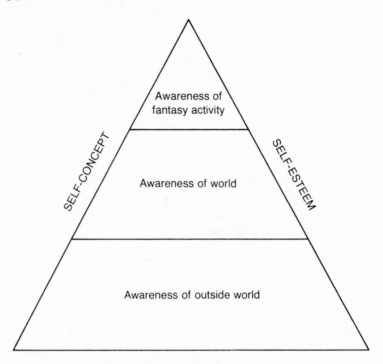

Fig. 9. Three levels of awareness.

Stevens (1971) has described three basic kinds of awareness: (1) awareness of the outside world, (2) awareness of the inside world, and (3) awareness of fantasy activity (Fig. 9).

1. *Awareness of the outside world* is what one sees, hears, smells, tastes, or touches. Nurses may see that an IV bottle is running low, smell the odor of a wound infection, hear the rolling of the dinner cart in the hallway, and touch a patient's warm, moist hand.

2. *Awareness of the inside world* means listening to what one's body is saying—aching, itching, tense, relaxed, or hungry. Nurses who have felt the tightness of neck tension and the sharpness of stomach hunger when they are late for dinner have experienced this second type of awareness. Awareness of the inside world includes physical manifestations of feelings and emotions, discomfort, and well-being.

3. *Awareness of fantasy activity* occurs when a person knows he is explaining, imagining, interpreting, guessing, thinking, comparing, planning, reminiscing, and anticipating. In formulating future plans or expressing wishes for certain patients (that Mr. G could get out of bed on his own), nurses are using fantasy activity.

When nurses monitor only the outside world, they are "turning off" to their own discomfort and bodily functions. How many times have nurses in intensive care units not taken a break during their 8 hour shift? Nurses who are completely absorbed in checking equipment such as cardiac monitors, IVs, catheters, or respirators are not tuned in to their own creative potential for improving the patient's condition. Instead of reacting only to the outside world of machines and the inside world of their own physical discomfort, nurses must develop their third level of awareness, which involves focusing on patient care needs and includes such activities as *anticipating* patients' needs and *explaining* procedures to the patient.

THE RELATIONSHIP BETWEEN SELF CONCEPT AND SELF ESTEEM

Self concept has been defined as the "unique set of perceptions, ideas, and attitudes which an individual has about himself" (Felker, 1974). Self concept can also be defined as the total picture one has of himself or as the individual's self image, whereas self esteem connotes how one *feels* about himself. It is the result of self concept and daily experiences. One's self esteem may be transitory: one may feel "the blahs" in the morning and then feel ecstatic in the afternoon. A person experiencing low self esteem will not act the same as a person feeling high self esteem in the same situation. For example, in dealing with death, nurses with a strong self concept may experience sadness, but nurses with a weak self concept often experience defeat.

USING SELF AWARENESS TO BUILD SELF CONCEPT AND SELF ESTEEM

An individual's view of himself is unique and often different from views held by others. The strength of one's self concept is dependent on optimal development of one's own awareness. Experiences that nurses have may often provide them with cues about their behavior. In certain situations one may judge himself to be competent or incompetent, good or bad, worthy or unworthy. Unless nurses are aware of the relationship between these messages and abilities, their self concept is forged not by their own self awareness, but by pressure exerted on them from the outside.

Low levels of awareness

An example of a low level of awareness is nurses' complaint that they are powerless to change their role in the health care delivery system. These nurses appear to be aware of only the outside world. They have low self esteem and a self concept that tells them that they are powerless.

High levels of awareness

A fully functioning level of awareness is demonstrated when nurses bring about constructive changes in hospital policies. By using a deep awareness of the outside world and by using the fantasy activities of explaining, defining, and comparing, nurses can develop a strong self concept and can indeed use personal power in constructive ways.

THREE KEYS FOR BUILDING POSITIVE SELF CONCEPT AND HIGH SELF ESTEEM
Key 1: Nurses can praise themselves

Self praise needs practice. Praising oneself may be a unique activity for nurses. It is not something that will come easily, but it will benefit everyone. To feel more comfortable with this activity nurses need to practice. They can do this by noting places where self praise might have been appropriate and then play "What I should have said to myself." If nurses believe that a patient's complaint of dizziness may be a side effect of a medication and convince the physician to change the medication, they can then feel good about themselves and offer self praise.

Another way to practice self praise is with families or friends.

Nurses can praise themselves in areas where objective criteria are absent. Nurses may not have to argue about whether the task they have done or the product they have made is in fact "good." It will be necessary for them to look at the type of evaluation they have made. However, the object of this key is not to develop objective criteria of self evaluation, but to develop an openness for expressing self praise and satisfaction. Nurses might express how they feel about something they have done or made, such as "I really felt good that I was able to finish my charting early and had time to spend with the terminal patient on the unit." By expressing self satisfaction they are giving themselves positive reinforcements and seeing themselves in a more positive manner.

Nurses can praise themselves for their role in task situations and environmental situations. In the task situation, nurses might express pleasure in doing a good job. In the personal area nurses can express approval about their appearance, their friendliness and warmth, or some other personal quality. In the environmental category they can express satisfaction for contributing to a production or smoothly running unit. Nurses can express praise within any of these three categories for a variety of reasons. There are basically five reasons for giving praise: (1) praise for mental attitudes or conditions—feelings and ideas, (2) praise for choice of materials, (3) praise for results achieved, (4) praise for methods used in achieving an end result, and (5) praise for reactions to end results (Felker, 1974).

Nurses can begin self praise by praising their work and then move to praising their personal qualities. It is more threatening to have someone dispute the image one has of himself as a person then it is to have someone dispute the evaluation one has of his work. Therefore, when nurses are using self praise, they need to begin with things that are not highly personal so that possible attacks on their self concept will be minimized. They can praise their accomplishments first and then move on to their personal qualities. They might say, "I felt proud to finish that dressing change without causing the patient to even grimace," when speaking of an accomplishment. Praise of a personal quality would be a statement such as, "I'm pleased that I have lots of patience and empathy for patients who frequently complain about their discomfort."

Nurses should make negative instances very specific. Nurses who criticize themselves over and over again may eventually feel they are "not good enough" or "worthless" or a "failure." When nurses do something that doesn't please them, they can say such things as, "I didn't regulate the IV drip properly this time." They can give themselves a chance to better themselves by saying such statements as, "Tomorrow, I'll correctly regulate the microdrip on that IV, now that I've learned how to do it."

Nurses should not expect immediate and dramatic changes in themselves.

Self concept is a fairly stable variable, since it is one of the basic mechanisms that humans use to interpret what happens to them. If nurses see themselves as failures, they are likely to interpret any difficulty as confirmation of the "fact" that they are failures. In this way their self concept moves from being a product to a producer. Changes may occur in how nurses see themselves, but these changes only occur over time.

Key 2: Nurses can set realistic goals

Goal setting is important because the goal often operates as the standard by which nurses evaluate themselves. If the goal is unrealistically low, the achievement of the goal is not an accomplishment. Nurses may see that they have met the goal, but they can also see that the goal was set so low that anyone, "even me," could reach it. If the goal is set unreasonably high, a similar process of perceived failure will occur. In this case nurses will regard the goal as appropriate and their performance as a failure. An example of an unrealistically high goal would be for nurses to expect to spend 20 minutes alone talking with each of their patients every day. An example of an unrealistically low goal would be for nurses to spend at least 5 minutes talking to one of their patients every day.

Realistic goals have three characteristics: (1) they are individual; (2) they are made in relation to past performance; and (3) they have both an outcome and an end in view (Felker, 1974).

Personal goals. Nurses are more committed to reaching their aspirations when they, and not someone else, have established their own personal goals. If people have no part in setting their goals, it's easy for them to lack commitment

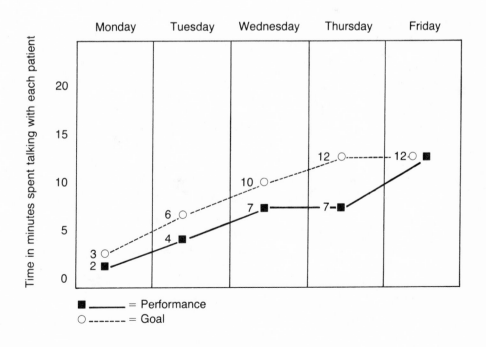

and to blame others if they fail. Instead of spending energy justifying failure to reach a goal, nurses can use energy in evaluating the reasonableness of their goal with such statements as, "Was the goal too high?" "How much lower would be realistic?"

Goals based on performance. Goal-setting is made in relation to past performance. The most reasonable type of goal setting occurs when the goal is slightly higher than previous performances and when it is attainable. If nurses never complete their patient care on time, a goal for one day may be to finish one bed bath without being interrupted.

Attainable goals. The third characteristic of realistic goal setting is an application of the first two characteristics. In realistic goal setting, there must be both an end goal and an end-in-view or goals-in-view. Having short range, attainable goals-in-view allows nurses to see that they are dealing with something possible, and it prevents them from being overzealous goal setters. By keeping goals small and attainable on a daily basis, they will increase the number of times they can praise themselves and receive compliments from others.

Nurses may want to keep a weekly chart of how many of their daily goals are reached. Their chart should include aspects of performance, a starting point, a final goal point, and an indication of the small steps in between. An example of such a chart is given above. It plots differences between performance of nurse-patient interaction and goals so that nurses can see how well they meet goals. From such a tool, nurses can adjust their performance to attain their goals.

Key 3: Nurses can evaluate realistically

One of the common characteristics of persons with negative self concepts is that they make unrealistically high demands upon themselves. People with low self esteem often judge themselves on the basis of unattainable goals of perfection. If nurses evaluate themselves against some unrealistic goal, they may perceive many of their efforts as failures. If they see their efforts as failures, self reinforcement and self praise are inappropriate, because they are reinforcing failure behavior. Self praise and self reinforcement are only appropriate after success or progress toward success.

In order for self evaluations to improve one's self concept and self esteem, evaluations must be realistic and accurate. A realistic self evaluation does not use "perfection" as the yardstick by which to measure performance. A realistic self evaluation is based on past performance in that it examines the progress of initial behaviors with present behaviors. A realistic self evaluation must also be specific. Do nurses evaluate themselves realistically, or do they demand perfection with words such as, "I should be finished giving my morning medications in 30 minutes"? A realistic self evaluation might be, "I can complete administration of the morning medications in 45 minutes compared to the hour and a half I first required."

Nurses can adopt an evaluation system based on the conviction that any improvement is good and that the way to greater success and adequate performance comes about through small steps.

Positive self concept and high self esteem are assets

The three keys for improving self concept and self esteem provide nurses with a tool for enhancing and maintaining a positive approach to health care delivery. Improving self concept and self esteem also enables nurses to more effectively meet the goals of the health care system. If nurses have a positive self concept and high self esteem, they are better prepared to take responsibility for fulfilling their professional role within the organizational structure.

If nurses believe they are an important part of the organization, they will take pride in moving the organization forward toward the goal of quality health care.

EXERCISES
Getting in touch with self awareness levels

1. **Awareness.** Dosage: three times a day for 2 minutes each session. Take the time to pay attention to your awareness *now* and two other times today at work and at home. Be an observer of your awareness and notice where it goes. Say to yourself, "Now I'm aware of . . ." and finish this sentence with what you are aware of at the moment and then notice whether this is something outside, something inside, or a fantasy. Where does your awareness go? Are you mostly aware of things outside your body or sensations inside your skin?

   Now I am aware of . . .
   Now I am aware of . . .
   Now I am aware of . . .

   Now direct your attention to whichever area you are *least* aware of, inside or outside, and become aware of this. To what extent are you occupied with fantasies, thoughts, and images? Notice that while you are occupied with a thought or an image, your awareness of inside and outside reality decreases or disappears. Are you occupied with fantasies, thoughts, and images more at work or more at home?

2. **Awareness at home.** Dosage: 3 minutes when you first come home. Now sit down and close your eyes and experience what it was like to be there at work. Ask yourself the following questions:

   What was it like to be there?
   How do you feel there?
   How do people appear there?
   Who do you feel uncomfortable with there?
   What noises do you hear there?
   What colors do you see there?
   Are you able to leave what was there at work and be in the *here* of home?

3. **Awareness at work.** Dosage: 3 minutes when you first arrive at work. Look around you and get in touch with your surroundings. What do you experience here?

   What is it like to be here?

How do you feel here?

How do the people appear here?

With whom do you feel uncomfortable?

With whom do you feel comfortable?

What noises do you hear?

What colors do you see?

Practicing self praise

Dosage: 15 minutes at coffee break.

1. While you're sipping your coffee, write down (as quickly as possible) all the things you feel "good" about having done today.

   I feel good about . . .

   I feel good about . . .

   I feel good about . . .

2. Next write down how you contributed to making your ward run efficiently.

   I helped things run smoothly by . . .

   I helped things run smoothly by . . .

   I helped things run smoothly by . . .

3. Now write down what you like about yourself at work.

   I like the way I . . .

   I like the way I . . .

   I like the way I . . .

See if what you feel good about in no. 1 is also the role you like and use to make your unit run smoothly. Was it easier to praise your work than yourself?

Setting realistic goals

Dosage: every day

1. Every day before you start work write down one goal you have for that day that is unique to you.

   My personal goal for today is to . . .

2. Now, state your goal so that it is unique to you and is in relation to your past performance.

   The weaknesses I wish to build on today are . . .

   The strengths I wish to develop are . . .

3. Next state your goal so that it is personal, accounts for your past abilities, and sets an obtainable standard for today.

   Yesterday's performance tells me that my new goal for today is to improve . . .

Evaluating your performance

1. Dosage: every day after work.

   Examine how you are working now compared to one of your past performances.

   Compared to how I worked when I first started this job, I now . . .

   At the beginning of a shift I . . . compared to my performance of . . . at the end of a shift.

   Two weeks ago I . . . and now I . . .

2. Dosage: every time you face a unique task.

Evaluate how well you do separate tasks.

I can administer medications . . .

My nursing care consists of . . .

When communicating with physicians . . .

3. Dosage: every time you have a new task or try to change your work habits.

Evaluate your work in terms of how you are improving.

I am improving my . . .

The first step I've taken toward success in . . .

Today I successfully moved toward . . .

REFERENCES

Barksdale, L. S.: Building self esteem, Los Angeles, 1972, The Barksdale Foundation for Furtherance of Human Understanding.

Benner, P., and Kramer, M.: Role conceptions and integrative role behavior of nurses in special care and regular hospital nursing units, Nursing Research **21**:20-29, 1972.

Felker, D. W.: Building positive self concepts, Minneapolis, 1974, Burgess Publishing Co.

Kramer, M., and Baker, C.: The exodus: Can we prevent it? Journal of Nursing Administration **1**(3): 15-30, 1971.

McCloskey, J.: High staff nurse turnover rate attributed to low self-esteem, OR Reporter **9**:3, 1974.

Menzies, I.: Nurses under stress, International Nursing Review **7**(9):9-16, 1960.

Perls, F., Hefferline, R. F., and Goodman, P.: Gestalt therapy: Excitement and growth in the human personality, New York, 1951, Julian Press, Inc.

Stevens, J. O.: Awareness: Exploring, experimenting, Moab, Utah, 1971, Real People Press.

SUGGESTED READINGS

Benson, H.: The relaxation response, New York, 1975, William Morrow & Co., Inc.

Berne, E.: Games people play, New York, 1964, Grove Press, Inc.

Bloomfield, H.: TM, discovering inner energy and overcoming stress, New York, 1975, Dell Publishing Co., Inc.

Craig, J. H., and Craig, M.: Synergic power: Beyond domination and permissiveness, Berkeley, 1974, ProActive Press.

Hamachek, D. E.: Encounters with the self, New York, 1971, Holt, Rinehart & Winston.

Harris, T. A.: I'm ok, you're ok, New York, 1967, Avon Books.

Hesse, H.: Siddhartha, New York, 1951, Bantam Books, Inc.

Illich, I. D.: Celebration of awareness, New York, 1971, Doubleday & Co., Inc.

James, M.: The ok boss, Reading, Mass., 1975, Addison-Wesley Publishing Co., Inc.

James, M., and Jongeward, D.: Born to win: Transactional analysis with gestalt experiments, Reading, Mass., 1971, Addison-Wesley Publishing Co., Inc.

Johnson, D. W.: Reaching out, Englewood Cliffs, N.J., 1972, Prentice-Hall, Inc.

Jourard, S.: The transparent self, New York, 1964, Van Nostrand Reinhold Co.

Luft, J.: Of human interaction, Palo Alto, Calif., 1969, Mayfield Publishing Co. (National Press Books).

Steiner, C.: Scripts people live, New York, 1975, Bantam Books.

Power is derived from relationships with others.

MICHAEL KORDA

9 DEVELOPING INTERPERSONAL POWER THROUGH DISCLOSURE, FEEDBACK, AND REINFORCEMENT

Nurses are often perceived as members of a helping, caring profession. They serve as support systems to clients and their families as well as to members of the health care team. However, nurses also *need* support systems. Perhaps the most critical support system that can be developed is found among their colleagues in the health care environment. Other nurses can be the strongest source of interpersonal power for the nurse practitioner. Power derived from relationships with others is built through: (1) a strong self concept, (2) an awareness of interpersonal processes, and (3) a loving attitude.

A STRONG SELF CONCEPT: POWER BASE IN INTERPERSONAL RELATIONS

A person without a strong self concept and a positive view of self worth may experience difficulty in viewing others in a positive way. Acceptance of others begins with acceptance of self. One can develop a positive self concept and personal power through becoming aware of one's own strengths and weaknesses and taking actions to build on strengths and to decrease the weaknesses. This same process of assessment and emphasis on strengths applies to interpersonal relationships and helps develop interpersonal power. By turning one's attention toward interpersonal processes, one can contribute to developing a climate of trust and facilitating positive communication. Interpersonal relationships need a climate of trust to grow and develop. The leader with an active interest in colleagues recognizes that trust facilitates the development of interpersonal power and influence. The climate becomes pervasive: effective relationships of leader to followers, followers to leader, and followers to followers manifest themselves in a climate of trust. In such a climate the nurse leader can allay fears of betrayal, reduce anxieties, promote acceptance, and develop the support systems that are critical to productivity and work satisfaction.

TRUST

Because human relationships are extremely complex, the element of trust is a difficult concept to define. Deutsch (1962) and others have analyzed trust as having the following characteristics: (1) *an element of choice;* the choice of whether or not to trust another person can lead to either beneficial or harmful consequences with regard to a person's needs or goals; (2) *a consequence;* the consequences can be either beneficial or harmful and will influence the future behavior of another person. A person will suffer more if the consequences are harmful than he will gain if they are beneficial. However, if the consequence is beneficial, the person will feel relatively confident that the other person will behave in a way that will again be beneficial. For example, when a mother leaves her child with a babysitter, she is making a trusting choice and predicting that no harm will come to her child; she will probably use the babysitter again if her predictions were borne out.

The key to building trust is being trustworthy. The expression of warmth toward another person in a relationship builds a high level of interpersonal trust. In making a disclosure about oneself to another person, one shows that he expects the confidant to respond with acceptance and support. In the next chapter we will discuss credibility and trustworthiness, but basically the congruence and consistency of verbal statements and nonverbal cues such as expression and tone of voice will affect another person's perception of trustworthiness. If an individual says he likes another person but is frowning, his statement will not be seen as trustworthy. In fact, his sincerity might be generally questioned.

Two basic types of behavior that will destroy trust

Declining to reciprocate when self disclosure occurs. If a leader remains closed while another person is sharing, an opportunity to build mutual trust has been forfeited. In maintaining reserve while another person talks candidly, the willing discloser is made to feel exposed and vulnerable.

Expressing rejection, ridicule, or disrespect after another person's self disclosure. Sometimes feelings of rejection or ridicule are expressed subtly. A long sigh, indicating boredom or lack of interest, may be devastating to the person disclosing personal information. Explicit forms of rejection might include using sarcasm, making a joke at the expense of another, belittling the importance of a person's self disclosure, moralizing, or being judgmental. For example, a person who shares a bad experience with a confidant does not want to hear, "Well, you got what you asked for!" A remark such as this spells rejection. In the future, the person making the disclosure may avoid anything beyond the most casual small talk, and the potential for a trusting interpersonal relationship may have been destroyed. The leader who deals ineffectively with subordinates cannot expect followers to provide accurate information or ideas because people will remember the offhanded way in which their communication was treated.

Building a climate of trust

A climate of trust implies a self fulfilling prophecy: people who expect trustworthiness in others usually find others worthy of trust. Conversely, people who have little confidence in others as being trustworthy will not act in a trusting manner and will find that others do not trust them. One's assumptions about other people and one's own behavior, as an expression of those assumptions, make a difference as to how other people will respond. In the educational development of children it has been found that if a child is treated as if he is intelligent he will behave intelligently. Assuming other people are trustworthy reinforces and creates positive energy fields within which people can work. The basis for strong interpersonal power sources thrives in such an atmosphere.

Subordinates and colleagues weigh clues from the nurse leader in their first contact. Subtle signals tell them whether they should be open or guarded in their interpersonal relations. If colleagues regard the nurse leader as threatening, they will spend emotional energy in their own defense. If, on the other hand, they see the leader as encouraging and supportive, they will tend to be more open. They will develop a feeling of trust—a feeling that the nurse leader will not knowingly or deliberately embarrass them or put them down. When feelings of trust are shared, energy can be spent in achieving goals, communication will be more direct and open, and information will be more relevant and accurate. A safe atmosphere is one in which people feel that they can share control over what happens.

Constructive steps must be taken to develop a climate of trust. For example, a leader can encourage subordinates, colleagues, or superiors to express concerns. By taking an interest in these statements and discussing them as part of the situation, the nurse leader encourages open communication. While showing an attitude of support and protection of subordinates' feelings, the nurse leader can return confidence by being open and honest. When something goes wrong, the leader should focus on *what happened* rather than *who did it*. This approach applies systematic problem solving by defining the problem, rather than making hasty conclusions about the cause. The leader develops interpersonal power through a participative approach. Getting the group involved in the problem solving process and giving them positive feedback encourages subordinates to work with the leader in getting the task accomplished. Success in this effort requires a balance: the leader must stimulate the development of colleagues and therefore should encourage independence rather than overdependence. That is, the leader should be careful to allow authority to vest with the lowest common denominator possible to get the job done. For example, if a problem exists at the unit level, problem solving should entail the head nurse and members of the unit rather than top management.

Nurse leaders should express their own self doubts and concerns in a natural way and be candid about the person with whom they are communicating. A person in a leadership position is never really "off the record" and should not risk starting or repeating rumors and gossip.

Leaders cannot compromise standards of honesty. They must let subordinates and colleagues know what they really want from them in asking for opinions. Do they really want a person to claim enthusiastically that a plan is feasible if indeed it is not? Through honesty the nurse leader can help people move along the scale from guardedness to openness. However, the leader should understand people will never be completely open with an authority figure in some situations. Complete openness might invite an attempt to discuss intimate personal or family problems that might be inappropriate. Therefore, people in positions of leadership, authority, or responsibility may have to maintain some social distance.

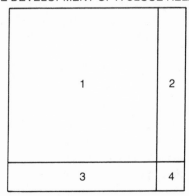

FEEDBACK

Known to self   Unknown to self

DISCLOSURE

Known
to others

1. Free to self and others	2. Blind to self, seen by others
3. Hidden area: self hidden from others	4. Unknown self

Unknown
to others

AT THE BEGINNING OF A RELATIONSHIP

1	2
3	4

AFTER THE DEVELOPMENT OF A CLOSE RELATIONSHIP

1	2
3	4

Fig. 10. The Johari Window—identification of areas of the self through feedback and disclosure.

Risk taking. Restraints individuals place on themselves in communicating with others can be more stringent than those imposed by supervisors or organizational structure. Each person has "hang-ups" about openness with other persons. In order to be open in communicating with others and to develop the climate of trust required as a foundation for interpersonal power, the nurse leader must be willing to take risks in moving toward openness. Usually openness is not only accepted but appreciated because it encourages a more productive atmosphere in which organizational tasks and goals are achieved, and people feel more satisfied and committed.

THE JOHARI WINDOW

Luft and Ingham (1955) have developed a model for looking at openness in human relationships. The Johari Window has two dimensions that differentiate between (1) things that a person needs to know about himself and certain things that one does not know about himself and (2) things that people know and do not know about another person. Fig. 10 illustrates the basic areas of the self described in the Johari Window.

In Area 1 is found information known both to oneself and to others, which is called public information. This includes feelings, opinions, and ideas about which a person chooses to be open, as well as things that cannot very well be hidden such as age, looks, and the like. (Many people spend a great deal of time and money trying to conceal these things about themselves.)

Area 2, the *blindspot*, comprises things that are known to others but not to oneself. These may include habits and abilities of which a person is unaware. For example, a speaker may nervously be playing with keys in his pocket. This is part of what others know about the speaker but may remain unknown to himself. Habits and characteristics often have an impact that may or may not be useful in relationships with others. A person who continually interrupts probably does not realize it; another person may not realize that he has the ability to make others want to help; or a person may never seem to be interested in the feelings of others or in what they are saying. These characteristics can be helpful or harmful.

Area 3 is comprised of things known to oneself but concealed from others. Some things in this area are concealed because a person does not known how to tell others; some are kept guarded because a person feels he would be viewed badly by others if these things were known. Feelings, doubts about oneself, secret hopes and dreams, the things one knows about another person that limit effectiveness unknown to the other person may be in this area. This area has been called the *facade*.

Area 4, the *unknown*, consists of those things that a person does not know about himself nor do others know. These may include forgotten experiences that may have been extremely influential, or unconscious needs or motives of which one is unaware. These things are normally left alone. But greater awareness can occur through various introspective experiences. It is generally found that the larger the Area 1, the more effective one can be in interpersonal relations. If Area 1 is wide, the individual can freely pass on his own ideas and feelings, experiment with new behaviors, express self doubts and concerns, and be open with other people in many ways. The more open one can be and the more he can bring to bear on his own capabilities, the less energy needed to expend in defense. Generally at the beginning of a relationship, the Area 1 arena is very small. As trust is developed and feedback is accepted and sought, Area 1 is pushed wider and wider until it forms the basis of the relationship. That is, the two basic ways of expanding the arena of interaction with other people are: (1) to develop more trust in the relationship, and (2) to develop methods of obtaining accurate feedback from others. Building a relationship, therefore, involves working to enlarge the free area, while decreasing the blind and hidden areas. Self disclosure and feedback should be kept in balance, which most people find difficult to do.

The nurse leader can use the Johari Awareness Model to increase understanding of interpersonal relationships and to become more effective in relationships with others. From our discussion of the model, portrayed in Fig. 10, one sees that the relative shape and size of the four parts or quadrants continually change because the model describes dynamic interpersonal processes. When two basic interpersonal processes, exposure (self disclosure) and feedback are used, the size and shape of the quadrants change. In the theory supporting the model, it is assumed that as the first quadrant (things known to self and to others) increases in size, the relationship will become more productive and rewarding. A person's asking for someone else's awareness—feedback—can be thought of as encouraging others to share information and suggests the asker's willingness to share information in return.

Feedback and disclosure have been studied in an organizational setting to discover the extent to which the formal lines of authority influenced their occurrence (Hall, 1974). Managers who were studied showed a consistent overreliance on feedback, as opposed to disclosure. In reference to the Johari Model, any overuse of one process at the neglect of another may result in an imbalance in the relationship. For example, participants may experience tension when the self-other awareness is extremely uneven. Productive relationships become more difficult as the first quadrant (things known to self and to others) diminishes in size and shape and other quadrants become dominant.

In Hall's study the extent to which managers used self disclosure and feedback was influenced by the status of the person in the interaction. Relationships with subordinates and colleagues were not significantly different from each other but were indeed different from relationships with superiors. As the authority of the person dealt with increased, the managers' disclosures decreased. Nurse leaders may find that subordinates behave in a guarded, cautious manner. Through the use of self disclosure and active seeking of feedback, a nurse leader can encourage group members to behave more openly. Frankness contributes to productive relationships and to a climate of trust in the organization.

Among the managers Hall studied, feedback was recognized as a reliable source of information and was employed most in colleague relationships. In dealing with subordinates, top management personnel reported least reliance on feedback. This fact may or may not be related to the results of a recent cross-cultural survey. Of the managers sampled from organizations in Japan, Great Britain, and the United States, approximately 74% referred to communication breakdown as the single most troublesome stumbling block to corporate excellence (Blake and Mouton, 1968). Managers who seldom use feedback from subordinates encourage a relationship with a large Blindspot. In relations with persons of equal or greater authority in the organization, their relationship shows a dominant Facade.

Differences in power among persons in an organization tend to reduce openness. Managers willingly act openly with people with whom they are communicating when they have authority over those people. This tendency may not reflect a lack of interpersonal trust as much as a lack of security within the organizational hierarchy.

Through awareness of interpersonal processes the nurse leader will be able to recognize and isolate the causes of tense, guarded relations. Usually these problems come from some combination of two types of felt restraints: (1) structural or cultural forces that lend intimidating values to authority positions in the eyes of subordinates, and (2) self imposed habits of guarded communication nurtured by a sense of insecurity or fear of rejection. Neither of these barriers to communication is insurmountable, and each can be minimized by creating a climate of trust.

SELF DISCLOSURE

Self disclosure can be thought of as a tool or mechanism in which a person shares awareness with others. In order to develop a strong interpersonal power base, people need an opportunity to know each other. To like a person, to ascribe support and power to another person, and to be his friend, one must know something about that person. And to be able to know that person, one must also know about oneself. In order to be free to disclose oneself to another person, one must accept and appreciate that self. According to one authority, a close personal relationship cannot develop without self disclosure (Jourard, 1964). A personal relationship and the power derived from that relationship grow as two people become more self disclosing and open about themselves. The person who feels he cannot reveal himself and cannot become close to others will not have the experience of being valued by others for who he is. Two people who stay silent about their reactions and feelings stay strangers.

Self disclosure has been defined as the process of revealing how one is reacting to the present situation. Inherent in revealing one's reactions are one's feelings and understandings. To be self disclosing means to share with another person how one feels about something that person has done or said and how one feels about events that are taking place. Self disclosure does not mean revealing many intimate details of past life. It does not mean making highly personal confessions, nor does it mean stating negative reactions to another person. Personal history is only helpful if it clarifies why a person reacts in a certain way.

An important concept in understanding self disclosure comes from balance theory. This comprehensive theory of group formation proposed by Newcomb holds that there is a symmetry to attraction among people (Newcomb, 1961). For example, if A likes B, then B probably likes A (Heider, 1944, 1946, 1958). The balance is upset when A also likes C but B does not. This imbalance requires a change in the relationship to restore balance. Balance theory holds that the attraction of one person to another is based on similar attitudes toward the same objects and common goals. We expect the people whom we admire, care for, or like to approve and agree with the things we like and to be sympathetic with opinions we hold. In an interpersonal relationship if one person acts in a self disclosing way, this behavior encourages the other person to act in a similar manner. The amount of self disclosure on the part of each person in a relationship will influence the other. The more one discloses, the easier the other person will find it to return the openness.

Willingness to engage in self disclosure has been studied in terms of the type of person who is most willing to be open. Research indicates that a person who is competent, open, and socially extroverted tends to be more willing to self disclose. These people are often more intelligent than self concealing peers. The self disclosing person has greater awareness of others, and his perceptions usually indicate a fairly close congruence between the way he is and the way he would like to be. He generally views his fellow man as good rather than evil. In times of stress he wants to communicate intimately with another person. Unless self disclosure has occurred prior to periods of stress, the interpersonal power base may be insufficient to enable people to be supportive when they most want to. It is important to be open with other people not only when trying to develop an interpersonal power base but also when building meaningful relationships.

The relevance of self disclosure

Self disclosure must be appropriate to the interpersonal relationship and to the situation. It is possible to disclose too much. In developing an interpersonal power basis, it is not wise to reveal too much about one's reactions too fast. The following guidelines offer some help to the leader trying to determine when self disclosure is appropriate:

1. Self disclosure should not be a random or isolated act but part of an ongoing relationship as it develops.
2. Self disclosure, when offered, should be reciprocated. Appropriate self disclosure concerns what is going on within and between persons in the present time, but does not delve into the past unless particular events relate directly to the present situation.
3. Self disclosure should be used only when it creates a reasonable chance of improving the relationship and should be considered in light of the effect that it will have on another person.
4. Generally, self disclosure occurs more rapidly in crisis situations and gradually moves to deeper levels as interpersonal power bases are developed.

Although most powerful interpersonal relationships are built through self disclosure and feedback, there are times when the sharing of some reactions would be inappropriate.

A person's ability to disclose himself to others depends on his own self awareness and self acceptance. As we have noted, a strong power base is necessary for effective self disclosure.

Positive self disclosure

Rarely do people openly discuss their reactions to others' behavior. Most people withhold their feelings about another person, even in intimate relationships because they are afraid of hurting another person for whom they care. Withholding feelings may be done to avoid making an intimate associate angry or because one fears rejection. In such situations one may feel that he does not know how to give feedback or disclose himself constructively. Therefore, the individual often says nothing, which makes the other person unaware of reactions to his behavior. Similarly, a person may continue to be ignorant of the effect of his own actions on another person. Many relations that could be more productive and enjoyable gradually deteriorate under the accumulated load of annoyance, hurt feelings, and misunderstandings.

Earlier studies of the self disclosure and feedback behaviors of people in leadership positions and others in an organizational setting were discussed. Most people, regardless of position, were more willing and likely to seek feedback than to make self disclosure. The relative status of the people involved also influenced the degree of self disclosure: leaders rarely chose self disclosing behavior in dealing with subordinates. But the nurse leader who wants to develop interpersonal power, as an adjunct to building a climate of trust, cannot avoid self disclosure. Strong relationships with others depend on it. Nurse leaders might recognize that they need to take the initiative in this type of behavior, particularly in dealing with subordinates who usually show reluctance to make self disclosing statements.

Effective self disclosure

The following points can increase the nurse's effectiveness in using self disclosure and in improving interpersonal relationships.

Self disclosure must be based on a desire to improve interpersonal relationships. Self disclosure is not an end in itself but a means to an end. The act of self disclosure shows that one values a relationship with another individual, and that he wishes to improve it because it is important. The individual is willing to take risks such as being rejected.

Self disclosure should not be aimed at making the other person change. At its best, self disclosure becomes feedback and the relationship becomes a learning situation for participants. The attitude should not be one of pointing out who is wrong and who is right. Focus should be on the relationship and the situation at a particular time. Attitudes and feelings should be expressed and described as temporary and capable of change. Instead of saying, "I'll never be able to stand you when you get impatient," a person might say, "Today I am irritated by the way you reacted this morning. Why do you act like that?" This approach shows that the person is responding to events, which can change, rather than to the person.

Be aware of timing. Reactions to behavior or factual situations should be shared as soon as possible after their occurrence so that those involved know exactly what behavior is being discussed. Most people are intuitively aware of this behavioral principle of reinforcement. That is, one does not discipline a small child the day after he has run out into the street because he may not understand the reason for the discipline and will learn nothing from it. So it is in work relationships in health care delivery settings. The leader should not wait a month before complaining about the actions of a colleague, peer, or superior.

Paraphrasing techniques or understanding responses can help one respond to comments being offered as feedback, to make sure that these comments are being understood in the way intended. Self disclosure and solicitation of feedback are more helpful if they deal with *specific* rather than *general* topics. A practical way to check the receiver's perceptions of what one is thinking, to avoid false assumptions about the other's feelings, is to ask questions: "Did my last statement bother you?" "Can you tell me what that remark made you think?"

In self disclosure and feedback situations, it is best to avoid making judgments about the other person. Name-calling or trait labelling, making accusations, imputing undesirable motives to the other, putting people down, delivering commands and orders, and using sarcasm will not help build strong interpersonal relations. For the person doing the name-calling they may offer great relief, but these outbursts contribute nothing to the growth of the relationship.

The most useful kinds of information that can be shared are behavioral descriptions that help a person sharpen his observational skills. Bailey and Claus (1975) contend that a problem can be described as a discrepancy between what *is* happening and what *should be* happening. In these terms, a problem solver is able to deal with closing a gap rather than jumping to conclusions. Effective feedback deals with visible evidence or behavior that is objectively observable by anyone who understands the operational definitions of the terms involved.

FEEDBACK

The purpose of feedback is to provide another person with constructive information to enable him to become aware of his behavior and the effects of the behavior on another individual. To be effective, feedback should be given in a nonthreatening way. This allows the other person to decrease defensiveness. The more defensive a person is, the less likely he is to perceive information that may be helpful to him.

Effective feedback

Helpful, nonthreatening feedback results when certain basic considerations are observed.

Express feedback in terms of behavior rather than identifying it with the person. It is more important to describe what a person does than to comment on what the person is. Language used in giving feedback, therefore, should be heavy in adverbs that relate to actions rather than nouns that explain qualities of a person. It is quite different to say that Miss J. talks considerably during staff meetings than to say that she is a "loudmouth." The person providing feedback should consider the amount of information that the receiver can use, rather than the amount that one might like to give. One should avoid the "blitz" approach of trying to overload a person with information. A person will be selectively perceiving those things that he wishes to hear and that will meet his immediate needs. The giving of feedback requires skill, understanding, tact, and respect for oneself and for others.

The content of feedback should emphasize description rather than judgment. Description keeps a person in an observational framework and helps to maintain a noncritical stance. An atmosphere of judgment encourages the person being observed to jump to conclusions and interpret judgments within his own frame of reference, which may be irrelevant to the given situation. Descriptions of behavior are best stated in terms of performance rather than subjective impressions indirectly stated. This means that one stresses quantity, which is objective and measurable, rather than quality, which is subjective and judgmental. It is more helpful to describe where a person's behavior falls on a continuum from low participation to high participation, than to assess it as being "good" or "bad" participation. Thinking in terms of a behavioral continuum frees one from thinking in categories, which may not reflect reality. Feedback should deal with behavior related to a specific reality. Feedback should deal with behavior related to a specific situation. It is important to observe behavior in the here and now rather than in the abstract. One's understanding of behavior is increased when it is tied to time and place.

Feedback should aim for the sharing of ideas and information rather than giving advice. Sharing of ideas leaves the other person free to decide for himself in light of his own goals and particular situation; advice tells a person what to do with the information. Feedback should be directed toward exploration of alternatives rather than answers or solutions. By focusing on a variety of procedures and means for accomplishing a particular goal, one is less likely to accept premature answers or solutions that may not fit the problem. Kepner and Tregoe (1965) warn against jumping to conclusions concerning the cause of a problem rather than looking at the actual facts surrounding the situation.

Feedback should deal with observations rather than inferences, on what is said rather than why it is said. Observable behavior refers to what one can see or hear. Inferences or conclusions about a person contaminate the observation and cloud the feedback. The person giving feedback may find it difficult to resist stating conclusions impulsively. Since feedback should encourage two-way communication, as well as learning and growth for both participants in the relationship, responses given primarily to meet emotional needs should be minimized. The primary purpose of giving feedback is to meet the needs of the receiver; however, feedback should not be forced on another person. Appropriate feedback offered at an opportune time is the key to using feedback as a tool.

Interpersonal power is based on feedback

Developing effective interpersonal power bases depends on one's personal power and self awareness, both of which depend on receiving feedback from other people. The quality of the feedback one receives from other persons may reflect how much one discloses to others. An awareness of the consequences of one's behavior helps one decide whether these consequences match one's intentions. Interpersonal effectiveness has been defined as the degree to which the consequences of one's behavior match one's intentions. The process of self awareness and attempting to understand interpersonal relations assist the person in a leadership position to enhance interpersonal power. Each time one interacts with another person, one makes some impact. Ideas may be stimulated, impressions and observations aroused, and feelings and reactions triggered. Sometimes the impression is what one wanted to engender. But at other times one may find that people react to behavior differently from what one might expect. For example, an expression of warmth could be viewed as condescending, or anger could be seen as a joke. Interpersonal effectiveness depends on one's ability to communicate clearly and to create a particular impression in order to influence the other person. Disclosing one's intentions, receiving feedback about one's behavior, and modifying one's behavior until other individuals perceive it as intended are some ways of improving interpersonal effectiveness.

Besides overt forms of self disclosure, people also reveal themselves in indirect ways. For example, they make disclosures about themselves in the jokes they tell, the things they find beautiful or moving, the books that interest them, the movies they see, the clothing they wear, facial expressions, and other ways. All these actions and expressions of attitudes tell other people something about them.

REINFORCEMENT

Reinforcing positive behaviors in others is a basic tenet of behavioral modification psychology. The concept is based on the premise that when an action is rewarded, the person receiving the reward will tend to repeat the act. The reward acts as a reinforcement for the behavior. This notion came from Skinner (1953) and is referred to as operant conditioning reinforcement theory. Skinner's theory maintains that to teach a person a particular verbal, manual, or psychomotor response to a situation one waits for that situation to occur, or arranges a situation so that the desired behavior occurs, and then promptly reinforces it through a reward. This action is called shaping behavior and is the method by which animals learn to perform complex tasks. For example, dogs are taught to jump through flaming hoops. The conditioning begins when the dog points his nose toward the hoop and is rewarded. As he walks toward the hoop, he receives successive rewards until finally he inches closer to the act desired and is rewarded promptly after the desired behavior.

The same principle has application to human behavior. If we are to develop strong interpersonal power bases, it is important that we reward each other for positive behavior. Nurses in particular should realize that they must support one another in the health care delivery system and reward supportive behavior when it occurs. Rewards can take many forms other than remuneration for services. Giving attention, recognizing years of service, and giving other special awards comprise a few of the ways organizations can reward their employees.

Principles have been observed that hold rather consistently in the process of reinforcement. If one behavior is asked for but another occurs, the second behavior will become part of the person's repertoire if it is reinforced. Policy statements, procedures, and other stated expectations may not have any effect in an organization, for example, if other behaviors occur and are rewarded. The nurse leader may formally state that a ward clerk or secretary in the organizational setting is expected to be helpful and supportive. But if the leader rewards the clerk who is not being helpful and supportive to other members of the group, then the clerk will continue the behavior, even though policies and statements in public may prohibit such behavior. A climate of trust cannot develop in conditions of leader duplicity.

Another principle relates to what happens when there is no reinforcement. As one might suspect, unrewarded actions do not continue. If a behavior does not appear to be useful or has no consequences when it occurs, it will stop occurring. A head nurse may find that a staff nurse needs support and asks for help in dealing with a difficult patient. If the leader does nothing to assist the nurse, she may not ask for help from the head nurse again.

A third principle indicates that rewards should closely follow the desired behavior in order to have an impact. When consequences are removed in time from an action, they will have less effect on influencing a repetition of the action. For example, if a faculty member has worked hard as a chairman of a certain committee and has not been commended by a department chairman for the time and energy expended, she may not wish to serve as a chairman again.

Stanford University conducted a series of studies several years ago on reinforcing certain types of behaviors in the classroom on the part of both teachers and students. Graduate students working on the studies applied their findings to their own classroom experiences and found that by simple behaviors and gestures students could encourage a teacher to say certain types of things in a lecture. Students would nod or look interested by giving certain positive attending responses whenever the teacher said "lunch" or talked about a certain topic. When another topic was discussed, they would look sleepy. As a result the desired behavior was shaped and recurred at remarkable frequency. This informal type of research generated considerable enthusiasm for the application of various types of behavioral modification techniques in classroom situations found to be effective in formal studies.

One study showed that a teacher's use of higher order questions, which is a very complex cognitive skill, could be reinforced by giving teachers positive feedback on their behavior (Claus, 1968). A nurse on a unit could easily use this approach. Every time a patient showed interest in feeding himself, the nurse might praise him. In fact, most nurses intuitively use this principle when they are trying to encourage a patient to do something for himself. They praise him when he does what they want him to do; they do nothing when he does not. That is effective. Nurses can shape behavior of supervisors in a similar manner. If a physician talks to a nurse in a certain desired way, the nursing staff might give support and positive reinforcement, rather than being defensive, arguing, or being negative. With positive reinforcement the behavior pattern will change considerably faster than it would if the physician were influenced only by a negative stimulus. By complaining, nurses will further solidify the physician's previous pattern of behavior and his cognitive set toward nurses.

The basis of reinforcement theory is a simple rule: Behavior is influenced by its consequences. Because nurse leaders are in a position that allows them to make decisions about consequences, they may choose to apply reinforcement theory in their actions. Attitudes that the leader adopts toward subordinates and others in using reinforcement theory are of utmost importance. These attitudes can also be applied to help people achieve personal growth and to increase their interpersonal skills so that they will find more happiness and satisfaction in their interactions with others. The nurse leader interested in building a climate of trust may want to concentrate on using reinforcement theory to help individuals and groups accomplish their goals. (The exercises at the end of this chapter deal with steps in building the strengths of another person.) Leaders should be careful not to use reinforcement principles as a means of manipulation. If they do, their motives will be obvious, a climate of tension and insecurity will be created, and the development of interpersonal skills will be curtailed.

Effective reinforcement

The procedure for applying reinforcement theory to affect behavior consists of three parts: (1) set a goal or objective, (2) arrange an outcome or consequence, and (3) observe any difference in the frequency of the response.

Specifying objectives. At the beginning of a relationship with another person, particularly a work relationship in an organizational setting, objectives are needed. Both people must understand clearly what they are trying to accomplish, how they will go about the task, and whether they are attaining the objective as they proceed. An objective is a result of what the behavior is expected to achieve. An objective should describe behavior that can be observed or measured. A department chairman in a university setting might set the following objective for faculty: "Serve on at least two departmental committees." Anyone can count the number of committees and know if faculty members are meeting this objective. But if the objective had been expressed vaguely in such terms as "Participate in university service," the objective is neither specific nor meaningful.

Arranging consequences. Basically two categories of consequences may be used to influence the occurrence of a specific behavior: (1) consequences that provide encouragement and support and (2) consequences that discourage an act through disapproval or indifference. The nurse leader who has open interpersonal relationships with staff members and colleagues will recognize that there are individual differences in how consequences are perceived. What one person experiences as support and encouragement may be perceived as demoralizing by someone else.

Observing differences in frequency of response. When one depends on memory alone, it is easy to misjudge the frequency of another person's behavior. Similarly, it is possible and common to misjudge or misinterpret the effects that arranged consequences are having on another person's behavior. A typical example is the teacher who interrupts what she is doing to tell a restless student to behave. These continual reminders have been found to aggravate the problem by increasing the inappropriate behavior. Through keeping records of behavior the teacher will discover this pattern. Nurse leaders may want to depend on records to observe the number of times the person they are trying to help actually engages in the pinpointed behavior. The "weepy" receptionist may enjoy being told that she is overly sensitive to casual criticism. But only when the leader keeps records will these patterns emerge.

THE IMPORTANCE OF A POSITIVE APPROACH

Positive energy provides momentum to the development of interpersonal power. Negative energy can sap or deplete a power base and short circuit the progress and constructive strength of interpersonal relationships. Nurse leaders who are intent on developing and using interpersonal power in their professional lives must keep a positive energy flow going. We have described a climate of trust as a good conductor of positive energy and have outlined some techniques for developing a climate of trust. Once that climate begins to be felt, effort is needed to maintain a positive mental outlook—an attitude of seeing the glass of water not filled to the brim as half-full rather than half-empty. Nurses with such a frame of mind will have a positive viewpoint of their own professional skills and the capabilities of collegues and staff within the institution.

If nurses feel downtrodden and powerless, this becomes a self fulfilling prophecy: they will be ineffective in the organization and in interpersonal relationships. Others will feel the same way. But if they see every situation or problem as an opportunity rather than as a defeat, the situation becomes very different. If nurse leaders feel powerful, others will perceive this attitude and be influenced to feel powerful themselves. If nurse leaders like people, they will perceive this acceptance of them and will likewise be accepting, eventually finding self disclosure as a basis for building a relationship.

The nurse is the central person in health care delivery

Nurses with a positive attitude realize that they are the hub around which the wheel of institutional health care delivery revolves. If they see themselves as occupying this critically powerful position, with access to many communication channels, they will appreciate the potential leadership and power that accrue to the person in a central leadership position. Within the organization they will be able to facilitate the needs of many subgroups because of the information resources to which they have access. If nurses see themselves in this critical position and are positive about their use of power, they will be able to bring about change in the health care system. But this effort will require positive energy, interpersonal power of great magnitude, and a realization that nurses can bring healing energy not only to clients but to organizational systems.

EXERCISES
Group exercise

1. Divide into pairs. Make a list of behaviors that you could engage in that would provide strengthening consequences for the person with whom you want a better relationship.
2. List behaviors that would provide weakening consequences.
3. Discuss with your partner how the effect of these consequences would be influenced by your place in the organizational hierarchy. Suppose you were the superior. Would you have more or less freedom to choose effective consequences?
4. Return to the larger group to share your suggestions. Discuss with the group ways in which subordinates are able to apply reinforcement theory in relations with superiors.
5. How might the use of reinforcement principles affect the climate of trust?

Individual exercise

1. Reinforcement of the strengths of another person requires practice. Think of a person you know: (1) who has relationship skills but lacks the self confidence to use them, and (2) whom you think you could help. Keeping in mind that you want to express support, write a brief description of the strengths you see in that person.

   _____

   _____

   _____

   _____

2. We discussed some of the reasons, cultural and personal, for which people in organizational settings find self disclosure difficult. Many people have similar problems in interpersonal relationships. Thinking of the person you are trying to help, describe the barriers that interfere with the use of interpersonal skills. We referred earlier to the fear of rejection, lack of a strong self concept, or absence of a positive attitude as typical stumbling blocks. List below the barriers that seem to be troubling the person you want to help.

   _____

   _____

   _____

   _____

3. What could you do to provide support for this person? We mentioned self disclosure, expression of sincere interest, and an active seeking of feedback as possible supporting behaviors. As you recall, we also mentioned the importance of individual differences in the way that these behaviors are perceived. Positive, strengthening consequences would likely follow from these behaviors.

   _____

   _____

   _____

   _____

REFERENCES

Bailey, J. T., and Claus, K. E.: Decision making in nursing: Tools for change, St. Louis, 1975, The C. V. Mosby Co.

Blake, R. R., and Mouton, J. S.: Corporate excellence through grid organizational development, Houston, Texas, 1968, Gulf Publishing Co.

Claus, K. E.: The effects of modeling and feedback variables on higher-order questioning skills, doctoral dissertation, Stanford University, Ann Arbor, Michigan, 1968, University Microfilms, no. 69-207.

Deutsch, M.: Cooperation and trust: Some theoretical notes. In Jones, M. R., editor: Nebraska symposium on motivation, Lincoln, Nebraska, 1962, University of Nebraska Press.

Hall, J.: Interpersonal style and the communication dilemma: I. Managerial implications of the Johari Awareness Model, Human Relations 27(4):381-399, 1974.

Heider, F.: Attitudes and cognitive organization, Journal of Psychology 21:107-112, 1946.

Heider, F.: Social perception and phenomenal causality, Psychological Review 51:358-374, 1944.

Heider, F.: The psychology of interpersonal relations, New York, 1958, John Wiley & Sons, Inc.

Jourard, S.: The transparent self, New York, 1964, Van Nostrand Reinhold Co.

Johnson, D. W.: Reaching out: Interpersonal effectiveness and self-actualization, Englewood Cliffs, N.J., 1972, Prentice-Hall, Inc.

Kepner, C. H., and Tregoe, B. B.: The rational manager, New York, 1965, McGraw-Hill, Inc.

Luft, J., and Ingham, H.: The Johari Window, a graphic model of interpersonal awareness, University of California at Los Angeles, Extension Office, 1955, Proceedings of the Western Training Laboratory in Group Development.

Newcomb, T. M.: The acquaintance process, New York, 1961, Holt, Rinehart and Winston.

Skinner, B. F.: Science and human behavior, New York, 1953, The Free Press.

SUGGESTED READINGS

Bavelas, A.: Communication patterns in task-oriented groups. In Cartwright, D., and Zander, A., editors: Group dynamics—Research and theory, New York, 1968, Harper & Row, Publishers.

Berlew, D. E.: Leadership and organizational excitement. In Kolb, P. A., Rubin, I. M., and McIntyre, J. M., editors: Organizational psychology: A book of readings, Englewood Cliffs, N.J., 1974, Prentice-Hall, Inc.

Beyers, M., and Phillips, C.: Nursing management for patient care, Boston, 1971, Little, Brown and Co.

Chapanis, A.: Interactive human communication, Scientific American 232:36-42, 1975.

Deutsch, M., and Krauss, R. M.: Theories in social psychology, New York, 1965, Basic Books, Inc., Publishers.

Francis, D., and Woodcock, M.: People at work: A practical guide to organizational change, La Jolla, 1975, University Associates.

Gibb, J. R.: Defensive communication. In Kolb, P. A., Rubin, I. M., and McIntyre, J. M., editors: Organizational psychology: A book of readings, Englewood Cliffs, N.J., 1974, Prentice-Hall, Inc.

Hall, J.: Interpersonal style and the communication dilemma: I. Managerial implications of the Johari Awareness model, Human Relations 27(4):381-399, 1974.

Keefe, W. F.: Open minds: The forgotten side of communication, New York, 1975, AMACOM.

Kolb, D. A., and Boyatzis, R. E.: On the dynamics of the helping friendship, In Kolb, D. A., Rubin, I. M., and McIntyre, J. M., editors: Organizational psychology: A book of readings, Englewood Cliffs, N.J., 1974, Prentice-Hall, Inc.

Longest, B. B., Jr.: Improved upward communication can reduce role ambiguity, Hospital Progress 56(2):61-65, 1975.

Lum, J. L. J.: Interaction patterns of nursing personnel, Nursing Research 19(4):324-330, 1970.

Marram, G.: The comparative costs of operating a team and primary nursing unit, Journal of Nursing Administration 6(4):21-24, 1976.

Massarik, F., and Wechsler, I. R.: Empathy revisited: The process of understanding people. In Kolb, D. A., Rubin, I. M., and McIntyre, J. M., editors: Organizational psychology: A book of readings, Englewood Cliffs, N.J., 1974, Prentice-Hall, Inc.

McGregor, D.: Difficulties in communication. In Davis, K., editor: Organizational behavior: A book of readings, ed. 4, New York, 1974, McGraw-Hill, Inc.

Miles, R. E.: Human relations or human resources? In Kolb, D. A., Rubin, I. M., and McIntyre, J. M., editors: Organizational psychology: A book of readings, Englewood Cliffs, N.J., 1974, Prentice-Hall, Inc.

Rogers, C. R., and Roethlisberger, F. J.: Barriers and gateways to communication. In Kolb, D. A., Rubin, I. M., and McIntyre, J. M., editors: Organizational psychology: A book of readings, Englewood Cliffs, N.J., 1974, Prentice-Hall, Inc.

Schaefer, M. J.: How should we organize? Journal of Nursing Administration 6(2):12-14, 1976.

Smith, K. H.: Changes in group structure through individual and group feedback, Journal of Personality and Social Psychology 24(3):425-428, 1972.

Taylor, D. A., and Altman, I.: Self-disclosure as a function of reward-cost outcomes, Sociometry 38(1):18-31, 1975.

Tobin, H.: Quality staff development—a must for change and survival: Standard IX, Journal of Nursing Administration 6(4):39-42, 1976.

Tolor, A., and others: The effects of self-concept,

trust, and imagined positive or negative self-disclosures on psychological space, Journal of Psychology **89:**9-24, 1975.

Van Dersal, W. R.: How to be a good communicator—and a better nurse, Nursing **4**(12):58-64, 1974.

Zalkind, S. S., and Costello, T. W.: Perception: Implications for administration. In Kolb, D. A., Rubin, I. M., and McIntyre, J. M., editors: Organizational psychology: A book of readings, Englewood Cliffs, N.J., 1974, Prentice-Hall, Inc.

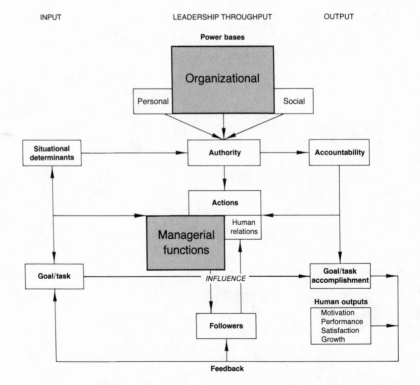

INPUT   LEADERSHIP THROUGHPUT   OUTPUT

Power bases

Organizational

Personal   Social

Situational determinants   →   Authority   →   Accountability

Actions

Managerial functions   Human relations

Goal/task   *INFLUENCE*   Goal/task accomplishment

Human outputs
Motivation
Performance
Satisfaction
Growth

Followers

Feedback

Only power can get people into a position where they may be noble.

ALFRED KAZIN

10 ORGANIZATIONAL POWER THROUGH EFFECTIVE MANAGEMENT

Management has been defined by a leading authority as "the organ of leadership, direction and decision in our social institutions" (Drucker, 1974). If indeed management is the organ of leadership and influence, then it behooves nurse leaders to know something about fundamentals of management and to acquire managerial skills.

It is not within the scope of this chapter to detail management concepts, tasks, practices, and responsibilities. Rather, it is the intent of the authors to: (1) describe the linkage and relationship between power bases inherent in organizations, and the use of managerial skills through *action;* and (2) present a broad overview of the management processes and skills so that managerial actions are effective. Our basic assumption relative to power and management is that if nurse managers have managerial *abilities* and motivational forces within themselves (the *will* to manage), and if indeed these power forces produce results within organizational settings, nurses can indeed influence individuals to be more productive and to achieve a high level of performance in health care and nursing educational institutions.

Competent nurse managers who deal intelligently with people, who operate on facts and take actions are a dynamic, positive force in health care organizations. Conversely, if nurse managers deal unwisely with people, take actions based on inadequate information, or operate from motives of prestige and self interest rather than concern for human welfare, they may indeed be doomed for failure.

To assist the reader to understand our approach to developing effective managerial *actions* and to provide the reader with a linkage system to the Claus-Bailey Power/Authority/Influence Model, a conceptual framework is presented.

SOURCES OF ORGANIZATIONAL POWER

Within organizations there are a number of complex power bases operating. The focus, however, in this discussion will be on the official or legitimate power and authority that are vested through the organization as well as the authors' tripartite model of power as: strength, energy, and action.

Much of the power derived from the formal authority of the organization is engendered in the managerial position. Through the organization, managers have been given the following powers: (1) formal authority to make decisions or take actions, (2) authority to enforce policies or procedures, (3) authority to acquire and control information and data, (4) the official title as the "person in charge," (5) legitimate access to people more powerful or of higher status, and (6) legitimate control of human and material resources.*

Although the power of management is legitimized by the organization, a critical concept relative to organizational power is that management derives power *not from command* over people but from assuming *responsibility* for carrying out functions and contributing to goals.

DEVELOPING A PHILOSOPHY OF MANAGEMENT

Most nurse leaders in management positions recognize the importance of developing a philosophy of nursing. It is usually a first step when planning or evaluating a nursing service or a school of nursing. Of equal importance to the nurse manager is the formulation of a philosophy of management. Without a

---

*Adapted from Drucker, 1974, p. 174

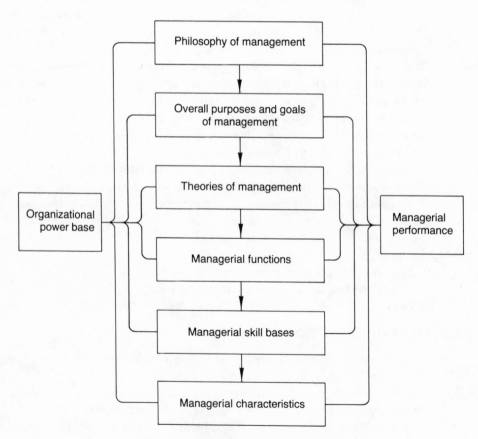

Fig. 11. A framework for management.

frame of reference against which management problems can be approached, there will be inconsistencies in judgemental skills, conflicts, crisis, and needless expenditure of time and energy (Fig. 11).

An author in the discipline of management shared his philosophy of management in its simplest form, "Do unto others as you would have them do unto you" (Appley, 1974, p. 127). Drucker also takes a simplistic philosophical approach in the following statement: "Management by objectives and self control may properly be called a philosophy of management" (Drucker, 1974, p. 442).

Although writing well-integrated statements on one's management beliefs may appear easy, a more challenging task is to make them operational. The philosophy must be reflected in the manager's *actions* and emanate as a mirror of his inner beliefs. To formulate a philosophy without truly believing in it and incorporating it into one's daily activities is a useless exercise. Furthermore one must recognize that once formulated, a philosophy cannot be static. A philosophy should be an emerging, dynamic point of reference.

It is not our intent to formulate a philosophy for the readers but rather to point out the necessity for such a framework in the hope that nurse managers will feel the need and deem it for such importance in their own situation that they will accept the task as a challenge and incorporate a meaningful managerial philosophy as an integral part of their management practices.

PURPOSES OF MANAGEMENT

In addition to deriving legitimate power from the organization the leader/manager can derive an important element of power from managerial skills. However, managerial patterns of action should be based on sound purposes.

Primary purposes of management are to achieve organizational goals and to provide opportunities for individuals to grow personally and professionally. Such overall purposes enable managers to use organizational power and to release the *power of others*. Blake and Mouton (1964) point out that when a manager creates an atmosphere in which people feel they have personal power, genuine communication will transpire and people will assume more responsibility, be more productive, and achieve goals.

Nurses in the role of manager will find that managerial functions involve both an art and a science: the art consists of using power bases and personal skills effectively, applying scientific principles to their work, and having a dedication to people and their welfare. Many of the personal skills are based on power coming from a strong self concept, strength, energy, and *ability*.

MANAGEMENT THEORIES

To further assist nurse managers, a number of theories of management have been researched and developed. One authority on management theories has defined a theory as "simply a more or less complete explanation of how and why someone or something behaves, occurs, or responds as he or it does under a given set of circumstances" (Miles, 1975, p. 32). Since management theories may or may not be influenced by one's philosophical views, it is important to differentiate theories from basic beliefs or life values. Three managerial theories formulated by Miles are summarized.

Traditional theory of management

Traditional theories of management are grounded in the works of Taylor and Weber who were leaders of the scientific management school during the beginning of the twentieth century (Taylor, 1967). Managers who subscribe to this traditional theory view their primary task as that of closely supervising and controlling subordinates, who work primarily for monetary gain. Policies and procedures are developed by top management, and work routines are established and enforced. A need for order, stability, and authority based on science characterizes managers who operate along a traditional theory of management.

Human relations theory

The human relations theory developed in response to criticisms leveled at traditional theorists. It was felt that *people* could not be standardized and that people were indeed human beings with needs, feelings, and desires. Managers who subscribe to this theory attempt to make each worker feel useful, involve them in management decisions, and work toward building collaboration and high morale. Basic assumptions are that individual needs and goals are of more importance in motivating people to work than money and that high morale is a major goal.

Human resources theory

One of the basic tenets of the human resource theorists is management's need to recognize the potential for growth in people and to provide training and continuing education for members of an organization. These theorists built on the work of human relations theorists but advocated using the full range of capabilities of subordinates. They emphasized facilitating performance rather than enforcing controls. In essence, they contended that the manager's basic task is to encourage participation through creating an environment in which members will contribute to efficiency of the organization. "Self direction," "self control," "mutual goal setting," and "wise use of human resources" are key concepts. The work of Maslow and the development of his human need hierarchy exerted a great deal of influence on the human resources theorists (Maslow, 1954).

MANAGEMENT FUNCTIONS

There appears to be a diversity of opinions among behavioral scientists as to how major management functions and activities should be classified. Drucker contends that there are five basic operations that a manager is responsible and accountable for and that results in the integration of material and human resources into a viable growing organism (Drucker, 1974). These five activities include: (1) setting objectives, (2) organizing, (3) motivating and communicating, (4) evaluating, and (5) developing people, including himself. Although the authors are in accord with Drucker's schema, they have adopted a more traditional approach in presenting the functions of management within a framework for *action*.

The four basic *functions* of management subscribed to by the authors and supported by Barnard (1938), Stieglitz (1961), and others, include activities of: (1) planning, (2) organizing, (3) directing, and (4) controlling. It is within these four broad basic managerial functions that management tasks and managerial skills will be discussed.

Regardless of the categorization of functions, it is important to point out that functions are performed within the context of a particular organization, department, or unit as well as with members within a particular situation. Although there are considerable overlapping and interaction among the four functions, each of the functions will be summarized briefly within theories of human relations and human resources.

PLANNING

Nurse managers must plan so that managerial activities have purpose, continuity, and consistency in order to meet the needs and goals of the organization and its members. The outcomes of planning result in *actions* taken by nurse managers that produce clearly defined objectives, identification of tasks or activities to be done, assignment of competent people to perform the tasks, provision of structure and material resources, and formulation and control of policies and procedures if necessary.

In general, all plans are derived from organizational goals and are differentiated from one another according to the frequency with which they are used and the problems presented.

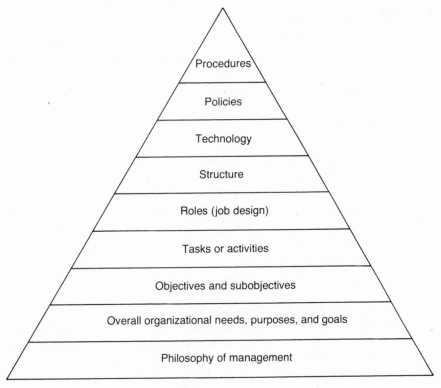

Fig. 12. Bailey-Claus organizational planning model.

To assist nurse managers in the planning process, a model has been developed by the authors. The model presented in Fig. 12 can serve as a guide to help the leader/manager conceptualize step by step activities for which he is responsible and accountable. The model in its hierarchical arrangement serves to: (1) make explicit where a new director of nursing service, dean of a school of nursing, or other nurse manager might begin in the orientation process to a new organization and to assist in the planning function; (2) provide nurse managers who may be developing a new health care delivery service or a new nursing education program with an orderly way to proceed; and (3) assist nurse managers to identify problem areas in the organization. For example, when new and extended roles for nurses evolved in the last decade, such as the clinical nurse specialist, a number of problems arose in the practice setting. These problems were related primarily to the fact that the organizational structure did not provide the clinical nurse specialists with clear lines of authority, responsibility, and accountability. As a consequence many organizations were forced to decentralize and provide a different structure in order to resolve the problem.

Planning for action

Action processes of decision making and delegation both require careful planning. The manager's responsibility for decision making requires a high order of competence if a manager is to perform effectively in making decisions and taking actions. A step by step procedure for making defensible decisions and for taking actions has been presented by Bailey and Claus (1975).

Participation of subordinates

Human relations theorists contend that managers involve subordinates in planning primarily for the purposes of obtaining cooperation and thus improving the work group morale. Managers who operate under the aegis of this theory, however, do not view subordinates as having important input in the decision making process but rather involve them to reduce resistance to decisions made by the manager.

Conversely, managers who subscribe to *human resources* theory involve subordinates in joint planning and encourage a high degree of subordinate participation for the purpose of improving both individual and organizational performance. The *nature* of the interactions between subordinates and manager is equally as important as the amount of participation.

It has been suggested by Miles (1975) that most managers who involve subordinates in the functions of management operate within the framework of both human relations and human resources theory but for different reasons.

Benefits of planning

Planning raises the level of rationality within an organization. Without planning, managers are compelled to react to problems or situations that often reach the level of a crisis (Hicks, 1972). Furthermore, when planning activities involve subordinates, and managers use both human relations and human resources theory, cooperation and morale of subordinates will probably be high and the performance of individuals and the organization will improve.

ORGANIZING

Technically speaking, organizing involves the *act* of assigning tasks and formal rules to various members in an organization; *designing* a structure; and formalizing policies and procedures in an effort to legitimize bases of power, authority, responsibility, and accountability. Thus, organizing is viewed as encompassing more than delegating tasks and supervising subordinates. Inherent in the process of organizing others is a basic need to have a psychological understanding of motivation, perception, and individual differences, and to incorporate psychological understanding into the actions taken by managers. Through *organizing* nursing personnel and nursing activities so that tasks can be accomplished and goals can be achieved, nurse managers can indeed move an organization forward.

Involving subordinates

Inherent in the function of organizing as well as carrying out other managerial functions is the nurse manager's ability to actively involve subordinates in managerial functions, create a climate of trust, and build a high level of morale throughout the organization (McClelland and Burnham, 1976). By taking actions to provide active participation and specifying what is expected of subordinates, nurses will feel that they are playing a vital role in the ongoing activities rather than merely doing a "job." Subordinates need to feel that they have had some input and are in agreement with the formal goals and ongoing activities of the unit or department as well as of the organization. Therefore by organizing and involving subordinates the nurse manager can accomplish what has been called the "engineering of consent," which means that subordinates have participated in the organization of tasks at hand and there has been some mutual agreement in the decision. For example, if the modality of nursing care in an acute care center is being changed from team nursing to primary care and the nurses at the unit level have not been involved in the decision to reorganize patient care services, the new plan will probably be ineffective (Bailey and Claus, 1975).

A major responsibility of nurse managers is to organize in such a way as to maximize the strengths and competencies of nurses and at the same time encourage cooperation. Nurse managers must use their influence strategies to induce collaborative behavior. They need to build on their own strength, energy, and ability and take actions to enable others to use these powers.

Technological tools in organizing

In addition to organizing human resources nurse managers should be apprised of technological tools that can assist them in carrying out managerial function and should use them. With the increase of clinical and administrative data it is essential that some form of automation be initiated. Physiological monitoring, establishment of medical data bases, programs for staffing, instructional programs, patient billing, and organizing, computing, storing, and retrieving student and faculty data are a few examples of how computers are being integrated into health care and educational systems in an effort to organize.

Since computerization is a reality in hospitals, as well as in many aspects of daily living, nurse managers must increase their knowledge of computer systems and take actions to incorporate them (Collen, 1974).

DIRECTING

Directing can be conceived as the managerial function that transforms organized plans into action through the use of human and material resources. It is also concerned with the *manner* by which organizational goals are attained. All management functions contribute to leadership skills, but directing perhaps comes closest to being synonymous with leadership. A manager may be adequate or inadequate, but a leader must lead. Similarly the task of directing must be done effectively if it is to be done at all. An effective manager is one who is able to direct subordinates without coercion or a display of undue authority. In directing others, the nurse manager should be tactful and assertive, as well as display confidence and strength. Tasks that are delegated to others should be challenging and suited to the person's capabilities.

Directing as a management function emphasizes the importance of dual responsibilities. Nurse leaders in top management positions are responsible to both the organization and the individual members. According to one authority, an important principle of direction is that "the more effective the directing process, the greater will be the contribution of subordinates to organizational goals" (Koontz and O'Donnell, 1972, p. 513).

The five main activities of directing are also important elements of leadership. They are *action* oriented and include the following: (1) setting goals, (2) using motivational forces within subordinates, (3) communicating with subordinates, (4) appraising and counseling, and (5) building and maintaining morale.

Directing, like leadership, depends on the relations between leader and subordinates. In directing, the leader's primary role is to involve subordinates in goal setting, make clear to the group what the goals are, and direct and evaluate goal attainment.

Guidelines that may be helpful to the nurse manager in the function of directing and taking actions include the following:

1. People respond best when they are directed by a single superior. This guideline is often referred to as the principle of unity of command.
2. Managers should have as much personal contact with subordinates as possible to enable subordinates to feel that the manager is interested in them and their work. Interacting with subordinates also enables the manager to gain valuable information about the subordinate and his role.
3. Techniques of directing should vary according to the people, the tasks, and factors in the internal and external environments.

Goal setting

Since goal accomplishment is the desired output in the Power/Authority/Influence Model and is also considered the ends through which organizational functions are aimed, the setting of goals is one of the most critical aspects of management. "Management by objectives" has become a password in many organizations (Odiorne, 1969).

Goals represent the basic plan of an organization. It should be pointed out that in addition to the overall goals of an organization, departments or units may also have goals that might be quite different but that will make a contribution to the organization. Setting goals requires both analytical and synthesizing skills. Although goals and objectives are sometimes used interchangeably, there are basic differences. Objectives are *specific,* whereas goals are *broad statements* of direction. For example, the goal of nursing service might be "to provide quality patient care at a reasonable cost," whereas an objective on a nursing service unit might be "to introduce primary care nursing on Ward Ten in 3 months." Through achieving objectives it is also possible for a department of nursing service to attain overall goals of the health care organization and for a school of nursing to meet educational needs of students.

Participative approach to goal setting

McGregor (1960), Drucker (1974), Odiorne (1969), and others suggest a participative approach in developing goals and objectives. They also contend that it is important for individual objectives to be an integral part of goal setting. When individual and organizational objectives are congruent, both are more readily obtained. In setting objectives it is helpful to use the following guidelines: (1) objectives should be specific; (2) objectives should be measurable; and (3) objectives should be attainable.

Using motivational forces

One of the primary tasks of management in carrying out the function of directing is to arouse motivational force *within* subordinates so that they will move toward organizational and personal objectives. Motivation can be viewed as an intangible—an attempt to explain actions. Managers should know why subordinates act in a certain way and what they want, need, and expect. If indeed managing is "making things happen" or "getting things done through the efforts of others," the manager's skill in understanding and using forces *within* subordinates will not only achieve goals but tend to bring out the best in people.

Theory X and Theory Y. McGregor (1960), late professor of management at Massachusetts Institute of Technology, studied numerous theories of motivation and contended that the assumptions management makes about human beings and work profoundly influence the organization. McGregor proposed two contrasting sets of assumptions about human beings and work. Theory X, according to McGregor, typified basic tenets held by most corporate managers. Theory X assumptions are summarized as follows:

1. Human beings inherently dislike work and will opt for avoiding work whenever possible.
2. Recognizing this inate dislike for work, supervisors must control, direct, and coerce subordinates, or threaten punishment in order to get people to achieve organizational goals.
3. Workers want security more than anything else; have little ambition, and avoid responsibility, preferring to be told what to do.

These assumptions appear to account for the organizational attitudes and atmosphere in many settings. Theory X assumptions dominated management thinking for many decades. Attempts at more humanistic approaches to management have often failed because of the complexity of bureaucratic organizations and because bureaucratic systems resist change (Hicks, 1972).

McGregor found evidence that a different managerial approach in dealing with people in organizations was needed, which he called "Theory Y." Basic assumptions about human beings and work according to McGregor's Theory Y are briefly summarized as follows:

1. Work, both physical and mental, is as natural for people as are play, relaxation, and rest.
2. When a worker is committed to objectives, he will use self direction and self control. Therefore, coercion, direction, and the threat of punishment will not necessarily be effective in getting the worker to meet organizational objectives.
3. Rewards associated with objectives can inspire workers to become more committed to organizational objectives and will move them toward goal attainment. Self actualization can be a result of effort expended on organizational objectives.
4. The average worker will seek out responsibility. Those who avoid responsibility have probably acquired this characteristic from experience rather than from nature.

Nurse managers probably recognize some elements of their own assumptions and values in both Theory X and Theory Y. Regardless of one's theories, the well known psychological fact remains: people react the way we expect them to, partly because our attitudes influence our perception to such a great extent. This observation about human behavior is known as the self fulfilling prophecy and proceeds in approximately this fashion: (1) a person assumes something to be true; (2) he acts in compliance with the assumption; (3) the action causes a reaction in another person or situation; (4) whatever the reaction, it is viewed as a confirmation and validation of the initial assumption.

Applied to motivation, this phenomenon causes people to do what the leader or manager expects. Maslow (1954) recognized the close relation between motivation and the self fulfilling prophecy several decades ago. He observed that a widespread assumption was that most workers' behavior resembled that of sheep needing a shepherd to follow. The truism he refers to is closely related to McGregor's Theory X. It maintains that only a small number of workers can handle self rule and independent judgment. But Maslow maintained that this view was merely the outcome of the self fulfilling prophecy. He believed that most people are not stupid and do not behave as the "herd" idea would have one believe. Rather, because people become accustomed to being led and to having their decisions made for them, they become progressively less able to function autonomously and less able to make decisions and direct themselves. The result, obviously, is a belief that is self fulfilling.

Current concepts in management support a movement toward Theory Y. Research suggests that the leader who wants to exert influence and to move the organization forward will provide workers with more autonomy, self direction, and a reward system commensurate with objectives.

Communication

Although communication is discussed in Chapter 11, the importance of two-way communication cannot be overemphasized. Communication channels that proceed from the unit level to top management as well as from the top level to lower levels are essential. Such two-way communication facilitates feedback, provides the manager with an important source of information, creates an atmosphere of trust, and promotes the use of motivational forces within subordinates.

Appraising and counselling

Appraising and counselling are also closely related to the giving of feedback. The performance of every person in the organization is vitally important to the overall functioning of the organization. A nurse manager must have the courage to make subordinates aware of their own strengths and weaknesses in order to help them grow and to strengthen the climate of trust. It is the primary task of managers to set standards and to analyze, appraise, and interpret performance to subordinates.

As forms of help, appraisal and counselling must be offered with tact and consideration. An effective manager attempts to let subordinates determine the kind and amount of help that they want, insofar as it is possible (Berlew, 1974). With planning and direction, a leader can make help available to those who seek it. The way in which help is given has tremendous importance because it influences the degree of subordinates' dependence on the leader. The manager should attempt to help subordinates achieve self control rather than dominate them through tight punitive control measures. Evaluation of subordinates is one of the weakest processes in management.

Building and maintaining morale

Building and maintaining morale have been discussed at length in the context of building of work groups (see Chapter 13). To summarize, high morale in a group facilitates communication, contributes to energetic and effective performance, and enhances creativity.

CONTROLLING

Controlling has been defined as "the measurement and correction of the performance of activities of subordinates in order to make sure that enterprise objectives and the plans devised to attain them are being accomplished" (Koontz and O'Donnell, 1972, p. 582).

Elements of control

There appear to be three basic elements implied in the definition of control: (1) control sets the objectives and standards by which performance is guided; (2) control both measures and evaluates performance in reference to these standards; and (3) control, in the form of control decisions, proposes remedial or corrective action.

Approaches to controlling

In carrying out the function of control, nurse managers might approach the function of controlling by asking themselves the following questions: (1) how often and where should performance be reviewed; (2) by whom should appraisals be made; (3) once evaluative reports are prepared, who should have access to them and to whom should they be sent; and (4) in what way can the process be conducted equitably and promptly at an expense that is reasonable for the organization (Newman, Sumner, and Warren, 1967, p. 676). When these questions have been asked and answered, the nurse manager will have guidelines for the next steps.

A number of other approaches to problems of control can be used. Control in some cases comes directly from people who participate in the work process. In some situations a nurse manager will feel obliged to allow considerable participation by subordinates in decisions relative to control. Some authorities maintain that the manager is indeed obliged to continually expand the control available to subordinates. This control, the argument goes, should increase in keeping with the growing experience and ability of group members (Miles, 1975).

The nurse manager will discover various types of control that are available and necessary to meet organizational needs: quality control, manpower control, and cost control.

Requirements of adequate control

The following ten requirements of adequate control have been offered by Koontz and O'Donnell (1972). Controls should: (1) reflect the nature and needs of the activity, (2) report deviations promptly, (3) be forward looking, (4) point up exceptions at critical points, (5) be flexible, (6) reflect the organizational pattern, (7) be economical, (8) be objective, (9) be understandable, and (10) lead to corrective action.

Control measures

Major traditional control devices consist of the following: policies and procedures, budgeting and reporting, and evaluating employee performance. Each of these measures will be briefly presented.

Policies. The primary function of policies is to serve as a control mechanism to reduce the amount of time and effort spent on problem solving and decision making tasks. They are usually developed for activities that are expected to recur regularly and to serve as guidelines for action. Because policies come from a managerial activity of the leader and have to be acted on by followers, the leader may choose to involve subordinates in the formulation of policies to guide their performance.

If nurse managers solicit input from colleagues or subordinates in formulating policy, they should do so only if they sincerely plan to follow through, evaluate the ideas, and give feedback to the group.

Procedures. Although related to policies, procedures are more specific. Many routine activities of a somewhat mechanical nature can be facilitated by formal procedures. A primary purpose of developing procedures is to enhance efficiency within the organization and to control for inefficiency. Through procedures, the manager assists subordinates to use time more efficiently, achieve greater productivity, and save the organization money. The ability to recognize the need for a procedure constitutes a managerial skill. Consider, for example, the use of procedures to reduce the work load of committees. Nurses often spend a great deal of time in committee meetings when sometimes the work of the committee could be supplemented by a formalized procedure. For example, a well defined grievance procedure will save time, reduce anxiety, and resolve conflict in a more efficient and satisfactory manner.

Budgeting. One of the most widely used devices for managerial control is budgeting. It also represents an element of the planning function in that it is a plan for the allocation of resources. The purpose is to assist the manager to: (1) determine what resources should be expended, (2) by whom, (3) for what, and (4) where. As a measure of control, the budget serves to ensure the manager that the results (allocations of resources and expenditures) conform to plans.

For too long, the responsibility for budgeting and reporting practices has been assigned to individuals other than the nurse manager. But this practice is slowly changing as a result of better prepared nurses and the expectations that nurse managers become more responsible and accountable.

Measurement. Effective management is action oriented. It is implementing the philosophy, goals, and objectives of both the individuals and the organization, assuming responsibility for the actions taken and for *measuring* the results. Thus evaluation can be viewed as one of the most important tasks of management and unfortunately one of the weakest links in health care and educational systems.

Evaluation has been defined as "the use of criteria as well as standards for appraising the extent to which particulars are accurate, effective, economic or satisfying" (Bloom, 1965, p. 185).

Steps in the evaluative process. Two basic steps are crucial to the evaluation process: (1) criteria and standards of performance should be established; and (2) a procedure for measuring the results must be developed. Standards are actually the criteria against which performance can be measured. For example, most nursing services have developed standards for patient care that describe how patient care activities should be performed. These standards can be used to determine how *effectively* the nurse is carrying out patient care activities, and can serve as an evaluation tool.

Guidelines for developing standards. To assist nurse managers in developing standards, the following procedures can serve as guidelines:

1. Identify activities or tasks being performed on a nursing unit or in a nursing department where control is needed.
2. If possible, use existing standards that might already have been developed such as the standards of care developed by the National League of Nursing.
3. If these standards do not seem appropriate, involve subordinates in the development of standards and seek the advice of experts.
4. Experiment with the standards on one or more units and analyze the results.
5. Modify the standards as indicated by the pilot program.
6. Review and revise standards at regular intervals.

Measuring performance. Drucker (1974) contends that the first requisite to measurement is analytical ability. He also states that:

> Measuring demands that measurement be used to make self-control possible rather than abused to control people from the outside and above—that is, to dominate them. It is the common violation of this principle that largely explains why measurement is the weakest area in the work of the manager today. As long as measurements are abused as a tool of control . . . measuring will remain the weakest area in the manager's performance (Drucker, 1974, p. 401).

For performance to be measured effectively, observed behaviors must be compared with the standards that have been developed. Analytical tools for measurements might include such procedures as the nursing audit, personal observations, rating scales, interviews, surveys, problem-oriented records, peer reviews, task-analysis method. Measures used should depend on whether the purpose of the measurement is to evaluate the performance of the nurse or to serve as a quality control system of health care services. Whatever the purpose of the measurement, only by the manager's ability to bring the evaluation and measurement process into being by taking actions for setting standards and measuring them can the skill and performance of members in an organization reach high levels of attainment.

PERSONAL DIMENSIONS OF THE IDEAL MANAGER

Much has been written about desirable traits for leaders as well as managers. Drucker suggests behavioral characteristics of a manager that appear to be useful (Drucker, 1974, p. 616). The major dimensions of the ideal manager are conceptualized in Fig. 13. Needless to say, few if any managers fit the model. How-

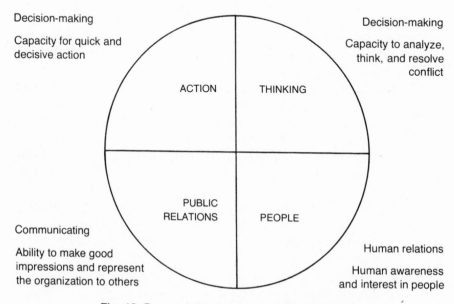

Fig. 13. Personal dimensions of an ideal manager.

ever failure to understand the importance of the personal characteristics of the leader/manager may contribute to ineffectiveness of top managers.

MANAGERIAL SKILLS

Managerial skills derive from knowledge of related process, from understanding and effectively using power, and from taking *responsibility* for achieving a high level of personal performance and for the performance of subordinates. Skills by nature are based on both information and practice. They require action.

Basic managerial skills of setting goals, involving subordinates in managerial functions, communicating effectively, making decisions, and using motivational forces to assist in developing and measuring performance of people exemplify critical managerial *actions;* they also present a challenge to managers to develop the abilities needed to carry out these responsibilities and to make a personal commitment to provide opportunities for growth, self realization, and effective use of power.

STUDY QUESTIONS

1. Describe your philosophy of nursing.
2. Describe your philosophy of management. Compare and contrast it with your philosophy of nursing.
3. What are the primary purposes of management?
4. Identify and define the functions of management.
5. Identify and describe three theories of management.
6. To which management theory do you subscribe? Why?
7. What is the relationship of the planning process to the decision making process?
8. (a) Why would you involve subordinates in managerial functions?
   (b) How would you involve them?
9. How can computer systems be used in health care organizations? in schools of nursing?
10. What are some of the major activities involved in carrying out the function of directing?
11. Define motivational forces? How can motivation be used at the unit or departmental level?
12. Compare and contrast Theory X with Theory Y.
13. As a manager would you subscribe to Theory X or Theory Y? Why?
14. Describe the function of controlling.
15. What are the requirements of adequate control? Give examples of each.
16. Differentiate policies from procedures. Give two examples of each from your practice setting.
17. What is the relationship of organizational power to social and personal power?
18. (a) Define power.
    (b) What are the bases of power?
    (c) What are the bases of authority?
    (d) How does developing managerial skills and skills in human relations relate to the development of power?

REFERENCES

Appley, I.: Formula for success: A core concept of management, New York, 1974, American Management Associations.

Bailey, J. T., and Claus, K. E.: Decision making in nursing: Tools for change, St. Louis, 1975, The C. V. Mosby Co.

Barnard, C. I.: The functions of an executive, Cambridge, Mass, 1938, Harvard University Press.

Berlew, D. E.: Leadership and organizational excitement. In Kolb, D. A., Rubin, I. M., and McIntyre, J. M., editors: Organizational psychology: A book of readings, Englewood Cliffs, N.J., 1974, Prentice-Hall, Inc.

Blake, R., and Mouton, J.: The managerial grid, Houston, Texas, 1964, Gulf Publishing Co.

Bloom, B.: Taxonomy of educational objectives: The classification of educational goals: Handbook I—Cognitive domain, New York, 1965, David McKay Co., Inc.

Collen, M. S.: Hospital computer systems, New York, 1974, John Wiley & Sons, Inc.

Drucker, P.: Management, New York, 1974, Harper & Row, Publishers.

Hicks, H. G.: The management of organizations: A systems and human resources approach, ed. 2, New York, 1972, McGraw-Hill, Inc.

Koontz, H., and O'Donnell, C.: Principles of management: An analysis of managerial functions, New York, 1972, McGraw-Hill, Inc.

Maslow, A. H.: Motivation and personality, New York, 1954, Harper & Row, Publishers.

McClelland, D., and Burnham, D.: Power is the great motivator, Harvard Business Review **54**(2):100-110, 1976.

McGregor, D.: The human side of enterprise, New York, 1960, McGraw-Hill, Inc.

Miles, R. E.: Theories of management: Implications for organizational behavior and development, New York, 1975, McGraw-Hill, Inc.

Newman, W. H., Sumner, C. E., and Warren, E. K.: The process of management, Englewood Cliffs, N.J., 1967, Prentice-Hall, Inc.

Odiorne, G. S.: Management decision by objectives, Englewood Cliffs, N.J., 1969, Prentice-Hall, Inc.

Stieglitz, H.: Corporate organization structures, New York, 1961, National Industrial Conference Board, Inc.

Taylor, F.: The principles of scientific management, New York, 1967, W. W. Norton & Co., Inc.

SUGGESTED READINGS

Arndt, C., and Huckabay, L.: Nursing administration: Theory for practice with a systems approach, St. Louis, 1975, The C. V. Mosby Co.

Bailey, J. T., and Claus, K. E.: Decision making in nursing: Tools for change, St. Louis, 1975, The C. V. Mosby Co.

Chernick, D. A.: Attitudes of women in management—Job satisfaction: A study of perceived need satisfaction as a function of job level, International Journal of Social Psychiatry **20**(1-2): 94-98, 1974.

Eckvahl, V. R.: On-the-job management training, Journal of Nursing Administration **6**(3):38-40, 1976.

Etzioni, A.: Modern organizations, Englewood Cliffs, N.J., 1964, Prentice-Hall, Inc.

Fuller, M. E.: The budget: Standard V, Journal of Nursing Administration **6**(4):36-38, 1976.

Good, A. W.: Supervision: The key to good management, Journal of Rehabilitation **40**(6):13-14, 30-31, 42, 1974.

Hagan, E: Nursing leadership behavior, Institute for Research and Service in Nursing Education, New York, 1961, Columbia University Teachers College.

Hegyvary, S. T., and Haussman, R. K.: Monitoring nursing care quality, Journal of Nursing Administration **5**(5):17-26, 1975.

Kramer, L. A.: The audit and I, American Journal of Nursing **76**:1139-1141, 1976.

Likert, R.: The human organization, New York, 1967, McGraw-Hill, Inc.

Litchfield, E.: Theory formulation. Notes on a general theory administration, Administrative Science Quarterly **1**:3-29, 1956.

Magner, M. A.: A management course revisited: Misericordia Hospital Medical Center, Supervisor Nurse **6**(3):19, 1975.

McClure, M. L.: Entry into professional practice: The New York proposal, Journal of Nursing Administration **6**(5):12-17, 1976.

McClure, M. L.: Quality assurance and nursing education: A nursing service director's view, Nursing Outlook **24**(6):367-369, 1976.

Plachy, R. J.: If you lead, a union can't, Modern Health Care **2**:116, 1974.

Stevens, B.: The nurse as executive, Wakefield, Mass., 1975, Contemporary Publishing.

Tead, O.: The art of leadership, New York, 1935, McGraw-Hill, Inc.

Tobin, H.: Quality staff development—A must for change and survival: Standard IX, Journal of Nursing Administration **6**(4):39-42, 1976.

Wong, P.: Problem solving through "process management," Journal of Nursing Administration **5**(1):37-39, 1975.

Communication is organization in action.
WARREN BENNIS

11 DEVELOPING SOCIAL POWER THROUGH EFFECTIVE COMMUNICATION

Effective interpersonal communication is an important base to social power and is the key interpersonal skill upon which a nurse leader can build a power base in interacting with colleagues, subordinates, and superiors. Communication is the basis of most of interaction with others. All people have extensive experience in communication; practice begins even before a person can utter words. Through effective communication nurses can influence others, learn to understand each other, like each other, build trust, form and terminate relationships, learn more about themselves and how other people perceive them, and move organizations toward goal attainment.

Zoll (1974) states that the greatest problem in communication is the illusion of it. Communication gaps exist because people make assumptions about the meaning another person wishes to convey, which may or may not be correct. An individual often assumes that the communication he has in mind is transmitted to others in such a way that the meaning is clear. This assumption creates considerable problems in working relationships. It is unrealistic to assume that everyone understands the communication in the way it was intended. For example, Lewis Carroll's book, *Alice In Wonderland,* cites many interesting examples of difficulties encountered in communication. When Humpty Dumpty was talking to Alice, he stated that when he used a word it meant just exactly what he chose it to mean, nothing more nor less. This confused Alice because she did not know that it was possible to make words mean so many different things. Humpty Dumpty replied that the question was which was to be master and that was all. Another quote from Carroll's book, "Do you mean what you say or do you say what you mean?" is a classic example of how communication can be interpreted or misinterpreted by the receiver.

Many of us have experienced difficulty with various meanings that can be attached to the word. Even the simplest words, such as "run" can have many different meanings: the clock is running; my nose is running; Josh is running; he is running down the list; he is running him down; they are running the meeting; the movie runs for two hours; she is running for President; the line runs off the page; the committee ran up a big bill.

135

WHAT IS COMMUNICATION?

Communication is the process of sharing information whereby one person sends a message to another with the conscious intent of evoking a response. The message may be a verbal, nonverbal, or behavioral stimulus that the sender transmits to the receiver. For example, a person can say "Hello, how are you" to another person who can reply with a "hello," or a nod of his head, or merely make an inarticulate sound.

The means of conveying the message to the receiver is called the *channel* and may be in the form of sound waves produced by speech, light waves that are seen, or feelings that are transmitted through the electrical field of the atmosphere. Interpersonal communication channels take several forms: memos, meetings, conferences, letters, speeches, newspapers, notes, signs, magazines, textbooks, lectures, and so on. The content of communication can take many *forms:* requests, regulations, policies, procedures, orders, commands, rules, announcements, bulletins, direction, and instructions.

Fig. 14 represents a model of the process of interpersonal communication, the type of communication that is most effective in building a strong power base. The sender has both sending and receiving functions, as does the receiver. The sender intends to share information with the receiver and encodes this information into a message composed of some type of symbol and energy intended to be meaningful to the receiver. The receiver decodes this message into an understanding, an idea, feeling, or mental image. The receiver then may or may not respond to the message by means of an overt verbal response, a nonverbal response, or a feeling that can be roughly interpreted as vibrations. This message becomes feedback to the original sender and is decoded into an idea, feeling, or mental image that indicates whether or not the communication was effective.

Noise

Noise is defined by communication experts as any element that interferes with the communication process. In the sender, noise might refer to attitudes, prejudice, frame of reference, the inappropriateness of the language, or other

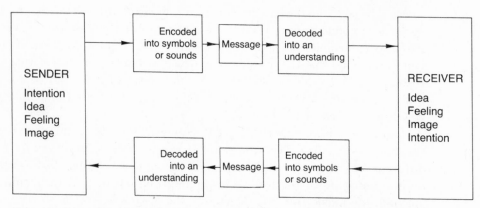

Fig. 14. The process of interpersonal communication. (From Claus and Claus, 1976.)

characteristics of the language. In the channel selected for communication, noise refers to environmental sounds or static, speech problems, distracting mannerisms, unreadable print, confusing words or symbols, and other similar external distractions from a wide variety of sources. For the receiver, noise refers to such things as attitudes, opinions, needs, expectations, background and experiences, and physical condition for receiving the message. To a great extent, the success of communication is influenced by the degree to which noise is overcome or controlled.

Effective communication exists between two persons when the receiver interprets the sender's message in the same way that the sender intended it. The only way for the sender to verify his effectiveness is to obtain feedback. In the process of feedback the receiver of a message communicates his understanding of a message back to the sender of the original message. This feedback assists the sender in modifying subsequent messages to correspond to the capabilities of the receiver to interpret the message appropriately.

While listening, the receiver continually (and involuntarily) filters what he hears or sees. Through this activity the receiver filters or processes the message through his experiences and perceives it in accordance with his own use of language, producing a message of a particular character. The receiver must interpret the intent of the message in reference to his own experience.

This complex process becomes even more difficult in the presence of either *interference* or *distortion*. Distortion is commonly caused by a lack of credibility on the part of the sender. Credibility is derived from the attitude of the receiver toward the trustworthiness of the sender's statement, an attitude that can be based on sources of power. The degree of a person's expertise in the subject under discussion, or his authority to make certain statements, typically influences the listener's attitude. Credibility is also based on the reliability of the information given, interpreted in relation to previous communications from that sender.

The perceived intentions of the sender are also important. If the sender is known to be selfish or willing to sacrifice the interests of others for petty interests of his own, then the credibility of that person's communication is low. On the other hand, credibility may be enhanced by the warmth perceived in the person who is communicating. Studies have shown that openness on the part of the sender engenders credibility more readily than closed or protected messages. The dynamic character of the sender is also important. Passive communication has been found to be considered less credible than dynamic communication. That is, a dynamic sender will likely be perceived as more credible than a passive sender. Peer opinion is also important concerning the credibility of the sender. If colleagues, superiors, or subordinates express the opinion that the sender is not trustworthy, the receiver tends not to believe what the sender has said.

Studies on sender credibility generally suggest that a highly credible sender is one who is perceived in a favorable light in all these dimensions. A sender who is perceived as having low credibility, on the other hand, is seen in a negative light. Therefore, if a sender wishes to increase his credibility, he should appear credible in terms of expertise, reliability, and motives.

Effective communication is based on credibility and the sender's ability to transmit clear messages to the receiver. Credibility thrives in a climate of trust. Studies of organizations show that a lack of trust may be a primary cause of communication distortion (Blake and Mouton, 1968). It reduces the information shared and causes suspicion about what little information is communicated. Increasing the communication between two individuals results in greater accuracy of understanding, but only when trust is high. Other reasons account for communication failures or disparities between what the sender meant to say and what the receiver thought the sender meant. The most common failures do not arise from word usage, grammatical form, lack of verbal ability, or even poor communication channels in organizations; rather, they are created by emotional or social sources of noise from a tense, anxious atmosphere. For example, in an insecure environment people simply do not listen to what others say (Gibb, 1961). Some people are so interested in their own communication or speaking that they listen only for openings in what another person is saying in order to make their contribution. Sometimes listeners are so sure that they know what the speaker is going to say that they distort the speaker's statements to match their expectations or interrupt the person and finish his sentence in the way that they assume it was to be given.

Other communication failures arise because individuals often listen in order to make judgments about the speaker and evaluate what he is saying (Rogers and Roethlisberger, 1952). This in turn makes the speaker guard his defenses. When a receiver constantly gives feedback such as "That's stupid," or "You're wrong," or "I do not agree with that," the speaker then guards himself and chooses words very deliberately. There are so many ways individuals can misunderstand each other that it is a wonder that effective communication takes place at all. A few simple practices, however, can encourage effective communication.

SENDING MESSAGES EFFECTIVELY

The sender can increase the likelihood that his message will be understood by paying attention to three dimensions of communication: his credibility, his ability to send a message understandable to the receiver and relatively free of noise, and his use of feedback from the receiver to verify that the optimal effects of the message were received.

Credibility

Several basic considerations can help the leader enhance the credibility of the messages sent in the organizational setting. These guidelines apply to communication in interpersonal relations and to the more public communication that the leader send throughout the organization.

1. The nurse leader should develop a climate of trust in communicating with others so that the communication being sent is supported. Conditions that are described as "communication problems" in an organization have been found to have little to do with communication, but come from an atmosphere of tension, suspicion, and distrust. The quality of personal relationships in an organization determines the effectiveness of the communication that takes place. The leader

can enhance this climate by expressing warmth and friendliness and by giving off positive energy when communicating with the receiver. To increase credibility in communicating, the nurse leader should be dynamic, emphatic, forceful, and perhaps even aggressive. A passive message may not be perceived as credible.

2. The leader as communicator should be dependable and consistent so that a receiver perceives the communicator as being predictable and dependable, thus encouraging the receiver to think of the information as reliable.

3. Finally, it is important to let the sender know that the leader's motives are unselfish. The leader should be open about the effect the message may have on the receiver.

Sending an understandable message

In an organizational setting the nurse leader will inevitably find that not every receiver understands messages correctly. But it is possible to improve one's chances of being understood, following these guidelines:

Use more than one channel of communication. The leader can increase the redundancy of a message and reduce the noise by using more than one channel of communication in combination such as memos, meetings, pictures, and written messages as well as the spoken words to repeat the message. Advertisers have been very successful in increasing the simplicity and redundancy of the message. Large sums are spent by advertisers working with consultants to develop the most effective "media mix" or combination of channels (print, radio, television, signs) for communicating a carefully planned message. In this respect, the nurse in the health care delivery setting can take a lesson from the advertisers in using more than one channel of communication to reinforce a message and to repeat the message to the same audience more than once.

Make the message as complete and specific as possible. Use of abbreviations or "in group" words will only create confusion. The receiver should have all the background information needed to understand the frame of reference and viewpoint of the sender. Details may be required to make a message clear. For example, reference to the "recent staff meeting" could be misleading without the helpful detail of the date of the particular meeting.

Take personal responsibility for the message. By claiming ideas and feelings expressed as personal, the nurse leader makes clear a desire to be open and credible.

Be consistent. Consistency in communicating makes a message more comprehensible and more convincing. That is, nonverbal and behavioral cues should be congruent. If the leader begins "I am confident that . . ." while facial expressions show anxiety and tension, confusing and conflicting signals are being transmitted to the listeners. When cues are inconsistent, the leader is similar to parents who confuse their children with the message, "Don't do as I do, do as I say."

OBTAINING OPTIMAL AND ACCURATE FEEDBACK

How can a leader find out if communication has really taken place? It is impossible to watch for action every time a communication is made. Therefore, the leader must discover and utilize ways of obtaining feedback from the intended receiver. Feedback is a process by which a sender perceives how the message is being decoded and received. One important aspect of feedback is the attitude of concern that the leader expresses by asking for feedback. When subordinates are asked to participate in the communication process, the climate of trust grows. The leader also benefits from the process by learning how to improve communication skills. The response received when asking for feedback may help the nurse leader to modify the message and communicate it more accurately. Inaccuracies in communication occur when the sender is unable to obtain information on how the message is being decoded. Open two-way communication may be required in order to develop a strong interpersonal power base. The sender of the communication should be able to check with the receiver and confirm that messages are being received properly so that misunderstandings do not grow and thus weaken the power base. When people work closely together, as do professionals in the health care delivery setting, effective communication facilitates the accomplishment of group tasks and the attainment of group and organizational goals.

Feedback implies two-way communication, based upon the model discussed earlier. One-way communication often occurs when the sender cannot determine how the receiver is decoding the message. Two-way communication requires continual use of feedback. Obtaining feedback on a one-to-one basis from another person by talking to that person occurs relatively naturally in many relationships and work situations. Getting feedback from larger numbers of people when they are not in face to face situations with the leader is more difficult.

Earlier some useful channels and forms of communication in organizational settings were listed: channels such as memos, meetings, and letters; and forms such as requests, regulations, rules, and bulletins. In most organizational settings the channels and forms of upward communication are few, and most communication activity is primarily oriented in a downward direction. To be effective in communication (especially if the goal is two-way communication), the nurse leader must understand this tendency. Nurses in positions of authority learn very quickly that rarely if ever will subordinates call a meeting to find out what a person was trying to say. It takes considerable courage to tell a supervisor that one does not know what he is talking about or what is expected. Some subordinates may even find it difficult to say "Let me see if I understood what you said. Is this it? . . ." Therefore, the responsibility for good communication belongs to the person trying to communicate.

In receiving or trying to obtain feedback about communication, the nurse leader should constantly ask questions: (1) How can I get feedback to see if my mental images were transmitted correctly? (2) How important is it that the mental image transmitted is received? What will be the consequences if it is not? (3) Is it important that everyone understand? Who should understand? (4) Can or should I use several channels of communication at the same time? (5) How should I space my messages? and (6) How can questions, doubts, or other concerns about the intended communication be reported back without distortion?

Just as the accuracy of a message can be increased by communicating it through a variety of channels, so too can feedback be made more exact if it is available through several communication channels. Feedback need not be only verbal. Facial expressions, posture, gestures and other nonverbal cues when asking questions are often more effective than verbal expressions in determining how the message is being interpreted by the receiver.

To the perceptive leader certain kinetic behavior or "body language" reveals the attitudes of people more precisely than voiced remarks. In a given situation some enactments of speech and body language are accepted (contextuals) and appropriate to the circumstances. Other behaviors seem out of place in a context and operate to impede the social transaction taking place. Inappropriate behaviors (transcontextuals) provide the leader with immediate feedback concerning communication problems. Listeners who look down, look away, or momentarily let their eyes go out of focus show that they are out of touch. A person making a remark about himself may appear to address his remark to the floor. Very often confessions or insinuations are stated in this style. A particularly commonplace transcontextual behavior among listeners is making a remark such as "I see what you mean," and then gesturing to cover or rub the eyes. Very often people cover their eyes when they are refusing to accept something that has been pointed out to them (Scheflen, 1972).

LISTENING AND RESPONDING

Speaking precisely and listening carefully present a challenge to most people. Often a sender does not organize thoughts before speaking, includes too many ideas, introduces many unrelated topics, and thus makes comprehension difficult. The sender may also ignore answering points made by the previous sender and therefore fail to respond to what has been said. How many times in a classroom or debate have we heard someone launch his own discussion of what he wants to say rather than responding to the previous speaker? The receiver, on the other hand, often does not give his undivided attention. It is a common practice for one to keep thinking about answers to expected questions instead of paying full attention. One often tends to listen to details rather than the essential message.

A good interpersonal relationship and power base cannot be developed unless a nurse leader can learn to listen and respond to other people. The style of listening and responding will determine whether the relationship and consequent power are distant and impersonal or close and strong. If power is to be derived from a close personal relationship, it is important to hear and understand communications when they are made. By letting the sender of a communication know that what he is saying is not being understood, a message of caring and wanting to understand is transmitted. By failing to listen and responding irrelevantly, the receiver communicates disinterest and insensitivity.

Types of response

Rogers (1965), a noted psychologist, conducted a series of studies on how individuals communicate with each other in face to face situations. He found that five types of statements are incidental and of no real importance. From his observations of individuals in different settings such as businesses, homes, parties, conventions, and other places, Rogers found that in descending order of frequency, responses could be characterized as follows:

Evaluative. The evaluative response, which is used most frequently, reveals that the receiver has assessed or judged the merits of the sender's information in terms of its rightness, appropriateness, or effectiveness. When, for example, a nurse supervisor asks colleagues for opinions of a new work schedule, a receiver's evaluative response might be "You're really proud of this aren't you?"

Interpretative. In using an interpretative response, a receiver expresses the intention of telling or explaining to the sender what the message really says. In this way the listener may imply in a helpful way what the sender might think about the situation at hand. The nurse leader can develop interpersonal power with subordinates by giving interpretative responses. A subordinate might confide self doubts to the nurse leader and receive an interpretative response such as, "You think you are effective as a clinician but can't feel enough positive signals from the people in your work group."

Supportive. The receiver is supportive in an effort to soothe or reduce the highly charged state of the sender's feelings and to convey a message that he need not feel as he does. For example, nursing students may confide to a faculty member that they lack confidence about a new work assignment. In this situation a supportive response could be "Well, it will mean hard work for you, but your preparation in that area is particularly strong, don't you think?"

Probing. When a receiver wants to direct a conversation to solicit more information from the sender, a probing response can be used. Questions of the sender can be solicited. As the central person in a communication network, the nurse leader will often face probing responses, particularly when there is regular and frequent communication with the staff.

Understanding. An understanding or paraphrasing response, which is the least used response, shows the sender that the receiver wants to find out whether he has understood the sender's message correctly. This type of response enables the nurse leader to develop effective communications through setting a climate of trust and openness, and thus serve to build a strong interpersonal power base.

A major barrier to close relationships on which power can be built is a tendency to judge, evaluate, approve, or disapprove of the statements made by another (Rogers, 1965; Rogers and Roethlisberger, 1952). The tendency to make evaluative responses to others' communication is common in many conversations or two-way communication. In situations such as health care delivery settings where patient anxiety is intense, the presence of strong feelings and emotions increases this tendency. The stronger the feelings, the greater the tendency of two persons to evaluate each other's statements, each from his own point of view. When a receiver gives understanding responses, more effective communication occurs and the evaluative tendency is reduced or avoided. An understanding response communicates the desire to understand the sender. It helps the sender and the receiver appreciate each other's point of view.

Paraphrasing. A typical understanding response is a paraphrase. That is, a skillful paraphrase helps the receiver determine whether he is in the sender's frame of reference with regard to the message. Paraphrasing is very difficult. However, when it is done with care and tact, the effects are powerful. When a message is paraphrased, it tends to reduce the sender's fears of revealing too much information and thereby decreases defensiveness. But paraphrasing can also be dangerous. If it is done carelessly, the sender may think that the receiver is correcting his language or improving it to show that he did not really say what he meant.

The phrasing used in making an understanding response is a fundamental aspect of listening in a positive, constructive way. The manner in which the response is phrased can vary as follows:

1. *Content, or words used.* By reiterating the same words that the sender has used, the receiver does not facilitate communication and does not really express his understanding. Taking the time to choose one's own words to restate the message shows interest. Indeed, it has been found that a simple repetition of the sender's words impedes understanding.

2. *Depth.* The significant aspect here is the similarity in depth between the message and the sender's response. A sincere and serious statement deserves something better than a flippant or sarcastic response. The most effective understanding is one that can draw the sender to a greater depth than his original statement.

3. *Meaning.* Because paraphrasing can be a difficult exercise, one might change the sender's meaning by omitting what seems a small point or adding what seems implicit in the original communication.

4. *Language.* To preserve accuracy in communication, the receiver should keep to simple language in rephrasing what he heard.

Rogers found that if a person used one category of responses as much as 40% of the time, other people would see him as *always* responding that way, illustrating a process similar to stereotyping. Overuse of certain responses can be remedied by becoming aware of one's responses to others' communication.

An effective leader should become proficient in using all five types of responses. Many relationships or conversations are best begun by using the understanding response until a level of trust has been established. The use of other categories of response may then become easier. When confrontation or a sensitive issue is at hand, it is helpful to paraphrase or restate what a person has said before attempting to express one's own point of view.

Selective perception

In responding to another person's communication, one tends to select part of his message in responding and not respond to other parts. Nearly everyone responds in this manner. Our perceptions have to be selective because any single message has so many levels of meaning, possible interpretations, and so many aspects—verbal, nonverbal, and behavioral—that it is inconceivable to expect a receiver to respond to all of them. Most communication is so complex that we have to be selective in what we perceive and how we respond. Selective perception, however, becomes a source of noise and distortion in communications. Factors that influence one's perception of messages include: expectations, needs, wants, desires, opinions, attitudes, and beliefs. For example, if one expects a person to be unfriendly, he will be sensitive to anything that can be perceived as rejection, unfriendliness, or aggressiveness. If past experience has led an individual to believe that certain people will be hostile, he will be sensitive to any expression of hostility. This selective perception and supersensitivity will make a person almost completely blind to expressions that could be taken as friendly and helpful. A person's wants and needs influence what is preceived in interpersonal communication. Maslow (1954) and Herzberg (1959) have proposed models that describe levels of needs that tend to filter people's perception. In Maslow's hierarchy, needs serve as motivators of human behavior and, in the sense of communication, as means by which people selectively perceive those items of the communication that meet their needs.

Maslow (1954) outlined an overall theory of human motivation. On the basis of clinical experience, he proposed that people's motivational needs were best described in hierarchical arrangement (Fig. 15). Basically, Maslow believed that once a given level of need was satisfied, it ceased to motivate a person. In order for the person to be motivated, the next level of need, in ascending order, would have to be activated. These needs, being motivators, influence the selective quality of perception in communication. The person who is distracted because of hunger, for example, may be more interested in watching the clock during a pre-luncheon meeeting than in contributing to the discussion taking place.

Another theory of motivation, closely related to Maslow's, is Herzberg's (1959) two-factor theory. From a motivational study of accountants and engineers Herzberg concluded that sources of satisfaction in a job were related to

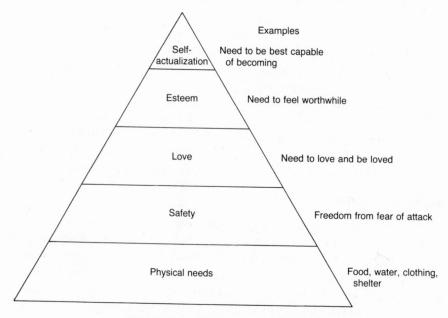

Fig. 15. The Maslow needs hierarchy.

job content, and dissatisfaction to job context. He referred to the satisfying elements as *motivators* and the dissatisfying ones as *hygiene factors* (Fig. 16). These factors of work satisfaction are known as Herzberg's two-factors of motivation.

In some respects the two-factor theory resembles the need hierarchy described by Maslow. Hygiene factors are more or less equivalent to the lower level needs in the hierarchy. Although effective in preventing dissatisfaction, these factors cannot in themselves provide satisfaction. Rather, they can boost motivation to a hypothetical starting point. But only the motivators are able to motivate people in work situations. In terms of this theory, a person cannot be motivated unless he finds the content of his job challenging.

Like Maslow, Herzberg believes that human motivation also influences perception. A person who finds his job challenging and feels motivated will at times show interest in the way he perceives communication. A young faculty member who is undergoing a pre-tenure review, might overhear a conversation about a "ten year plan" and misunderstand it as "tenure plan" because of the strength of the motivation for professional advancement.

Studies of learning have shown that people learn and remember material consistent with their attitudes, beliefs, and opinions. Similarly, these attitudes,

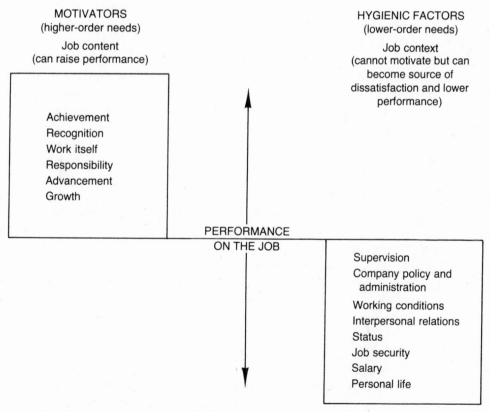

Fig. 16. Herzberg's two-factor motivation-hygiene theory of needs-motivation. (From Herzberg, Mausner, and Andrews, 1959.)

beliefs, and opinions may indeed affect what he is learning because of selective perception. A person in a leadership position who wishes to develop power on an interpersonal basis should be aware of the influence of selectivity in perception. Nurse leaders must also remain flexible in terms of perception and realize that they may have misperceived a message. Interpretations of messages should be tentative until confirmed by the sender. For this reason a nurse leader must negotiate the meaning of a message before responding to it.

PATTERNS OF COMMUNICATION: TWO-WAY VERSUS ONE-WAY

The nurse leader frequently participates in task-oriented groups. In a leadership role, facts and information are critical to the communication process. Relevant information should be collected in an efficient manner. Sometimes the gathering of facts and reliable information from subordinates will require two-way communication. Throughout a two-way communication process the leader must be aware that two-way communication takes longer, is less efficient, and may be more disorganized than one-way communication. However, it is likely to be accurate and to enhance the confidence of the receiver. In the health care delivery setting, where a climate of trust is important to staff and patients, the nurse leader often finds two-way communication necessary, despite the effort it demands. Indeed, it is the sender, the leader, who generally experiences greater frustration in two-way communication. The source of the frustration frequently centers around the leader's awareness that the messages have been misunderstood by the group.

The study of communication patterns in work groups provides provocative suggestions about the advantages of the nurse leader's central role in the health care delivery setting. Because the leader's role attracts information from many sources, the leader may be able to inspire the group to arrive at creative solutions while maintaining a generally high level of job satisfaction.

Recent social science research has begun to question assumptions about the relation of communication patterns in a task group to the particular specifications of the task at hand (Bavelas, 1968). Traditionally, the view expressed in the literature on management has been that the optimal communication patterns in such groups depended on the task. But observers have noted that work groups regularly communicate in patterns that are different from those formally expressed. Indeed, in most groups one observes a gradual shift toward the class of communication patterns that will allow information to flow as early and easily as possible. When a group operates independently of outside control, internal social processes account for the patterns of interaction. However, when it exists within a larger organization, a group cannot develop patterns as spontaneously.

Although nursing groups or health care groups are expected to maintain formal patterns of communication, studies have begun to explore the possibly limiting effect of such formal patterns. In any group within an organization a communication pattern simply describes who may communicate with whom. Fig. 17 shows several variations on how five individuals may be linked. In pattern A each person can communicate directly with two people in the group, and in C

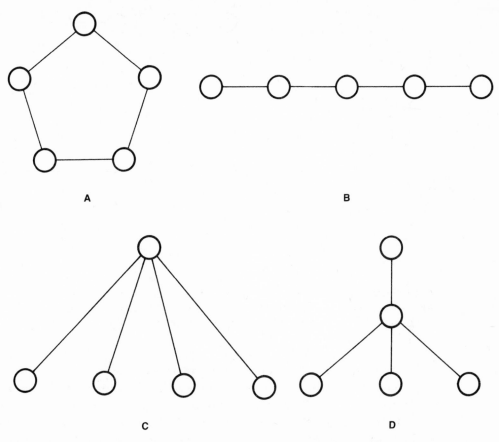

Fig. 17. Some different communication patterns. Each line represents a communication linkage.

and D, by comparison, only one person in the group can communicate with all the others. These differences, in a real situation, are perceived as differences in "distance" between people in an organization.

When various communication patterns in groups are studied, the purpose is to discover what difference, if any, these patterns make. In one such experiment a task was studied that required group communication and cooperation for problem solution (Bavelas, 1968). Patterns of communication were examined in terms of the emergence of leadership patterns. Fig. 18 shows different ways in which leaders emerged. The findings suggested that it was the person in the most central position who was most likely to be recognized by others as the leader. A related phenomenon was that persons in the least central positions were observed to be lowest in morale.

The implications of these findings are extremely interesting in light of the nurse leader's role. The nurse leader is often at the center of a communications network with access to more sources of information than anyone else. Another study of task groups showed that "keymen" or people who emerge as leaders in groups (only 20% of participants) are differentiated from others in their designation of the key role for themselves (Guetzkow, 1968). They were more

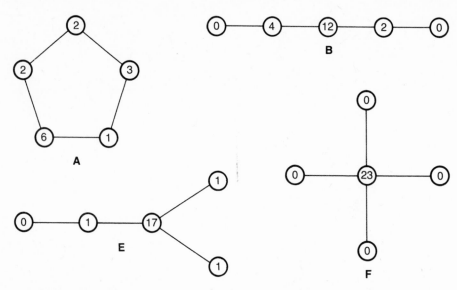

Fig. 18. Emergence of recognized leaders in different communication patterns. The number at each position shows the total number of group members who recognized the individual in that position as the leader in Leavitt's experiment (1951).

perceptive in assessing their situation in the organization than people who did not become leaders. Nurse leaders, therefore, might look upon their centrality in the information network as an opportunity to improve their own power bases. Using the information they receive, they might choose to assert their capabilities and enhance the leadership available. Organizatonal power appears to go to those who seek and use information about their own access to that power.

The prospects for improving the present state of social selfunderstanding depends on certain adequate intercommunication (Bavelas, 1968). It is imperative that every effort be made to enhance communication in health care systems.

The nurse leader who can communicate effectively has a powerful tool that can be used to influence individuals or groups toward greater personal satisfaction.

EXERCISES
Observing communication behavior

Select a group to observe, or place yourself in crowded surroundings where a number of conversations are taking place at once. Using the checklists provided here, record the number of times you observe each type of communication behavior. After a week discuss the general patterns you have observed.

Checklist for ineffective communication

1. The receiver does not give his attention to the message, does not listen.

2. The receiver makes the sender defensive by listening only to be able to make judgments or evaluate.

---

3. The receiver understands the words that are used but does not "get the message."

---

4. The sender uses vague referents such as pronouns to describe his own opinions and reactions.

---

5. The receiver misunderstands the message by changing it to what he expected to hear.

---

6. Other behaviors that are ineffective in communication.

Checklist for effective communication

1. The receiver makes an understanding response by paraphrasing what the sender says.

---

2. The receiver refrains from making judgmental statements or evaluations of what the sender has said.

---

3. The listener tries to discover the underlying meaning of the message and is not distracted by specific words.

---

4. The receiver makes tentative responses until he has discussed with the sender how best to interpret his meaning.

---

5. Other effective communication behaviors.

REFERENCES

Bavelas, A.: Communication patterns in task-oriented groups. In Cartwright, D., and Zander, A., editors: Group dynamics: Research and theory, ed. 3, New York, 1968, Harper & Row, Publishers.

Blake, R. R., and Mouton, J. S.: Corporate excellence through grid organizational development, Houston, Texas, 1968, Gulf Publishing Co.

Claus, K. E., and Claus, R. J.: Signage: Planning environmental visual communication, Palo Alto, Calif., 1976, Institute of Signage Research.

Gibb, J. R.: Defensive communication, Journal of Communication 11(3):141-148, 1961.

Guetzkow, H.: Differentation of roles in task-oriented groups. In Cartwright, D., and Zander, A., editors: Group dynamics: Research and theory, ed. 3, New York, 1968, Harper & Row, Publishers.

Herzberg, F., Mausner, B., and Snyderman, B. B.: The motivation to work, ed. 2, New York, 1959, John Wiley & Sons, Inc.

Johnson, D. W.: Reaching out: Interpersonal effectiveness and self-actualization, Englewood Cliffs, N. J., 1972, Prentice-Hall, Inc.

Leavitt, H. J.: Some effects of certain communication patterns on group performance, Journal of Abnormal and Social Psychology 46:38-50, 1951.

Maslow, A.: Motivation and personality, rev. ed., New York, 1970, Harper & Row, Publishers.

Rogers, C.: Dealing with psychological tensions, Journal of Applied Behavioral Science 1(1):6-25, 1965.

Rogers, C., and Roethlisberger, F. J.: Barriers and gateways to communication, Harvard Business Review 30(4):46-52, 1952.

Scheflen, A. E., with Scheflen, A.: Body language and social order: Communication as behavioral control, Englewood Cliffs, N.J., 1972, Prentice-Hall, Inc.

Zoll, A. A., III: Explorations in managing, Reading, Mass., 1974, Addison-Wesley Publishing Co.

SUGGESTED READINGS

Bernal, H.: Power and interorganizational health care projects, Nursing Outlook 24(7):419-421, 1976.

Brehm, J. W., and Mann, M.: Effect of importance of freedom and attraction to group members on influence produced by group pressure, Journal of Personality and Social Psychology 31(5):816-824, 1975.

Lassey, W. R.: Introduction: Communication and leadership. In Lassey, W. R., editor: Leadership and social change, Iowa City, 1971, University Associates.

Pym, B.: The making of a successful pressure group, British Journal of Sociology 24(4): 448-461, 1973.

Van Dersal, W. R.: How to be a good communicator—and a better nurse, Nursing 4(12):58-64, 1974.

Vickers, G.: Changing patterns of communication, Futures Conditional 3(2): Item 2.

Wallston, K. A., and Wallston, B. S.: Nurses' decisions to listen to patients, Nursing Research 24(1): 16-22, 1975.

Wood, M. T.: Power relationships and group decision making in organizations, Psychological Bulletin 79(5): 280-293, 1973.

The flow that pushes the problem has the answer in it.
People under pressure have more going for them.

ROBERT NADEAU

12 RESOLVING CONFLICT

JOCELYNE M. NIELSEN, R.N., M.S.

CONFLICT AND NURSING

As members of a nurturing profession, concerned primarily with patient welfare, nurses often feel an important dimension of their role is to "keep and peace" and avoid conflict. Because of these feelings, the term "conflict" has a negative connotation for nurses. However, conflict should be looked at from a broader perspective. Nurse leaders must recognize that conflicting situations can be constructive as well as destructive and that conflict exists in health care and educational institutions whenever there is a lack of: (1) goal clarity, (2) well-defined tasks, (3) role clarity, and (4) clearly stated policies and procedures.

To gain a better understanding of what conflict and conflict resolution are all about, a first step is to define what is meant by concepts presented in this chapter and, second, to learn how one might approach conflict resolution in more creative and constructive ways.

Definition of terms

A *conflict* is a clash, a struggle that occurs whenever the harmony and balance among thoughts, feelings, and behavior are threatened. This disturbance gives rise to incompatible activities and interferes with desired goals (Deutsch, 1969).

A conflict may be within a person or a group. Such conflicts are called *intrapersonal or intragroup conflicts* and relate to personal and group dynamics. This chapter focuses on interpersonal and intergroup conflicts and the disagreement and struggle between two or more persons or groups of persons. An important assumption is that conflict exists whenever people relate to each other for the purpose of attaining a goal and that nurse leaders have choices of making the situation either constructive or destructive.

A *constructive* approach is one that embodies creativity in the resolution of conflict and one that contributes to the growth and understanding of the individual and the group to which one belongs.

A *destructive* approach is one that has the tendency to expand conflict and bring negative consequences for the individual and the group. Frequently nurse leaders have blocks in their personal and interpersonal spaces that prevent them from the creative resolution of conflicts. However, because of professional education and experiences with patients, faculty, members of the health care team, and their own daily living, nurses have knowledge and skills that often contribute to resolving conflicts. Some nurse leaders have experienced success in dealing with conflict and can build on these experiences. Nurse leaders who have not experienced success may find that numerous relationships, both personal and collegial, terminate because of unsuccessful resolution of conflicts, which results in ineffective leadership. A clearer notion of what conflict resolution is all about will assist them to approach conflict in a more creative and effective way.

Role of the nurse leader in conflict

Nurse leaders are expected to give guidance to colleagues, subordinates, and clients, and to participate in conflict resolution with subordinates and superordinates. There is a desperate need in educational and health care institutions for creative leadership to influence the educational process of nurses and the delivery of health care through innovations. Nurse leaders must be able to analyze, understand, and intervene in conflict. Direct involvement in a conflict may vary, depending on the type and magnitude of the conflict as well as the position held by the nurse leader in the situation.

If the elements of conflict are well understood at the top management level in schools of nursing or nursing service agencies, if there is good communication at a feeling level among the members of the group, and if the goals, tasks, roles, and procedures are clearly defined, nurse leaders will facilitate and influence group members to move toward more effective education for students and toward quality nursing care. It is the goal of this chapter to assist the reader to gain new insights into the process of conflict and its resolution.

Conflict in a systems framework

Within a systems framework, three elements or subsystems interact in a conflict situation: (1) cognitive (information, communication), (2) affective (sub-

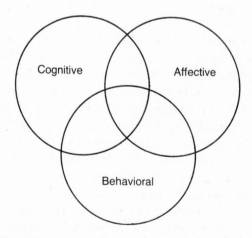

Fig. 19. Interactive elements in a conflict situation.

jective knowledge, feelings), and (3) behavioral components (reactions) (Boulding, 1957). See Fig. 19.

These elements interact with each other to form a total system that aims at maintaining consistency and balance. When conflict arises, each party is confronted by another system made up of a communication process, information, feelings, and reactions. The state of the system is perceived through these interactive elements. A simple example illustrates this model. A head nurse at a large, complex acute care center complained with anger to the director of nurses, "If Sandra Collings does not agree with our staffing policy, she should resign." The head nurse reacted with strong emotions to some information received about Sandra Collings from the evening charge nurse. Sandra had requested an extra day off for a special trip out of state. The head nurse reacted by taking the issue to the director. In this situation, cognitive, affective, and behavioral components demonstrate the total system represented by the head nurse.

Conditions that predispose to conflict

Conditions that predispose to conflict are lack of clarity concerning goals, tasks, roles, and procedures. Conflict arises primarily from differences or disagreement. Differences may occur in the areas of: (1) information or belief; (2) interests, desires, or values; (3) competition, rivalry, or scarcity of resources. When conflicts arise from disagreements, they involve one or more of the following: (1) means and ends, (2) power and control issues, (3) competitive and cooperative approaches, (4) rationality and irrationality, (5) subjective and objective reality, (6) cognitive and affective aspects. These lists are not exhaustive, but demonstrate the numerous dimensions of living that predispose to conflict.

Productive or constructive outcomes of conflict

Conflict has a number of positive functions. It has been described as "the root of personal and social change." Conflict may also stimulate problem solving and the generation of creative solutions; it can be a source of personal enjoyment and fulfillment, and it allows for the development of personal identity. Productive conflict resolution at the individual level can be conceived as creative thinking. At the social level conflict resolution is comparable to cooperative group problem solving.

CREATIVE CONFLICT RESOLUTION—A CONSTRUCTIVE APPROACH

A creative approach in conflict resolution is similar to the description of creative thinking that includes the following phases: (1) an initial period of problem recognition with sufficient desire to solve it; (2) a period of concentrated effort to solve the problem through routine and habitual action; (3) a period of withdrawal caused by the frustration experienced at the failure of customary actions; (4) an incubation period that leads to reformulation of the problem from a different perspective to bring about a new presentation; (5) a moment of insight in which a tentative solution appears; and (6) a final solution, which is then elaborated, tested, and communicated.

To foster the creative process in the resolution of conflict, one must develop an appropriate state of arousal or tension about the problem, reformulate the problem if necessary, and brainstorm for ideas, which can be combined with flexibility to arrive at novel patterns or solutions.

Within the context of nursing and hospital systems, creative conflict resolution may be difficult to generate unless nurse leaders approach conflict resolution in a creative way. Human needs of patients and personnel in the health care system are of such magnitude and importance in today's world that nurse leaders must become creative in setting up the environment as well as in creatively resolving conflicts.

Interpersonal conflicts

Interpersonal conflicts can be minimized in educational institutions and health care settings if the goals are clear, the tasks well-defined, and roles are delineated. In the hospital nursing situation, conflicts between nurses may arise because of unclear goals. For example, the establishment of priorities by the team leader in the care of patients may result in conflict. Different members of the team may have other priorities. Personal needs of nurses such as time for vacations and education are problems faced by directors of both schools of nursing and nursing services. Conflicts frequently occur in both educational settings and inservice agencies because nurses have different expectations than their superordinates, because policies have not been formulated, or because policies are unclear.

Failure in handling these types of interpersonal conflicts may lead to destruction of relationships. Conversely, constructive resolution of conflict leads to the growth of the individual involved. It brings about increased self confidence and greater ability to take risks and to handle stress. "A relationship has to withstand the stress involved in a conflict to be a lasting one" (Johnson, 1972).

Resolving interpersonal conflict. In resolving conflict, the trust level in the relationship and the degree of understanding between the parties is of utmost importance. An increase in both trust and understanding is a definite sign of progress toward the resolution sought.

Where does one begin in learning to resolve conflict? This is a question frequently asked by students and other interested groups. An examination of one's own present and past styles of conflict management might be a beginning point. Conflicts experienced with spouse, siblings, parents, teachers, employers, and others can provide information on conflict management. Recall of personal experiences can develop awareness of effective or ineffective actions in resolving the conflict and may also reveal personal bias.

A second step might be the establishment of effective communication with the other party. Without effective communication trust cannot develop. The development of a climate of trust can be a long and difficult process. A gradual building of trust will set the tone for forthcoming cooperative solutions.

Working with a conflict. There is a human tendency to strike out at people who cause pain or discomfort. To approach conflict in a way that is derogatory to the other person's behavior will only contribute to anger and defensiveness. For example, when Head Nurse Stewart was told by the night nurse that a patient complained to her because he did not have his linen changed during his morning care, the head nurse jokingly responded, "You always tend to get hysterical over small problems." The night nurse left the nurses' station angry and upset.

It is important to define the events leading to the conflict and to narrow the dimensions of the conflict. The more clearly the conflict is defined, the easier it is to resolve. Since several approaches may be used in conflict resolution, it is important to select the most appropriate strategy. One may choose a win-lose approach, or one may choose a creative, cooperative, problem solving approach. The win-lose approach frequently brings resentment and hostility toward the winner and a breakdown in communication. Competitive modes of communication to deceive and manipulate are used in a win-lose approach, and distrust and dislike are some of the outcomes.

The cooperative, creative problem solving approach tends to lead to a more effective solution to the problem. This approach is characterized by a sense of well-distributed power and an appropriate use of power. It brings about creative sharing and personal growth of the participants. Cooperative strategy and style have not been consistently valued in our industrialized society. However, in the last decade there has been an increased interest in studying and humanizing the work environment, which has led to an increased awareness of newer and more appropriate alternatives to conflict resolution at both the interpersonal and the organizational levels.

Conflict within an organizational context

Conflict within an organization can be seen as a dynamic process underlying a wide variety of organizational behaviors. It can also be seen as an episode that can be evaluated in terms of functions and dysfunctions within the organization. Five stages of conflict episode have been identified: (1) latent conflict (conditions), (2) perceived conflict (cognitive), (3) felt conflict (affective), (4) manifest conflict (behavior), and (5) conflict aftermath (conditions).

These stages are similar to the systems approach discussed earlier. An examination of the stages gives the nurse-leader some definite and specific events that might be used as guidelines in understanding a conflict episode.

1. *Latent conflict.* This source of conflict is present when the demands of participants for resources exceed what is available (for example, when most nurses wish to work on the day shift). It may also occur when participants either seek to control some activities of others or are removed from a position of control. This affects the individual's need for autonomy. An example of such latent conflict is often found among professional nurses who pursue independent roles vis-a-vis physicians. Another source of latent conflict may occur when goals are divergent and parties must cooperate and reach a consensus. For example, a group of head nurses may be in a latent stage of conflict if they are unable to agree on allowing special compensatory leave for nurses working on intensive care units. The above examples and conditions may remain at a latent stage of conflict through effective leadership, communication, and creative problem solving.

2. *Perceived conflict.* A state of perceived conflict exists when parties misunderstand each other and perceive a conflict when no latent conflict conditions are present. Poor communication may contribute to such conflict stage. For example, the shift system in a hospital often contributes to perceived conflicts because of the lack of adequate communication between shifts. Conversely, some latent conflict does not reach the awareness of participants. A latent conflict may be perceived only when it becomes a strong threat. A conflict relating to a central value of one's personality would be a strong threat. Personal conflicts tend to be suppressed since they are usually only mildly threatening to other individuals in the organization. There is a tendency to perceive some latent conflicts among employees of a hospital as personal, which may suppress latent organizational conflicts. Statements such as "It is a personality conflict," or "We could never resolve this problem with such a person—she should resign," might be reflective of limited perception of possible latent organizational conflicts.

3. *Felt conflict.* The perception of a latent conflict may produce tension and anxiety in participants who feel that their identity is threatened. This is called personalization of conflict. Individuals who tend to feel victimized and have low self esteem might personalize conflict. Such a process is seen as dysfunctional. The organizational structure should provide for the individual's expression of anxieties so that internal balance and harmony can be maintained.

4. *Manifest conflict.* A conflict is manifest when the behavior of some person or persons frustrates the goals of some of the participants. Open aggression, defensive acts, tactics such as apathy, rigidity, and withdrawal are some manifest behaviors of a conflict. Conflict resolution programs and approaches are usually applied between perceived, felt, and manifest conflict.

5. *Conflict aftermath.* A conflict genuinely resolved to everyone's satisfaction creates the basis for a more cooperative relationship. If the conflict is suppressed, the latent conditions may explode in more serious form until resolution or dissolution of the relationship.

The recognition of the above stages and the acquisition of skills by nurse leaders to intervene at the five stages of conflict might contribute to clarification of organizational goals, tasks, roles, structure, policies, and procedures.

Three models to analyze organizational conflicts. When nurses are placed in a position of authority and responsibility, an understanding of social systems is requisite. The complexity of health care and educational institutions requires that nurse leaders have an understanding of social systems and their impact on the delivery of care. A bargaining model, bureaucratic model, and a systems model have been developed and reported by Pondy as one way to gain understanding of conflict (Pondy, 1967).

1. *Bargaining model.* This model relates to interest groups and competitive modes of behavior. Discrepancy between demands of competing parties and the available resources provides a source of potential conflict among interested parties. Attempts at increasing the resources or at reducing the demands of the groups in conflict are measures usually employed to resolve conflict at a bargaining level. Nursing leaders should view this process as part of a constructive and positive attempt to be democratic in the allocation of scarce resources within the

organizational context. The need for more qualified nursing staff to improve the quality of care is often a struggle in large institutions. Nurse leaders have difficulty coping with the amount of extra work required to gather the necessary data to convince the hospital board of the need.

2. *Bureaucratic model.* This model refers to problems of control. It is useful in examining conflict along vertical dimensions of a hierarchy. Conflicts may relate to authority and structure between superior and subordinate and between various roles. Different expectations over control and autonomy and the lack of assurance that superiors have the same goals as the subordinates are some examples of potential conflict situations.

Modern large hospitals are attempting to increase the involvement of the individual in activities of the organization. Decentralizing nursing departments and nursing care units and fostering participative management tend to reduce the autonomy and increase the interdependence of the participants. Such conditions create more intimate relationships and promote creative endeavors, but they also increase personal conflict.

3. *Systems model.* This model is concerned with problems of coordination and lateral conflicts among people at the same level of hierarchy. In a goal-oriented organization such as a hospital, lateral conflict often exists between physicians and nurses. The interdependency of their roles toward the well-being of patients is a potential source of lateral conflict. Since cooperation is essential between physicians and nurses, it is essential that a joint decision process be combined with creative approaches to resolve lateral conflicts.

BUILDING A PERSONAL POWER BASE FOR RESOLUTION OF CONFLICTS

An understanding of the concepts presented, whether they relate to interpersonal or organizational conflict situations, may not help nurse leaders to successfully resolve conflicts. A crucial factor in creative and constructive conflict resolution is the state of the nurse leader facing the conflict. There are personal characteristics or states that tend to bring about a sense of well-being in the ability to connect to one's higher self and to be open to the increased energy level that this centering state provides (Leonard, 1975).

SUMMARY

This chapter has emphasized the need for decreasing unnecessary conflicts by developing well-defined goals, clear tasks, explicit roles, and clearly stated policies and procedures. Nurse leaders also need to develop competence in conceptualizing conflict as a positive force and to develop skills at a personal level to resolve conflict effectively.

EXERCISES
Personal style of resolving conflict

1. Recall a conflict you have been involved in recently.
2. Was it constructive or destructive?

3. How would you characterize your style of handling the conflict?
4. How would you characterize the other person's style of handling the conflict?
5. List creative alternatives you did not generate at the time of the conflict that could have contributed to your and the other person's growth and would have positively affected your work setting.
6. What are you willing to try to improve communication during conflict?
7. What are you able to risk to develop more trust during a conflict?

Creative solution to a conflict

1. Recall a conflict where a creative or constructive solution was found and used.
2. Examine the process of finding the solution and describe how a creative solution was found. What made the solution possible?

Analyzing conflict

1. What is the information base available about the conflict?
2. How is the communication handled?
3. (a) What are your feelings toward a conflict?
   (b) What are the feelings of the other person in the situation toward the conflict?
4. (a) What do you know subjectively about the situation?
   (b) What does the other know subjectively about the situation?
5. (a) How are you reacting to the situation?
   (b) How is the other person reacting to the situation?
6. (a) What is your trust level toward the other person (high, medium, or low)?
   (b) What is the other person's trust level toward the other person (high, medium, or low)?

Organizational conflicts

1. Make a list of disagreements you have about quality patient care in your setting, which you personally feel would cause conflicts to occur if you were to mention them at work.
2. For each difficulty stated evaluate the following four questions: Could this disagreement be resolved if:
   (a) Nursing care goals were clearer?
   (b) Nursing care tasks were clearly defined?
   (c) Nursing roles were clearer?
   (d) Policies and procedures were clearly stated?
3. Brainstorm on the possible solutions related to clarifying goals, tasks, roles, and policies that would contribute to reducing conflicts.
4. State three consequences that negatively affect quality patient care because you "keep the peace" at work.
5. When would you feel comfortable about asking for a third party, a consultant or a mediator, to help you in resolving a conflict at work?

Five stages of a conflict episode

1. Give examples from your work setting that illustrate the five stages of a conflict episode. Select a different situation for each stage or use the same

situation: (a) latent conflict, (b) perceived conflict, (c) felt conflict, (d) manifest conflict, and (e) conflict aftermath.

7. For each example given above visualize a constructive solution. Always look for a solution from a "letting go" place inside yourself. Your state of relaxation and your sense of well-being will affect your choices of solutions.

8. Examine the three models presented to analyze organizational conflicts. Then, brainstorm with a colleague or a friend on possible structure of mechanisms that would creatively deal with such organizational conflicts on an ongoing basis.

REFERENCES

Boulding, K. E.: Organization and conflict, Journal of Conflict Resolution **1:**122-34, 1957.

Deutsch, M.: Conflict: Productive and destructive, Journal of Social Issues **25:**7-40, 1969.

Johnson, D. W.: Reaching out, Englewood Cliffs, N.J., 1972, Prentice-Hall, Inc.

Leonard, G. B.: The ultimate athlete, New York, 1975, The Viking Press, Inc.

Pondy, L. R.: Organizational conflict: Concepts and models, Administrative Science Quarterly **12:**296-320, 1967.

SUGGESTED READINGS

Assighori, R.: The act of will, New York, 1973, The Viking Press, Inc.

Benner, P.: Values clashes. In Davis, M., Kramer, M., and Strauss, A., editors: Nurses at work, St. Louis, 1974, The C. V. Mosby Co.

Bennis, W. G., and Thomas, J. M., editors: Management of change and conflict, London, 1972, Penguin Books Ltd.

Bondurant, J. V.: Creative conflict and limits of symbolic violence. In Bondurant, J. V., editor: Conflict: Violence and non-violence, Chicago, 1971, Aldine Publishing Co.

Bolton, C. K., and Lindberg, M. E.: Conflict: The conditions and processes in community organizations and interpersonal relationships, Monticello, Ill., May, 1971, Council of Planning Librarians Exchange Bibliography, no. 187.

Deutsch, M.: Conflicts: Productive and destructive, Journal of Social Issues **25**(1):7-41, 1969.

Fitts, W. H.: Interpersonal competence: The wheel model. Studies on the self concept, Nashville, Tenn., 1970, Counselor Recordings and Tests.

James, M., and Jongeward, W. D.: Born to win, Reading, Mass., 1971, Addison-Wesley Publishing Co., Inc.

Johnson, D. W.: The constructive use of conflict. In Johnson, D. W.: Contemporary social psychology, Philadelphia, 1973, J. B. Lippincott Co.

Leonard, G. B.: Sports and competition: Winning isn't everything. It's nothing, Intellectual Digest **3:**45-47, 1973.

Likert, R., and Bowens, D.: Conflict strategies related to organizational theories and management systems. In Likert, R., and Bowens, D.: Attitudes, conflict and social change, New York, 1972, Academic Press, Inc.

Mahl, G. F.: Psychological conflict and defense, New York, 1971, Harcourt Brace Jovanovich, Inc.

May, R.: Power and innocence, New York, 1972, W. W. Norton & Co., Inc.

Smith, C. G., editor: Conflict resolution: Contributions of the behavioral sciences, Notre Dame, 1971, University of Notre Dame.

Walton, R. E.: Interpersonal peacemaking: Confrontations and third party consultation, Reading, Mass., 1969, Addison-Wesley Publishing Co., Inc.

Watson, J.: The quasi-rational element in conflict, Nursing Research **25:**19-23, 1976.

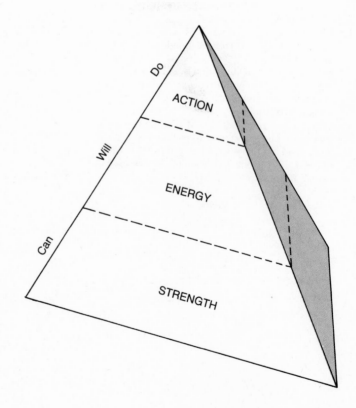

Power is the resource that makes it possible to direct and coordinate the activities of man.

PETER BLAU

13 WORKING EFFECTIVELY WITH OTHERS

BRIDGING THE GAP

If power is the resource that enables nurse managers to direct and coordinate nursing service or nursing education activities, then it behooves nurse managers to understand and to use the basic concepts of power in working effectively with others. We have defined power as the *ability* (based on *strength*) and *willingness* (based on *energy*) to act (which yields *results*).

PURPOSES OF WORK GROUPS

The primary *purposes* of work groups from the perspective of our definition of power and from our delineation of power bases are to:
1. Use the *ability* and *strengths* of a group of people who bring a wide range of knowledge, experiences, and judgment to bear on a problem or task through working from their personal, organizational, and social power bases.
2. Use the *willingness* of members of the work group, which is supported by positive *energy* to share information and opinions and to probe the *facts*.
3. Use group *actions* taken by the members to produce *results*.

WORK GROUPS DEFINED

We are defining the work group as a group of persons to whom some task, problem, or other activity has been assigned with the *expectation* that there will be some group *action* that produces *results*. We are assuming that whether a group is labeled a "task force," "committee," "team," or "commission," essentially our broad definition of work groups will be applicable.

THE NATURE OF WORK GROUPS

Since work groups vary in the nature of the assignment, in their permanency, and in the authority assigned to them, particularly in health care and educational systems, a great deal of confusion has resulted.

Authority based groups

Some work groups have been given authority to make decisions. For example, since decentralization of nursing services has taken place in many health care settings, activities such as budgetary planning, implementation, and control have been delegated to the unit. Since the activity involves the head nurse working with other members of the unit and involves decision making that affects subordinates, it is known as a *line* working group.

Work groups that recommend

A recommending work group is often appointed to deliberate on problems. They do not have the authority to decide, but merely make recommendations to a dean of a school of nursing or a director of nursing service who may or may not accept the recommendations. Since the authority relationship to the superior is advisory in nature, it is known as a *staff* work group.

Status of work groups

Work groups may be temporary or permanent. A work group may be appointed to study the philosophy of nursing service, then may be disbanded when the task is completed. A more permanent work group in an acute care setting might be a board of directors of a hospital, although even the membership on such a board is subject to change because of resignations and other contingencies.

USING ORGANIZATIONAL POWER BASES TO SATISFY NEEDS

One of the primary goals of health care systems is to deliver quality health care services. Since health care centers are increasingly complex, multidisciplinary by nature, technical-scientific in their orientation, and often bureaucratic in structure, it becomes difficult for individuals in a health care organization or an educational institution to understand their unique contribution in attaining organizational goals. It is even more difficult to understand their role as members of a group whether it be an administrative group consisting of a dean and assistant deans; a director of nursing service and assistant directors; or a head nurse working with other nurses, physicians, nutritionists, pharmacists, paraprofessionals, patients and their families, and a host of other related people.

To enable nurses to gain a better understanding of the needs of: (1) an organization, (2) a work group, (3) the individual, and (4) a task or assignment, these four basic needs will be reviewed briefly within the context of power bases—organizational, social, and personal.

Needs of the health care organization

To be effective, a work group must attempt to satisfy the needs of the organization within which the group functions. The organization has certain needs for which the work group is constituted. Sometimes the organization will formalize its needs overtly in statements of goals. For example, a large, complex acute care hospital on a health science university campus might have multiple goals pertaining to teaching, research, and patient care services. Bailey and Claus (1975) discuss the fact that organizations have need levels corresponding to individual need levels. These needs must be considered when a leader is building personal, organizational, and social power bases.

Within any organization, different types of groups will be apparent, which vary in the success with which they satisfy organizational needs. The sensitive leader can observe different degrees of competition and cooperation among members of these groups and capitalize on the strengths of the individuals.

Needs of the group

The second constellation of needs that must be considered in maintaining and building effective work groups is the group needs. People working on a task or project together need procedures for considering their need levels and for building strong relationships and power bases. The group needs to have a growing awareness of itself as a group and must notice its constantly changing interactions and relationships with other groups either within or outside the organization. The maintenance level of the group, which is discussed later, refers to the level of positive interaction that can be maintained as a group accomplishes a task. In order for a group to be successful, the maintenance level must be relatively high, and social, personal, and organizational power bases must be effectively utilized.

Individual needs

The productivity of a work group may be enhanced by paying particular attention to the need patterns of the individuals. These needs include physical needs, safety, love, esteem, and self actualization (Maslow, 1954). Miles (1959) reports that the source of an individual's motive for helping the group influences effectiveness. If an individual is concerned with what outsiders will think, then he will not act with commitment over a sustained period. Changes in behavior will probably be only haphazardly related to the group's task, will not be permanent, and will likely give the impression of confusion or even a lack of interest and understanding. But if a group member is motivated by a strong personal desire to do well, he can be an important asset to the group. If the leader or other group members recognize this desire and help that person improve his manner of working with them, a lasting and constructive change can come about. The strongly motivated person, given the help of insiders, will change his behavior in the group in systematic ways that are related to his job and to the group's task.

Needs for accomplishment

Some groups indeed are constituted solely for the purpose of accomplishing a given task. Once that task is accomplished, the group may be disbanded. In some cases groups must form to accomplish several types of tasks at one time, such as planning, implementing, and evaluating an orientation program for new faculty members. Whatever the nature of the task or the assignment, the important *need* is that the mission has been accomplished and that the results or outcomes are productive.

Ideally goals of the organization, group, and the individual coincide around the task or assignment so that each of these areas may be fulfilled with the accomplishment of the task. Fig. 20 illustrates the interactive relationship of the

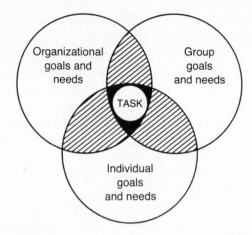

Fig. 20. Interactive relationship of various blocks of needs and tasks in group work.

various blocks of needs in a group around the tasks. Because organizational, group, and individual needs revolve around the accomplishment of a task, these needs must be considered by those who would build an effective group. As these four forces come into balance, the group becomes more mature and effective. Members of the group are able to consider the merits of suggestions without concentrating on the person who made the suggestion. Organizational growth and improved patient care follow when a group develops a sense of camaraderie and team spirit. When one or more of these major concerns is neglected, the efficiency of the entire group is impaired and its growth may be retarded or perhaps destroyed.

Nurse leaders, being members of several groups or committees in different roles, can benefit from the perspective in which they view individual needs. Overlapping work groups, according to recent research, enable group leaders to act as the "link" between various levels of organizational functioning (Lippitt, 1969). Nurses can develop their leadership skills through recognizing need levels in the many groups in which they participate, not necessarily only those groups in which they have been formally designated as the leader.

The effective functioning of a group may require a great deal of leadership action. That is, in some situations not one leader but many will be necessary. Within a group different members can and indeed ought to act as leader from time to time. Perhaps the group's formal leader may be the person who most clearly reflects the hospital's or the university's position. But that leader may depend on group members to contribute important information or help correct misunderstandings. With experience, most nurse leaders come to realize that in any group it is extremely unlikely to find one person able to satisfy all the leadership needs of the group. Whether in the role of leader or member of a particular group, the nurse with leadership skills can learn to balance levels of needs through remaining alert to the needs at work in all group responsibilities.

GUIDELINES FOR PRODUCING RESULTS

To assist work groups to collaborate and work together more effectively, the following guidelines have been proposed (Lippitt, 1969):

An understanding and commitment to group goals—willingness to use energy. Often ambiguity in goal orientation or unclear role expectations (related to hazy job descriptions) gives team members difficulty in functioning together. Most often these cause the troubles that are conveniently and wrongly attributed to personality problems within the group. If goals are clear, the group is more apt to be *willing* to use their *energy* to move the group forward.

Maximum utilization of the various resources of group members—ability based on strength. If each member of the group is to be a resource, he must have access to open communication channels to all other group members. Groups with many contributing members require enough personal trust among members to allow anyone in the group to speak freely. People must talk to people, rather than roles talk to roles.

Encouragement of flexibility, creativity, and sensitivity to the needs of members—actions that yield results. Support of group members for each other improves the group's *functioning* and makes participation a positive experience. Members have a sense of belonging and wanting to help other members. Encouraging ideas of others directly influences the group's creativity: some creative people work best when they can respond to other people's ideas. A creative group takes *actions* that yield *results*.

The practice of shared leadership—ability based on strength. It is extremely unlikely for one person to be able to satisfy all the leadership needs of a group. Part of a leader's responsibility is to provide group members with opportunities for personal development and growth, as well as to capitalize on their abilities and strengths. Procedures such as role reversal or revolving chairmanships allow group members to use their leadership abilities and contribute to their knowledge and experience.

Procedures to guide action and meet the particular problem or situation—actions to yield results. Almost any ongoing work group has trouble in differentiating various situations requiring decisions. Voting procedures are common in group decision making but have been found to be inappropriate for group *action* in some instances. In a spirit of shared leadership a group may want to reach its decisions by consensus. But the group might do better to first distinguish who has sufficient information to make a decision, who ought to be consulted before the group proceeds with a decision, and who ought to be told of a decision once it is made. Only in some cases will unanimous agreement be relevant. Many times a majority vote will be appropriate.

Utilizing the appropriate steps and guidelines for decision making—actions that yield results. The following steps have been delineated to assist nurses in the problem solving and decision making process (Bailey and Claus, 1975): (1) define overall needs, purposes, and goals; (2) define the problem; (3) specify constraints, capabilities, resources, and claimant groups; (4) specify the approach to problem solution; (5) state behavioral objectives and performance criteria; (6) list alternative solutions; (7) analyze options; (8) choose: apply decision rules; (9) control and implement decisions; and (10) evaluate the effectiveness of action.

POWER—A RESOURCE IN GROUP PROCESS

The group process is concerned with the interaction and forces between group members in a social situation. Within our definition of power, the group process can also be viewed as a vehicle for using the *ability, willingness,* and *actions* of a work group to produce the desired *results.* Specialists in group processes contend that certain behaviors of a group should be examined and considered as a prerequisite to effective *actions.* For example, sometimes only a few members of a work group will speak up in a frank manner. Similarly one or two people may tend to dominate the discussion. Often a group loses the ability to discriminate among issues. Too much time may be spent on details and too little time on critical matters that should receive the attention of the entire group. Groups tend to be easily sidetracked when there is no clear agenda. A leader trying to build strong power bases in groups will want to be aware of particular characteristics of the background and behavior of groups.

Willingness based on energy

The leader should remember that each person in a group is an individual. As an individual member of a group, a person brings to that group his own perceptions, orientations, and experiences. Some will bring positive energy and others negative. The attitude and experiences of each group member affect the behavior of all the participants. A group can experience the effects of being joined by a person who is tired and ineffective: the entire group may become listless and nonproductive. Positive energy is infectious, but so is negative energy. Energy promotes the willingness of a group to move toward accomplishing the work of the group.

Participation patterns based on strengths and ability

The communication failures and methods for increasing two-way communication that we have discussed also apply to group situations. Communication within group settings is often rambling and rarely succinct and to the point. Another level of participation accompanies nonverbal communication such as postures, facial expressions, or glances that can be either disruptive or helpful in spurring the group to positive action.

In some groups a pattern will emerge in the amount, order, and content of participation, corresponding to formal lines of authority. Members perceived to be of high status (physicians, for example) may be the first to speak up, have the most to say, and be most persuasive on every issue. But it is the group task or problem that determines which group member is the best source of information. Therefore, if patterns of participation simply conform to organizational ranking of members, the information needs of the work group may not be met. Moreover, the willingness of other group members to participate will wane as they feel less at liberty to express ideas of their own or to challenge what has been said. In such a situation the nurse leader should find ways to encourage more participation by building on *strengths* of group members. Nurses have knowledge and abilities that often need to be recognized and verbalized. Because nurses are being better educated and have a better self image, their participation patterns appear to be changing.

Group cohesion for action and results

Group productivity and morale depend on cohesion to a great extent. When a crisis or a difficult decision arises, a group's cohesiveness determines the effectiveness with which it functions and affects the results. Individual motivations and needs, strengthened by the cooperative situation in the group, are the basis of group cohesiveness. Cohesion has been found to depend very strongly on commitment to the goals of the group, on members wanting to belong, and on having respect for other members of the group. A desire to belong and to work with the group proves indispensable to collaboration. In most group situations one will notice subgroups based on friendship and interests. Group cohesion can be enhanced by subgroups in some cases. But it can be thwarted when interpersonal relationships isolate or shut out some members from the rest of the group. The leader can balance these factions by keeping group objectives and tasks prominent among group concerns.

Willingness and energy through the work environment

The climate or emotional setting of the group is an important factor in utilizing the willingness and energy of group members. Sometimes climate refers to freedom or informality or to rigid structures of operation. The work climate determines whether or not people are free to openly communicate with one another, make disclosures, seek feedback, or reinforce one another in positive behavior. The climate of trust discussed in an earlier chapter provides group members the means to more effectively use their energy.

Standards for group action

Any group in health care delivery needs standards by which to direct its operation. Standards should be developed from normative behavior, or what is desired as normative behavior over a period of time. Flexible standards and a situation in which there are relatively few deviations or discrepancies from the standards allow greater freedom of action. Standards that are narrowly defined work to increase deviations from the norm, creating a situation that may be harmful to group functioning. Normally group standards can be established fairly quickly. Various kinds of standards emerge in any work group, and these will affect patterns of work. These standards can be discerned by the leader and the group members alike. To help the work group function effectively, standards should be applied consistently and impartially. The group leader can cause work problems by setting standards and then allowing some people to violate them while holding others rigidly to them. Such behavior will cause subordinates to lose interest in their work, disrupt the group's productivity, destroy cohesion and group task orientation. Standards should be developed and used in such a way that groups can take positive action and produce results.

Procedures for action: team building

The leader of an effective work group must develop systematic procedures for building morale of a group and set the style for productivity and action. Many of these procedures derive basically from sensitivity training groups that were found to be particularly effective in accomplishing goals. Principles have evolved that apply to any organizational or group work effort. Basically the leader's responsibility is to periodically examine the extent to which the group functions effectively. Part of the leadership process requires that the leader solicit the help of group members in identifying barriers to collaboration and then to undertake the reduction and elimination of these barriers. Usually the process entails a series of meetings. The following procedures may assist the nurse leader in moving groups forward: (1) having regularly scheduled meetings, (2) making action lists of the strengths of group members that show how each member of a group can facilitate other members, and (3) holding intergroup sessions to include other units that may be affected by the group's behavior and accomplishments.

Goals for actions and results

Goals of a group can be set for an immediate short-range or can be very long-range. Effective groups continually check the validity and clarity of their goals and in so doing learn how to set goals in terms of behavioral objectives and how to evaluate them in terms of performance criteria and standards of behavior. In this way factual data are obtained to be used as the basis for decision making. The group leader will want to use goals to enhance a climate of trust, one that encourages self disclosure, feedback, and positive reinforcement. Such a climate will grow from a clear idea of where a group stands in relation to its goals and what needs to be done to obtain results.

Leader and follower interaction for results

The focus of this book is leader-follower interaction and the development of power that enables this to occur. Referring to the model in Chapter 1, you will recall that we differentiate between two types of leadership actions: managerial functions and human relations functions. If these actions are commensurate with group and organizational goals, the group being influenced will demonstrate a willingness to follow the group leader. According to the demands of the work situation, managerial functions and human relations can be assumed by either a single leader or the group. In a leaderless group these functions can be assumed by all the members or by certain members assigned responsibility for basic areas. The characteristics we have described affect work groups as they try to accomplish tasks required to meet the objectives mentioned earlier in this chapter.

A plan for action

An account of the experience of one health care group reports difficulties caused by regular weekly conference meetings of the entire work group (Rubin and Beckhard, 1972). The group found 90-minute meetings (the only gathering of the entire team) to be boring, unsatisfying, and a waste of time. The net effect of the sessions was to drain energy from participants and discourage the commitment required to solve patient problems, which was one purpose of the meetings. Action plans were then developed to improve meetings, including:

1. Forming an agenda planning committee, apparently in hopes of discouraging the rambling discourse so typical of meetings.
2. Rotating the chairmanship so that all group members could improve their skills at running a meeting. A form of role reversal, this technique encourages talkers to become listeners and encourages a breakdown of participation patterns based on formal status lines.
3. Assigning observers, also on a rotating plan, to help the team evaluate—immediately after the meeting—the influence and impact of its own group dynamics.

Functions of the leader in building effective work groups

Maintenance functions. Group maintenance functions have been described as those functions that concern themselves with the relationships and comfort of members of the group. That is, specific actions can create an atmosphere or climate of trust so that people want to work and appear to enjoy working in a particular group. The group leader should assume responsibility and be accountable for what transpires in work groups. The following responsibilities of a group leader have been summarized by Lippitt (1969), a leading authority on organizational development.

1. *Encouraging:* letting other group members know that the leader recognizes the value of what they can contribute, allowing them the opportunity to participate, being warm and responsive to their efforts and concerned with their growth and development.
2. *Expressing group feelings:* communicating feelings with others, becoming and staying sensitive to group moods and to relationships creating subgroups.
3. *Harmonizing:* alleviating tension by supportively listening to disagreements.
4. *Compromising:* offering to give in a little of one's own position, even if a conflict involves one's own status; using self restraint, tact and, self-discipline to promote cohesiveness within the group.
5. *Gate-keeping:* trying to facilitate the flow of information, to keep communication open; suggesting plans such as role reversal or rotating chairmanship to encourage participation of the full group in discussions.
6. *Setting standards:* articulating criteria to be met by the group; assessing group productivity and effectiveness of group dynamics by applying these standards.

Task functions. Task functions are those activities or problems that have been assigned to the group and on which group members are expected to take some kind of action—usually actions to reach a goal. When group members assume responsibility for both task and maintenance function, groups are likely to operate at maximum efficiency. Sometimes through effective leadership, groups satisfy maintenance and task functions simultaneously. For example, a group leader may request a member of a work group to obtain and share information that may be needed before the group can take further action. This could be a way of encouraging a group member to participate in group discussion (a maintenance function) and also to perform a needed task. It makes little difference which function is performed by which member, so long as appropriate functions are carried out and the leadership is provided. The leader acts as energizer, coordinating the efforts of the group members. The following task functions will assist the leader of the work group in carrying out the leadership role.

1. *Initiating and recommending group tasks.* The leader can more clearly define the problem that a group may have been given as a task. Steps can be proposed in solving a problem, and the work can be delegated by the leader.

2. *Gathering information for opinion seeking.* The leader can ask relevant questions from the group to gain input that the group's knowledge and experience can be shared.

3. *Information or opinion giving.* The leader can present the group with facts and data and use the group to critique the ideas.

4. *Clarifying or explaining.* At times groups may become confused if too many ideas are expressed or if group members digress. It is the leader's responsibility to clarify ideas.

5. *Summarizing.* One of the primary tasks of the leader is to summarize. Outlining what has been said in an organized manner is helpful to group members. Summarizing can also be used as an analysis of what appeared to be the most important actions taken by the group.

6. *Consensus testing.* Leaders need to send out "feelers" to discover whether the work group is approaching a conclusion. Asking members to comment on the degree of agreement within the group is often a useful technique.

THE ULTIMATE TASK OF NURSE LEADERS

The guidelines presented here can indeed assist nurse leaders to work effectively with others, since basically leadership is an interactive process—a shared relationship among dynamic systems of people and the organization. Nurse leaders can exert influence on members of the work group and in turn can be influenced by group members and the organization. Power, influence, and authority—these are the critical factors that nurses must understand and use to work effectively with groups and ultimately to accomplish their task. The ultimate task of the leader is to lead!

EXERCISES
Assessment of your team co-workers

Complete this questionnaire before and after the team building meetings.

1. What is your relation to the team?

     _____

     _____

2. What is your satisfaction with team's current functioning?

     _____

     _____

3. What are the goals of the team?

     _____

     _____

4. What are your personal goals?

     _____

     _____

5. How are decisions made that affect the team?

     _____

     _____

6. What are the problems of the team right now?

     _____

     _____

7. What personal problems relate to the team right now?

     _____

     _____

8. What action strategies are needed right now?

     _____

     _____

9. What are the feelings about the team building meeting?

     _____

     _____

My relationships with the other team members

Fill in the blanks below and then ask other members of your team to complete this form. You may want to invite the other team on your floor to try this exercise with their members.

1. Write the first names and titles of everyone on your team after each number. Next describe your relationship with each of these people.

     a. Name, title _____

          Relationship _____

     b. Name, title _____

          Relationship _____

     c. Name, title _____

          Relationship _____

2. Meet with your team and share your notes with each other. (You may or may not want a facilitator of group process present.)

3. After this meeting, write down the names and titles of your team members and again describe your relationship with each person. Note if there are any changes from your first perceptions.
4. During the next 2 weeks, keep a diary of how you work together as a team. Later you may want to share this diary with your team members in another team building meeting.

REFERENCES

Bailey, J. T., and Claus, K. E.: Decision making in nursing: Tools for change, St. Louis, 1975, The C. V. Mosby Co.

Lippitt, G. L.: Organizational renewal: Achieving viability in a changing world, New York, 1969, Appleton-Century-Crofts.

Maslow, A.: Motivation and personality, New York, 1954, Harper & Row, Publishers.

Miles, M. B.: Learning to work in groups, New York, 1959, Columbia University Press.

Rubin, I., and Beckhard, R.: Factors influencing the effectiveness of health teams, Milbank Quarterly **50**(3):317-335, 1972.

Lewis, H., and Streitfield, H.: Growth games, New York, 1971, Bantam Books Inc.

Luft, J.: Group processes: An introduction to group dynamics, ed. 2, Palo Alto, Calif., 1970, Mayfield Publishing Co.

Maier, N. R., Solem, A. R., and Maier, A. A.: The role-play technique: A handbook for management and leadership practice, La Jolla, Calif., 1975, University Associates.

Malamud, D. I., and Machover, S.: Toward self-understanding: Group techniques in self confrontation, Springfield, Ill., 1965, Charles C Thomas, Publisher.

Otto, H. A.: Group methods to actualize human potential: A handbook, ed. 2, Beverly Hills, Calif., 1970, Holistic Press.

SUGGESTED READINGS

Cartwright, D., and Zander, A., editors: Group dynamics—Research and theory, ed. 3, New York, 1968, Harper & Row, Publishers.

Fagan, J., and Shepherd, I. L.: Gestalt therapy now, Palo Alto, Calif., 1970, Science and Behavior Books.

Fromkin, H. L., and Sherwood, J. J., editors: Intergroup and minority relations, La Jolla, Calif., 1976, University Associates.

Johnson, D. W.: Reaching out, Englewood Cliffs, N.J., 1972, Prentice-Hall, Inc.

Knowles, H., and Knowles, M.: Introduction to group dynamics, New York, 1959, Association Press.

Pfeiffer, J. W., and Jones, J. E., editors: A handbook of structured experiences for human relations training, 5 vols., La Jolla, Calif., 1975, University Associates, Inc.

Stevens, B. J.: Use of groups for management: The organization of committees in a nursing division, Journal of Nursing Administration **5**(1):20-21, 1975.

Twenty exercises for trainers, Washington, D.C., 1972, National Training Laboratories Institute for Applied Behavioral Science.

REFERENCES

Annas, G. J., and Healey, J.: The patient rights advocate, Journal of Nursing Administration **4**(3):25-31, 1974.

Appley, I.: Formula for success: A core concept of management, New York, 1974, American Management Associations.

Argyle, M., and Kendon, A.: The experimental analysis of social performance. In Berkowitz, L., editor: Advances in experimental social psychology, vol. 3, New York, 1967, Academic Press, Inc.

Arndt, C., and Huckabay, L.: Nursing administration: Theory for practice with a systems approach, St. Louis, 1975, The C. V. Mosby Co.

Bailey, J. T.: Leadership in nursing, Echo—Nursing Change and Challenge **4**(2):6, 1974.

Bailey, J. T.: The critical incident technique in identifying behavioral criteria of professional nursing effectiveness, Nursing Research **5**(5):52-64, 1956.

Bailey, J. T., and Claus, K. E.: Decision making in nursing: Tools for change, St. Louis, 1975, The C. V. Mosby Co.

Bailey, J., McDonald, F., and Claus, K. E.: An experiment in nursing curriculums at a university, Belmont, Calif., 1972, Wadsworth Publishing Co. Inc.

Bales, R. F.: The equilibrium problem in small groups. In Parsons, T., Bales, R. F., and Shils, E. A., editors: Working papers in the theory of action, New York, 1953, The Free Press.

Bales, R. F., and Slater, P. E.: Role differentiation in small decision making groups. In Parsons, T., and Bales, R. F., editors: Family, socialization and the interaction process, New York, 1955, The Free Press.

Barker, R. G.: Ecological psychology, Stanford, Calif., 1968, Stanford University Press.

Barksdale, L. S.: Building self esteem, Los Angeles, 1972, The Barksdale Foundation for Furtherance of Human Understanding.

Barnard, C. I.: The functions of an executive, Cambridge, Mass., 1938, Harvard University Press.

Bass, B. M.: Some observations about a general theory of leadership and interpersonal behavior. In Petrullo, L., and Bass, B. M., editors: Leadership and interpersonal behavior, New York, 1961, Holt, Rinehart and Winston.

Bavelas, A.: Communication patterns in task-oriented groups. In Cartwright, D., and Zander, A., editors: Group dynamics: Research and theory, ed. 3, New York, 1968, Harper & Row, Publishers.

Bavelas, A., and others: Experiments on the alteration of group structure, Journal of Experimental Social Psychology **1**:55-71, 1965.

Bem, D. J.: Self-perception: An alternative interpretation of cognitive dissonance phenomena, Psychological Review **74**:183-200, 1967.

Benne, K. D., and Sheats, P.: Functional roles and group members, Journal of Social Issues **4**:41-49, 1948.

Benner, P., and Kramer, M.: Role conceptions and integrative role behavior of nurses in special care and regular hospital nursing units, Nursing Research **21**:20-29, 1972.

Bennis, W. G.: Leadership theory and administrative behavior: The problem of authority, Administrative Science Quarterly **4**:259-301, 1959.

Bennis, W. G.: The unconscious conspiracy, New York, 1976, AMACOM.

Bennis, W. G., Benne, K. D., and Chin, R.: The planning of change, ed. 2, New York, 1969, Holt, Rinehart and Winston.

Bennis, W. G., and others: Authority, power and the ability to influence, Human Relations **11**:143-155, 1958.

Berlew, D. E.: Leadership and organizational excitement. In Kolb, D. A., Rubin, I. M., and McIntyre, J. M., editors: Organizational psychology: A book of readings, Englewood Cliffs, N.J., 1974, Prentice-Hall, Inc.

Berne, E.: Games people play, New York, 1964, Grove Press, Inc.

Binderman, R. M.: The issue of responsibility in gestalt therapy, Psychotherapy: Theory, Research and Practice **11**(3):287-288, 1974.

173

Blake, R. R., and Mouton, J. S.: Corporate excellence through grid organizational development, Houston, Texas, 1968, Gulf Publishing Company.

Blake, R. R., and Mouton, J. S.: The managerial grid, Houston, Texas, 1964, Gulf Publishing Co.

Blau, P. M.: Exchange and power in social life, New York, 1964, John Wiley & Sons, Inc.

Bloom, B.: Taxonomy of educational objectives: The classification of educational goals: Handbook I—Cognitive domain, New York, 1965, David McKay Co., Inc.

Boulding, K. E.: Organization and conflict, Journal of Conflict Resolution 1:122-134, 1957.

Bowers, D. G., and Seashore, S. E.: Predicting organizational effectiveness with a four-factor theory of leadership. Administrative Science Quarterly 11: 238-263, 1966.

Brouwer, P. J.: The power to see ourselves, Harvard Business Review 54(1):66-73, 1976.

Butler, D. C., and Miller, N.: Power to reward and punish in social interactions, Journal of Experimental Social Psychology 1:311-322, 1965.

Cant, G.: Valiumania, New York Times Magazine, February 1, 1976, pp. 34-44.

Caplow, T.: Principles of organization, New York, 1964, Harcourt Brace Jovanovich, Inc.

Cartwright, D., and Zander, A.: The structural properties of groups: Introduction. In Cartwright, D., and Zander, A., editors: Group dynamics: Research and theory, ed. 3, New York, 1968, Harper & Row, Publishers.

Clark, P., and Wilson, J. Q.: Incentive systems, Administrative Science Quarterly 6:129-166, 1961.

Claus, K. E.: The effects of modeling and feedback variables on higher-order questioning skills, doctoral dissertation, Stanford University, Ann Arbor, Michigan, 1968, University Microfilms, no. 69-207.

Claus, K. E., and Claus, R. J.: Signage: Planning environmental visual communication, Palo Alto, Calif., 1976, Institute of Signage Research.

Collen, M. S.: Hospital computer systems, New York, 1974, John Wiley & Sons, Inc.

Cooper, R.: Day-surgery centers snip away red tape, put clamps on costs, The Wall Street Journal, January 23, 1976, p. 1.

Craig, J. H., and Craig, M.: Synergic power: Beyond domination and permissiveness, Berkeley, Calif., 1974, ProActive Press.

Dahl, R. A.: The concept of power, Behavioral Science 2:201-215, 1957.

Davis, M. S.: Variations in patients' compliance for doctor's advice, American Journal of Public Health 58:274-288, 1968.

Deutsch, M.: Conflict: Productive and destructive, Journal of Social Issues 25:7-40, 1969.

Deutsch, M.: Cooperation and trust: Some theoretical notes. In Jones, M. R., editor: Nebraska symposium on motivation, Lincoln, Nebraska, 1962, University of Nebraska Press.

Deutsch, M., and Krauss, R. M.: The effect of threat upon interpersonal bargaining, Journal of Abnormal and Social Psychology 61:181-189, 1960.

Dornbusch, S. M., and Scott, W. R.: Evaluation and the exercise of authority, San Francisco, 1975, Jossey-Bass, Inc., Publishers.

Driscoll, V. M.: Independence in nursing: Challenge or burden? Can we exist without it? Michigan Nurse 45:12-15, 1972.

Drucker, P. F.: Management, New York, 1974, Harper & Row, Publishers.

Drucker, P. F.: The effective executive, New York, 1967, Harper & Row, Publishers.

Dyer, W. G.: The sensitive manipulator, Provo, Utah, 1972, Brigham Young University Press.

Emerson, R. M.: Power-dependence relations, American Sociological Review 27:31-41, 1962.

Extending the scope of the nursing practice art, Washington, D.C., 1971, Department of Health, Education and Welfare.

Felker, D. W.: Building positive self concepts, Minneapolis, 1974, Burgess Publishing Co.

Fiedler, F.: A theory of leadership effectiveness, New York, 1967, McGraw-Hill, Inc.

Finkleman, A.: Commitment and responsibility in the therapeutic relationship, Journal of Psychiatric Nursing and Mental Health Services 13(1):10-14, 1975.

Fischer, C. S.: The effect of threats in an incomplete information game, Sociometry 32:301-314, 1969.

Fleishman, E. A.: Twenty years of consideration and structure. In Fleishman, E. A., and Hunt, J. G., editors: Current developments in the study of leadership, Carbondale, Ill., 1973, Southern Illinois University Press.

Fotheringham, W. C.: Perspectives on persuasion, Boston, 1966, Allyn & Bacon, Inc.

Free-enterprise the answer? Forbes Magazine, January 15, 1976, p. 40.

Freed, E. X.: Accountability in mental health care, Journal of Nursing Administration 5(7):36-37, 1975.

French, J. R. P., Jr., and Raven, B.: The bases of social power. In Cartwright, D., editor: Studies in social power, Ann Arbor, Mich., 1959, The University of Michigan Press.

Friedenberg, E. Z.: Coming of age in America, New York, 1965, Random House, Inc.

Friedlander, F., and Greenberg, S.: Effects of job attitudes, training, and organization climate on performance of hard-core unemployed, Journal of Applied Psychology 55:287-295, 1971.

Gibb, J. R.: Defensive communication, Journal of Communication 11(3):141-148, 1961.

Godfrey, M. A.: Your fringe benefits—How much are they really worth? Nursing 5(1):73-75, 1975.

Goodstadt, B., and Kipmis, D.: Situational influences on the use of power, Journal of Applied Psychology 54:201-207, 1970.

Gouldner, A. W.: The norm of reciprocity: A preliminary statement, American Sociological Review **25:**161-179, 1960.

Guetzkow, H.: Differentiation of roles in task-oriented groups. In Cartwright, D., and Zander, A., editors: Group dynamics: Research and theory, ed. 3, New York, 1968, Harper & Row, Publishers.

Hall, J.: Interpersonal style and the communication dilemma: (I) Managerial implications of the Johari Awareness Model, Human Relations **27**(4):381-399, 1974.

Harris, T. A.: I'm ok, you're ok, New York, 1967, Harper & Row, Publishers.

Heider, F.: Attitudes and cognitive organization, Journal of Psychology **21:**107-112, 1946.

Heider, F.: Social perception and phenomenal causality. Psychological Review **51:**358-374, 1944.

Heider, F.: The psychology of interpersonal relations, New York, 1958, John Wiley & Sons, Inc.

Hemphill, J. K.: Relations between the size of the group and the behavior of "superior" leaders, Journal of Social Psychology **32:**11-22, 1950.

Herzberg, F., Mausner, B., and Snyderman, B. B.: The motivation to work, ed. 2, New York, 1959, John Wiley & Sons, Inc.

Hicks, H. G.: The management of organizations: A systems and human resources approach, ed. 2, New York, 1972, McGraw-Hill, Inc.

Higbee, K. L.: Fifteen years of fear arousal: Research of threat appeals: 1953-1968, Psychological Bulletin **72:**426-444, 1969.

Hollander, E. P., and Julian, J. W.: Studies in leader legitimacy, influence and innovation. In Berkowitz, L., editor: Advances in experimental social psychology, vol. 5, New York, 1970, Academic Press, Inc.

House, R. J., and Dessler, G.: The path-goal theory of leadership: Some post hoc and a priori tests. In Hunt, J. G., and Larson, L. L., editors: Contingency approaches to leadership, Carbondale, Ill., 1973, Southern Illinois University Press.

Howells, L. T., and Becker, S. W.: Seating arrangement and leadership emergence, Journal of Abnormal and Social Psychology **64:**148-150, 1972.

Johnson, D. W.: Reaching out: Interpersonal effectiveness and self-actualization, Englewood Cliffs, N.J., 1972, Prentice-Hall, Inc.

Jourard, S.: The transparent self, New York, 1964, Van Nostrand Reinhold.

Kalisch, B. J.: Of half gods and mortals: Aesculapian authority, Nursing Outlook **23**(1):22-28, 1975.

Katz, D., and Kahn, R. L.: The social psychology of organizations, New York, 1966, John Wiley & Sons, Inc.

Kelley, H. H., and Thibaut, J. W.: Group problem solving. In Lindzey, G., and Aronson, E., editors: The handbook of social psychology, vol. 4, ed. 12, Reading, Mass., 1969, Addison-Wesley Publishing Co., Inc.

Kepner, C. H., and Tregoe, B. B.: The rational manager, New York, 1965, McGraw-Hill, Inc.

Kipnis, D., and Cosentino, J.: Use of leadership powers in industry, Journal of Applied Psychology **53:**460-466, 1969.

Kipnis, D., and Lane, W. P.: Self confidence and leadership, Journal of Applied Psychology **46:**291-295, 1962.

Kipnis, D., and Vanderveer, R.: Ingratiation and the use of power, Journal of Personality and Social Psychology **17:**280-286, 1971.

Kite, W. R.: Attributions of causality as a function of the use of reward and punishment, unpublished doctoral dissertation, Stanford, Calif., 1964, Stanford University.

Koontz, H., and O'Donnell, C.: Principles of management: An analysis of managerial functions, New York, 1972, McGraw-Hill, Inc.

Korda, M.: Power: How to get it, how to use it! New York, 1975, Random House, Inc.

Kramer, M.: Reality shock: Why nurses leave nursing, St. Louis, 1974, The C. V. Mosby Co.

Kramer, M., and Baker, C.: The exodus: Can we prevent it? Journal of Nursing Administration **1**(3):15-30, 1971.

Leavitt, H. J.: Some effects of certain communication patterns on group performance, Journal of Abnormal and Social Psychology **46:**38-50, 1951.

Leonard, G. B.: The ultimate athlete, New York, 1975, The Viking Press, Inc.

Lewin, K., Lippitt, R., and White, R. K.: Patterns of aggressive behavior in experimentally created social climates, Journal of Social Psychology **10:**271-299, 1939.

Likert, R.: The human organization, New York, 1967, McGraw-Hill, Inc.

Lindskold, S., and others: Factors affecting the effectiveness of reward power, Psychonomic Science **26:**68-70, 1972.

Lindskold, S., and Tedeschi, J. T.: Reward power and attraction in interpersonal conflict, Psychonomic Science **22:**211-213, 1971.

Lindskold, S., and Tedeschi, J. T.: Threatening and conciliatory influence attempts as a function of source's perception of own competence in a conflict situation, mimeographed manuscript, Albany, N.Y., 1970, State University of New York at Albany.

Lio, A. M.: Leadership and responsibility in team nursing, Nursing Clinics of North America **8**(6):267-281, 1976.

Lippitt, G. L.: Organizational renewal: Achieving viability in a changing world, New York, 1969, Appleton-Century-Crofts.

Lippitt, R., and White, R. K.: The social climate of children's groups. In Baker, R. G., Kounin, J. S., and Wright, H. F., editors: Child behavior and development, New York, 1943, McGraw-Hill, Inc.

Lipset, S. M., and Raab, E.: Watergate: The vacillation of the President, Psychology Today **7**(6):77-84, 1973.

Luchins, A. S., and Luchins, E. H.: On conformity with judgments of a majority or an authority, Journal of Social Psychology **53**:303-316, 1961.

Luft, J., and Ingham, H.: The Johari Window, a graphic model of interpersonal awareness, Los Angeles, 1955, University of California at Los Angeles, Extension Office, Proceedings of the Western Training Laboratory in Group Development.

MacLean, G., and Tedeschi, J. T.: The use of social influence by children of entrepreneurial and bureaucratic parents, mimeographed manuscript, Albany, N.Y., 1970, State University of New York at Albany.

Marlowe, D., Gergen, K. J., and Doob, A. N.: Opponent's personality, expectation, and interpersonal bargaining, Journal of Personality and Social Psychology **3:** 206-213, 1966.

Marram, G. D.: Visibility of work and the evaluation process: Evaluation and authority for nurses in hospitals and teachers in open and closed schools, unpublished doctoral dissertation, Stanford, Calif., 1971, School of Education, Stanford University.

Maslow, A.: Motivation and personality, rev. ed., New York, 1970, Harper & Row, Publishers.

McClelland, D., and Burnham, D.: Power is the great motivator, Harvard Business Review **54**(2):100-110, 1976.

McCloskey, J.: High staff nurse turnover rate attributed to low self-esteem, OR Reporter **9:**3, 1974.

McGregor, D.: The human side of enterprise, New York, 1960, McGraw-Hill, Inc.

Mechanic, D.: Sources of power of lower participants in complex organizations, Administrative Science Quarterly **7:**349-362, 1962.

Meininger, J.: Success through transactional analysis, New York, 1973, New American Library, Inc., Signet Books.

Menzies, I.: Nurses under stress, International Nursing Review **7**(9):9-16, 1960.

Meyers, M. S.: Every employee a manager: More meaningful work through job enrichment, New York, 1970, McGraw-Hill, Inc.

Miles, M. B.: Learning to work in groups, New York, 1959, Columbia University Press.

Miles, R. E.: Human relations or human resources? In Kolb, D. A., Rubin, I. M., and McIntyre, J. M., editors: Organizational psychology: A book of readings, Englewood Cliffs, N.J., 1974, Prentice-Hall, Inc.

Miles, R. E.: Theories of management: Implications for organizational behavior and development, New York, 1975, McGraw-Hill, Inc.

Miller, N., and Butler, D.: Social power and communication in small groups, Behavioral Science **14:** 11-18, 1969.

Miller, N., Butler, D., and McMartin, J. A.: The ineffectiveness of punishment power in group interaction, Sociometry **32:**24-42, 1969.

Mintzberg, H.: The nature of managerial work, New York, 1973, Harper & Row, Publishers.

Moos, R., and Insel, P., editors: Issues in social ecology: Human milieus, Palo Alto, Calif., 1974, Mayfield Publishing Co., National Press Books.

Moscovi, S.: Communication processes and the properties of language. In Berkowitz, L., editor: Advances in experimental social psychology, vol. 3, New York, 1967, Academic Press, Inc.

Mulder, M.: Power and satisfaction in task-oriented groups, Acta Psychologica **16:**178-225, 1959.

Newcomb, T. M.: The acquaintance process, New York, 1961, Holt, Rinehart and Winston.

Newman, W. H., Sumner, C. E., and Warren, E. K.: The process of management, Englewood Cliffs, N.J., 1967, Prentice-Hall, Inc.

Odiorne, G. S.: Management decision by objectives, Englewood Cliffs, N.J., 1969, Prentice-Hall, Inc.

Olye, I.: The healing mind, Millbrae, Calif., 1974, Celestial Arts.

Parsons, T.: On the concept of influence, Public Opinion Quarterly **27:**37-62, 1963.

Parsons, T.: Structure and process in modern societies, New York, 1960, The Free Press.

Passos, J.: Accountability: Myth or mandate? Journal of Nursing Administration **3**(3):16-22, 1973.

Peabody, R.: Authority in organizations: A comparative study, doctoral dissertation, Stanford, Calif., 1960, Stanford University.

Perls, F., Hefferline, R. F., and Goodman, P.: Gestalt therapy: Excitement and growth in the human personality, New York, 1951, Julian Press, Inc.

Pondy, L. R.: Organizational conflict: Concepts and models, Administrative Science Quarterly **12:**296-320, 1967.

Presthus, R.: Authority in organizations, Public Administration Review **20:**88-91, 1960.

Reiff, R.: The control of knowledge: The power of the helping professions, The Journal of Applied Behavioral Science **10**(3):451-461, 1974.

Ringer, R. J.: Winning through intimidation, Los Angeles, 1974, Los Angeles Book Publishers Co.

Roethlisberger, F. J., and Dickson, W. J.: Management and the worker, Cambridge, Mass., 1939, Harvard University Press.

Rogers, C.: Dealing with psychological tensions, Journal of Applied Behavioral Science **1**(1):6-25, 1965.

Rogers, C., and Roethlisberger, F. J.: Barriers and gateways to communication, Harvard Business Review **30**(4):46-52, 1952.

Rothbart, M.: Effects of motivation, equity and compliance on the use of reward and punishment, Journal of Personality and Social Psychology **9:**353-362, 1968.

Rubin, I., and Beckhard, R.: Factors influencing the effectiveness of health teams, Milbank Quarterly **50**(3):317-335, 1972.

Scheff, T. J.: Control over policy by attendants in a mental hospital, Journal of Health and Human Behavior **2**(2):93-105, 1961.

Scheflen, A. E., with Scheflen, A.: Body language and social order: Communication as behavioral control, Englewood Cliffs, N.J., 1972, Prentice-Hall, Inc.

Schlenker, B. R., and Tedeschi, J. T.: The exercise of social influence, Liege, Belgium, July, 1971, Paper presented at the Seventeenth International Congress of Applied Psychology.

Scott, W. R.: Professional employees in a bureaucratic structure: Social work. In Etzioni, A., editor: The semi-professions and their organization, New York, 1969, The Free Press.

Scott, W. R.: Reactions to supervision in a heteronomous professional organization, Administrative Science Quarterly 10:65-81, 1965.

Selznick, P.: TVA and the grass roots, Berkeley, Calif., 1949, University of California Press.

Shartle, C. L., and Stodgill, R. M.: Studies in naval leadership, Columbus, 1952, Ohio State University Research Foundation.

Shaw, M. E.: Communication networks. In Berkowitz, L., editor: Advances in experimental social psychology, vol. 1, New York, 1964, Academic Press, Inc.

Simon, H. A.: Administrative behavior, New York, 1957, Macmillan, Inc.

Simon, H. A.: On the concept of organizational goal, Administrative Science Quarterly 9:1-22, 1964.

Skinner, B. F.: Science and human behavior, New York, 1953, The Free Press.

Smith, D. H.: The classification of communication: Problems and a proposal, Pacific Speech 2:15-24, 1968.

Stevens, J. O.: Awareness: Exploring, experimenting, Moab, Utah, 1971, Real People Press.

Stieglitz, H.: Corporate organization structures, New York, 1961, National Industrial Conference Board, Inc.

Stodgill, R. M.: Handbook of leadership, New York, 1974, The Free Press.

Tannenbaum, R., Wechsler, I., and Massarik, F.: Leadership and organization: A behavioral approach, New York, 1961, McGraw-Hill, Inc.

Taylor, F.: The principles of scientific management, New York, 1967, W. W. Norton & Co., Inc.

Tedeschi, J. T., Schlenker, B. R., and Lindskold, S.: The exercise of power and influence: The source of influence. In Tedeschi, J. T., editor: The social influence process, Chicago, 1972, Aldine Publishing Co.

Walton, R.: Quality of working life: What is it? Sloan Management Review 15:11-23, 1973.

Ward, C. D.: Seating arrangement and leadership emergence in small discussion groups, Journal of Social Psychology 74:83-90, 1968.

Watson, D. L.: Effects of certain social power structures on communication in task-oriented groups, Sociometry 28:322-336, 1965.

Watson, D., and Bromberg, B.: Power, communication, and position satisfaction in task-oriented groups, Journal of Personality and Social Psychology 2:859-864, 1965.

Weber, M.: The theory of social and economic organization, Henderson, A. M., and Parsons, T., translators; Parsons, T., editor: New York, 1947, The Free Press.

Wood, M. T.: Power relationships and group decision making in organizations, Psychological Bulletin 79(5):280-293, 1973.

Zoll, A. A., III: Explorations in managing, Reading, Mass., 1974, Addison-Wesley Publishing Co., Inc.

SUGGESTED READINGS

Altman, I.: The environment and social behavior, Monterey, Calif., 1975, Brooks/Cole Publishing Co.

Appelbaum, A., and others: Dependency versus autonomy: The group conference method applied to an organizational problem, Bulletin of the Menninger Clinic **39**(1):47-66, 1975.

Arndt, C., and Huckabay, L.: Nursing administration: Theory for practice with a systems approach, St. Louis, 1975, The C. V. Mosby Co.

Ashley, J.: About power in nursing, Nursing Outlook **21:**637-641, 1973.

Assighori, R.: The act of will, New York, 1973, The Viking Press, Inc.

Bailey, J. T., and Claus, K. E.: Decision making in nursing: Tools for change, St. Louis, 1975, The C. V. Mosby Co.

Bass, B. M., and Franke, R. H.: Societal influence on student perceptions of how to succeed in organizations: A cross-national analysis, Journal of Applied Psychology **56:**312-318, 1972.

Bavelas, A.: Communication patterns in task-oriented groups. In Cartwright, D., and Zander, A., editors: Group dynamics—Research and theory, New York, 1968, Harper & Row, Publishers.

Benner, P.: Values clashes. In Davis, M., Kramer, M., and Strauss, A., editors: Nurses at work, St. Louis, 1974, The C. V. Mosby Co.

Bennis, W. G., and Thomas, J. M., editors: Management of change and conflict, Harmondsworth, England, 1972, Penguin Books Ltd.

Bensen, H.: The relaxation response, New York, 1975, William Morrow & Co., Inc.

Berlew, D. E.: Leadership and organizational excitement. In Kold, D. A., Rubin, I. M., and McIntyre, J. M., editors: Organizational psychology: A book of readings, Englewood Cliffs, N.J., 1974, Prentice-Hall, Inc.

Bernal, H.: Power and interorganizational health care projects, Nursing Outlook **24**(7):419-421, 1976.

Berne, E.: Games people play, New York, 1964, Grove Press, Inc.

Beyers, M., and Phillips, C.: Nursing management for patient care, Boston, 1971, Little, Brown and Co.

Bickman, L.: The social power of a uniform, Journal of Applied Social Psychology **4**(1):47-61, 1974.

Bloomfield, H.: TM: Discovering inner energy and overcoming stress, New York, 1975, Dell Publishing Co., Inc.

Bolton, C. K., and Lindberg, M. E.: Conflict: The conditions and processes in community organizations and interpersonal relationships, Monticello, Ill., May, 1971, Council of Planning Librarians Exchange Bibliography, no. 187.

Bondurant, J. V.: Creative conflict and limits of symbolic violence. In Bondurant, J. V.: Conflict: Violence and non-violence, Chicago, 1971, Aldine Publishing Co.

Brehm, J. W., and Mann, M.: Effect of importance of freedom and attraction to group members on influence produced by group pressure, Journal of Personality and Social Psychology **31**(5):816-824, 1975.

Cartwright, D., and Zander, A., editors: Group dynamics—Research and theory, ed. 3, New York, 1968, Harper & Row, Publishers.

Castenada, C.: Tales of power, New York, 1974, Simon & Schuster, Inc.

Chapanis, A.: Interactive human communication, Scientific American **232:**36-42, 1975.

Chernick, D. A.: Attitudes of women in management —Job satisfaction: A study of perceived need satisfaction as a function of job level, International Journal of Social Psychiatry **20**(1-2):94-98, 1974.

Clark, K. B.: Pathos of power, New York, 1974, Harper & Row, Publishers.

Coulton, M. R.: Labor disputes: A challenge to nurse staffing, Journal of Nursing Administration **6**(4):15-20, 1976.

Craig, J. H., and Craig, M.: Synergic power: Beyond domination and permissiveness, Berkeley, Calif., 1974, ProActive Press.

de Bono, E.: Lateral thinking for management: A handbook for creativity, New York, 1971, American Management Association.

de Bono, E.: PO: A device for successful thinking, New York, 1972, Simon & Schuster, Inc.

Deloughery, G. L., and Gebbie, K. M.: Political dynamics: Impact on nurses and nursing, St. Louis, 1975, The C. V. Mosby Co.

Deutsch, M.: Conflicts: Productive and destructive, Journal of Social Issues 25(1):7-41, 1969.

Deutsch, M.: Studies of interpersonal bargaining, Journal of Conflict Resolution 6:52-76, 1962.

Deutsch, M., and Krauss, R. M.: Theories in social psychology, New York, 1965, Basic Books, Inc., Publishers.

Dowling, W. F., and Wayles, L. R.: How managers motivate: The imperatives of supervision, New York, 1971, McGraw-Hill, Inc.

Dunnette, M. E., editors: Handbook of industrial and organizational psychology, Chicago, 1976, Rand McNally & Co.

Eckvahl, V. R.: On-the-job management training, Journal of Nursing Administration 6(3):38-40, 1976.

Eisenhower, L. A., editors: Building a faculty team, Nursing Outlook 24:437-440, 1976.

Elsberry, N. L.: Power relations in hospital nursing, Journal of Nursing Administration 2(5):75-77, 1972.

Etzioni, A.: Modern organization, Englewood Cliffs, N.J., 1964, Prentice-Hall, Inc.

Fagan, J., and Shepherd, I. L.: Gestalt therapy now, Palo Alto, Calif., 1970, Science and Behavior Books.

Fenn, M., Mungovan, R., and Towell, D.: Developing the role of the unit nursing officer, Nursing Times 71(7):262-264, 1975.

Fiedler, F. E.: The contingency model—A reply to Ashour, Organizational Behavior and Human Performance 9:356-368, 1973.

Fiedler, F. E.: Personality and situational determinants of leader behavior. In Fleishman, E. A., and Hunt, J. G., editors: Current developments in the study of leadership. Carbondale, Ill., 1973, Southern Illinois University Press.

Fiedler, F. E., and Chemers, M.: Leadership and effective management, Glenview, Ill., 1974, Scott, Foresman and Co.

Fitts, W. H.: Interpersonal competence: The wheel model; Studies on the self concept, Nashville, Tenn., 1970, Counselor Recordings and Tests.

Foster, C.: Development self control, Kalamazoo, Mich., 1974, Behaviordelia, Inc.

Francis, D., and Woodcock, M.: People at work: A practical guide to organizational change, La Jolla, Calif., 1975, University Associates.

Franklin, J. L.: Down the organization: Influence processes across levels of hierarchy, Administrative Science Quarterly 20:153-164, 1975.

Froman, L. A., and Cohen, M. D.: Threats and bargaining efficiency, Behavioral Science 14:147-153, 1969.

Fromkin, H. L., and Sherwood, J. J., editors: Intergroup and minority relations, La Jolla, Calif., 1976, University Associates.

Fuller, M. E.: The budget: Standard V, Journal of Nursing Administration 6(4):36-38, 1976.

Gahagan, J. P., and Tedeschi, J. T.: Effects of promise credibility, outside options and social contact on interpersonal conflict, mimeographed manuscript, Albany, N.Y., 1970, State University of New York at Albany.

Galloway, B. T.: The nurse as a professional manager, Hospitals 48:89, 1974

Gardner, J. W.: Self-renewal: The individual and the innovative society, New York, 1971, Harper & Row Publishers.

Gazda, G. M.: Human relations development: A manual for educators, Boston, 1973, Allyn & Bacon, Inc.

Gibb, J. R.: Defensive communication. In Kolb, P. A., Rubin, I. M., and McIntyre, J. M., editors: Organizational psychology: A book of readings, Englewood Cliffs, N.J., 1974, Prentice-Hall, Inc.

Good, A. W.: Supervision: The key to good management, Journal of Rehabilitation, 40(6):13-14, 30-31, 42, 1974.

Gore, W. J.: Administrative decision making: a heuristic model, New York, 1964, John Wiley & Sons, Inc.

Gortner, S. R.: Scientific accountability in nursing, Nursing Outlook 22(12):764-768, 1974.

Gray, L. N., and Mayhew, B. H., Jr.: Proactive differentiation, sequence restraint, and the asymmetry of power: A multidimensional analysis, Human Relations 25:199-214, 1972.

Greene, C. N.: The reciprocal nature of influence between leader and subordinate, Journal of Applied Psychology 60:187-193, 1975.

Griesinger, D. W., and Livingston, J. W., Jr.: Toward a model of interpersonal motivation in experimental games, Behavioral Science 18(3):173-188, 1973.

Hagan, E.: Nursing leadership behavior, New York, 1961, Columbia University Teachers College, Institute for Research and Service in Nursing Education.

Hall, J.: Interpersonal style and the communication dilemma: I. Managerial implications of the Johari Awareness model, Human Relations 27(4):381-399, 1974.

Hamachek, D. E.: Encounters with the self, San Francisco, 1971, Holt, Rinehart and Winston.

Harford, T., Solomon, L., and Cheney, J.: Effects of proliferating punitive power upon cooperation and competition in the triad, Psychological Reports 24:355-360, 1969.

Harris, T. A.: I'm ok, you're ok, New York, 1967, Avon Books.

Hegyvary, S. T., and Haussman, R. K.: Monitoring

nursing care quality, Journal of Nursing Administration 5(5):17-26, 1975.

Heimann, C. G.: Four theories of leadership, Journal of Nursing Administration 6(5):18-28, 1976.

Hersey, P., Blanchard, K. H., and LaMonica, E. L.: A situational approach to supervision: Leadership theory and the supervising nurse, Supervisor Nurse 7(5):17-22, 1976.

Herzog, A.: The B. S. factor, New York, 1974, Penguin Books.

Hesse, H.: Siddhartha, New York, 1951, Bantam Books, Inc.

Hollander, E.: Leaders, groups, and influence, New York, 1964, Oxford University Press, Inc.

Hollander, E. P.: Style, structure and setting in organizational leadership, Administrative Science Quarterly 16(1):1-9, 1971.

Hughes, C. L.: Goal setting: Key to individual and organizational effectiveness, New York, 1965, American Management Association.

Hunt, J. G., and Larson, L. L.: Contingency approaches to leadership, Carbondale, Ill., 1974, Southern Illinois University Press.

Illich, I. D.: Celebration of awareness, New York, 1971, Doubleday & Co., Inc.

Incident reporting—nurses' responsibility, The Regan Report on Nursing Law 13(8):1, 1972.

Insel, P., and Moos, R.: Psychological environments: Expanding the scope of human ecology, American Psychologist 29:179-188, 1974.

Insel, P., and Moos, R.: The work environment scale, Palo Alto, Calif., 1972, Stanford University Department of Psychiatry, Social Ecology Laboratory.

James, M.: The ok boss, Reading, Mass., 1975, Addison-Wesley Publishing Co., Inc.

James, M., and Jongeward, W. D.: Born to win, Reading, Mass., 1971, Addison-Wesley Publishing Co., Inc.

Johnson, D. W.: Reaching out, Englewood Cliffs, N.J., 1972, Prentice-Hall, Inc.

Johnson, D. W.: The constructive use of conflict. In Johnson, D. W., editor: Contemporary social psychology, New York, 1973, J. B. Lippincott Co.

Jourard, S.: The transparent self, New York, 1964, Van Nostrand Reinhold Co.

Kalisch, B. J.: Of half gods and mortals: Aesculapian authority, Nursing Outlook 23(1):22-28, 1975.

Kalisch, B. J., and Kalisch, P. A.: Is the history of nursing alive and well? Nursing Outlook 24:362-366, 1976.

Kaye, D.: The woman boss: Getting there is only half the problem, Mainliner 20(6):34-37, 1976.

Keefe, W. F.: Open minds: The forgotten side of communication, New York, 1975, AMACOM.

Kinsella, C.: Consultant's role must be clearly defined, American Nurse 7(12):12, 1975.

Kipnis, D.: Does power corrupt? Journal of Personality and Social Psychology 24(1):33-41, 1972.

Knowles, H., and Knowles, M.: Introduction to group dynamics, New York, 1959, Association Press.

Kolb, D. A., and Boyatzis, R. E.: On the dynamics of the helping friendship. In Kolb, D. A., Rubin, I. M., and McIntyre, J. M., editors: Organizational psychology: A book of readings, Englewood Cliffs, N.J., 1974, Prentice-Hall, Inc.

Kramer, M.: Reality shock: Why nurses leave nursing, St. Louis, 1974, The C. V. Mosby Co.

Kramer, L. A.: The audit and I, American Journal of Nursing 76:1139-1141, 1976.

Lassey, W. R., editor: Leadership and social change, Iowa City, Iowa, 1971, University Associates.

Leininger, M.: The leadership crisis in nursing: A critical problem and challenge, Journal of Nursing Administration 4(2):28-34, 1974.

Leonard, G. B.: Sports and competition: Winning isn't everything. It's nothing, Intellectual Digest 3: 45-47, 1973.

Lewis, E. P.: Accountability: How, for what, and to whom? Nursing Outlook 20(5):315, 1972.

Lewis, H., and Streitfield, H.: Growth games, New York, 1971, Bantam Books, Inc.

Likert, R.: The human organization, New York, 1967, McGraw-Hill, Inc.

Likert, R., and Bowens, D.: Conflict strategies related to organizational theories and management systems. In Likert, R., and Bowens, D.: Attitudes, conflict and social change, New York, 1972, Academic Press, Inc.

Lio, A.: Leadership and responsibility in team nursing, Nurse Clinics of North America 8(2):267-280, 1976.

Litchfield, E.: Theory formulation. Notes on a general theory administration, Administrative Science Quarterly 1:3-29, 1956.

Longest, B. B., Jr.: Improved upward communication can reduce role ambiguity, Hospital Progress 56(2):61-65, 1975.

Loring, R., and Wells, T.: Breakthrough: Women into management, New York, 1972, Van Nostrand Reinhold Co.

Luft, J.: Group processes: An introduction to group dynamics, ed. 2, Palo Alto, Calif., 1970, National Press.

Luft, J.: Of human interaction, Palo Alto, Calif., 1969, National Press.

Lum, J. L. J.: Interaction patterns of nursing personnel, Nursing Research 19(4):324-330, 1970.

MacDonald, M. R.: Matching personalities with position: A study of job satisfaction, Supervisor Nurse 6(4):43-50, 1975.

Magner, M. A.: A management course revisited: Misericordia Hospital Medical Center, Supervisor Nurse 6(3):19, 1975.

Mahl, G. F.: Psychological conflict and defense, New York, 1971, Harcourt Brace Jovanovich, Inc.

Mahoney, M. J., and Thoresen, C. E.: Self-control: Power to the person, Monterey, Calif., 1974, Brooks/Cole Publishing Co.

Maier, N. R., Solem, A. R., and Maier, A. A.: The role-play technique: A handbook for management and leadership practice, La Jolla, Calif., 1975, University Associates.

Make the most of your authority, Hospital Supervision **8**(24): 1975.

Malamud, D. I., and Machover, S.: Toward self-understanding: Group techniques in self confrontation, Springfield, Ill., 1965, Charles C Thomas, Publisher.

Marram, G.: The comparative costs of operating a team and primary nursing unit, Journal of Nursing Administration **6**(4):21-24, 1976.

Massarik, F., and Wechsler, I. R.: Empathy revisited: The process of understanding people. In Kolb, D. A., Rubin, I. M., and McIntyre, J. M., editors: Organizational psychology: A book of readings, Englewood Cliffs, N.J., 1974, Prentice-Hall, Inc.

May, R.: Power and innocence, New York, 1972, W. W. Norton & Co., Inc.

McClelland, D.: The two faces of power. In Kolb, D. A., Rubin, I. M., and McIntyre, J. M., editors: Organizational psychology: A book of readings, Englewood Cliffs, N.J., 1974, Prentice-Hall, Inc.

McClelland, D., and Burnham, D.: Good guys make bum bosses, Psychology Today **9**(7):69-70, 1975.

McClelland, D., and Burnham, D.: Power is the great motivator, Harvard Business Review **54**(2):100-110, 1976.

McClure, M. L.: Entry into professional practice: The New York proposal, Journal of Nursing Administration **6**(5):12-17, 1976.

McClure, M. L.: Quality assurance and nursing education: A nursing service director's view, Nursing Outlook **24**(6):367-369, 1976.

McGregor, D.: Difficulties in communication. In Davis, K., editor: Organizational behavior: A book of readings, ed. 4, New York, 1974, McGraw-Hill, Inc.

McMullan, D.: Accountability and nursing education, Nursing Outlook **23**(8):501-503, 1975.

Miles, R. E.: Human relations or human resources? In Kolb, D. A., Rubin, I. M., and McIntyre, J. M., editors: Organizational psychology: A book of readings, Englewood Cliffs, N.J., 1974, Prentice-Hall, Inc.

Millard, R. M.: The new accountability, Nursing Outlook **23**(8):496-500, 1975.

Miller, J. P., and Fry, L. J.: Social relations in organizations: Further evidence for the Weberian model, Social Forces **51**:305-319, 1973.

Miller, S.: Dialogue with the higher self, Synthesis **1**(2):122-139, 1975.

Misumi, J., and Seki, F.: Effects of achievement motivation on the effectiveness of leadership patterns, Administrative Science Quarterly **16**(1):51-59, 1971.

Modlin, H. C.: Science and technology versus ethics and morals, Bulletin of the Menninger Clinic **37**(2): 149-159, 1973.

Moustakas, C. E.: Finding yourself, and finding others, Englewood Cliffs, N.J., 1974, Prentice-Hall, Inc.

Mulder, M.: Power equalization through participation? Administrative Science Quarterly **16**(1):31-39 1971.

Mullane, M. K.: Nursing care and the political arena, Nursing Outlook **23**(11):699-701, 1975.

Nolan, M. G.: Wanted: Colleagueship in nursing, Journal of Nursing Administration **6**(3):41-43, 1976.

Novello, D. J.: The national health planning and resources development act, Nursing Outlook **24**(6): 354-358, 1976.

O'Reilly, C. A., III, and Roberts, K. H.: Information filtration in organizations: Three experiments, Organizational Behavior and Human Performance **11**(2):253-265, 1974.

Otto, H. A: Group methods to actualize human potential; A handbook, ed. 2, Beverley Hills, Calif., 1970, Holistic Press.

Parker, W. S.: Realities of responsibility, Nursing Times **67**(3):1053-1054, 1971.

Passos, J. Y.: Accountability: Myth or mandate? Journal of Nursing Administration **3**(3):17-22, 1973.

Patchen, M.: The locus and basis of influence on organizational decisions, Organizational Behavior and Human Performance **11**(2):195-221, 1974.

Peter, L. J., and Hull, R.: The Peter principle, New York, 1970, Bantam Books, Inc.

Pfeiffer, J. W., and Jones, J. E., editors: A handbook of structured experiences for human relations training, 5 vols., La Jolla, Calif., 1975, University Associates, Inc.

Pierce, S. F., and Thompson, D.: Changing practice: By choice rather than chance, Journal of Nursing Administration **6**(2):33-39, 1976.

Plachy, R. J.: If you lead, a union can't, Modern Health Care **2**:116, 1974.

Polk, B. B.: Male power and the women's movement, Journal of Applied Behavioral Science **10**:415-431, 1974.

Pollard, W. E., and Mitchell, T. R.: Decision theory analysis of social power, Psychological Bulletin **78**(6):433-446, 1972.

Pym, B.: The making of a successful pressure group, British Journal of Sociology **24**(4):448-461, 1973.

Reiff, R.: The control of knowledge: The power of the helping professions, Journal of Applied Behavioral Science **10**:451-461, 1974.

Riggs, J. L., and Kalbaugh, A. J.: The art of management: Principles and practices, New York, 1974, McGraw-Hill, Inc.

Rogers, C. R.: On becoming a person, ed. 2, Boston, 1961, Houghton Mifflin Co.

Rogers, C. R., and Roethlisberger, F. J.: Barriers and gateways to communication. In Kolb, D. A., Rubin, I. M., and McIntyre, J. M., editor: Organizational psychology: A book of readings, Englewood Cliffs, N.J., 1974, Prentice-Hall, Inc.

Rubin, I., and Beckhard, R.: Factors influencing the effectiveness of health teams, Milbank Quarterly **50**(3):317-335, 1972.

Sampson, R. V.: The psychology of power, New York, 1965, Pantheon Books, Inc.

Schaefer, M. J.: How should we organize? Journal of Nursing Administration **6**(2):12-14, 1976.

Schmalenberg, C. E., and Kramer, M.: Dreams and reality: Where do they meet? Journal of Nursing Administration **6**(5):35-43, 1976.

Shiflett, S. C., and Nealey, S. M.: The effects of changing leader power: A test of "situational engineering," Organizational Behavior and Human Performance **7**(3):371-382, 1972.

Sims, H. P., Jr., and Szilagyi, A. D.: Leader structure and subordinate satisfaction for two hospital administrative levels: A path analysis approach, Journal of Applied Psychology **60**(2):194-197, 1975.

Smith C. G., editor: Conflict resolution: Contributions of the behavioral sciences, Notre Dame, 1971, University of Notre Dame Press.

Smith, D. H.: Communication and negotiation. In Thayer, L. O., editor: Communication spectrum, Flint, Mich., 1968, National Society for the Study of Communications.

Smith, K. H.: Changes in group structure through individual and group feedback, Journal of Personality and Social Psychology **24**(3):425-428, 1972.

Smith, R. J., and Cook, P. E.: Leadership in dyadic groups as a function of dominance and incentives, Sociometry **36**(4):561-568, 1973.

Steers, R. M., and Porter, L. W.: Motivation and work behavior, New York, 1975, McGraw-Hill, Inc.

Steiner, C.: Scripts people live, New York, 1975, Bantam Books, Inc.

Stevens, B.: Management tools needed, American Nurse **7**(9):9, 1975.

Stevens, B. J.: Accountability of the clinical specialist: The administrator's viewpoint, Journal of Nursing Administration **6**(2):30-32, 1976.

Stevens, B. J.: AANA's standards of nursing services: How do they measure up? Journal of Nursing Administration **6**(4):29-31, 1976.

Stevens, B. J.: The nurse as executive, Wakefield, Mass, 1975, Contemporary Publishing, Inc.

Stevens, B. J.: Use of groups for management: The organization of committees in a nursing division, Journal of Nursing Administration **5**(1):20-21, 1975.

Stogdill, R. M.: Handbook of leadership: A survey of theory and research, New York, 1974, The Free Press.

Tannenbaum, A. S.: Social psychology of the work organization, Belmont, Calif., 1967, Wadsworth Publishing Co., Inc.

Taylor, D. A., and Altman, I.: Self-disclosure as a function of reward-cost outcomes, Sociometry **38**(1):18-31, 1975.

Tead, O.: The art of leadership, New York, 1935, McGraw-Hill, Inc.

Tedeschi, J. T., editor: The social influence processes, Chicago, 1972, Aldine Publishing Co.

Tedeschi, J. T., Bonoma, T., and Novinson, N.: Behavior of a threatener: retaliation versus fixed opportunity costs, Journal of Conflict Resolution **14**:69-76, 1970.

Terry, G. R.: Principles of management, ed. 6, Homewood, Ill., 1972, Richard D. Irwin, Inc.

Teulings, A. W. M., Jansen, L. O. O., and Verhoeven, W. G.: Growth, power structure and leadership functions in the hospital organization, British Journal of Sociology **24**:490-505, 1973.

Tobin, H.: Quality staff development—A must for change and survival: Standard IX, Journal of Nursing Administration **6**(4):39-42, 1976.

Tobin, H. M., and others: The process of staff development: Components for change, St. Louis, 1974, The C. V. Mosby Co.

Tolor, A., and others: The effects of self-concept, trust, and imagined positive or negative self-disclosures on psychological space, Journal of Psychology **89**:9-24, 1975.

Twenty exercises for trainers, Washington, D.C., 1972, National Training Laboratories Institute for Applied Behavioral Science.

Van Dersal, W. R.: How to be a good communicator—and a better nurse, Nursing **4**(12):58-64, 1974.

Vickers, G.: Changing patterns of communication, Futures Conditional **3**(2): Item 2.

Visitor's safety: Nurses share responsibility, The Regan Report on Nursing Law **13**(9):2, 1972.

Wallston, K. A., and Wallston, B. S.: Nurses' decisions to listen to patients, Nursing Research **24**(1): 16-22, 1975.

Walton, R. E.: Interpersonal peacemaking: Confrontation and third party consultation, Reading, Mass., 1969, Addison-Wesley Publishing Co., Inc.

Watson, J.: The quasi-rational element in conflict, Nursing Research **25**:19-23, 1976.

Wergin, J. F.: The evaluation of organizational policy making: A political model, Review of Educational Research **46**(1):75-116, 1976.

White, H. C.: Some perceived behavior and attitudes of hospital employees under effective and ineffective supervision, Journal of Nursing Administration **1**(1):49-54, 1971.

Whitehead, J. A.: Clinical responsibility and its proper reward, Nursing Mirror **13**(4):42-43, 1972.

Wong, P.: Problem solving through "process management," Journal of Nursing Administration **5**(1):37-39, 1975.

Wood, M. T.: Participation, influence, and satisfaction in group decision making, Journal of Vocational Behavior **2**(4):389-399, 1972.

Wood, M. T.: Power relationships and group decision making in organizations, Psychological Bulletin **79**(5):280-293, 1973.

Yinon, G., and Bizman, A.: The nature of effective bonds and the degree of personal responsibility as determinants to risk taking for self and others, Bulletin of the Psychonomic Society 4(2-A):80-82, 1974.

Zalkind, S. S., and Costello, T. W.: Perception: Implications for administration. In Kolb, D. A., Rubin, I. M., and McIntyre, J. M., editor: Organizational psychology: A book of readings, Englewood Cliffs, N.J., 1974, Prentice-Hall, Inc.

INDEX